Appreciating the Theater: Cues for Theatergoers

Appreciating the Theater: Cues for Theatergoers

Julian M. Kaufman

Hofstra University

DAVID McKAY COMPANY, INC. · NEW YORK

APPRECIATING THE THEATER:
CUES FOR THEATERGOERS

LIBRARY OF CONGRESS CATALOG CARD NUMBER: 73-124549

MANUFACTURED IN THE UNITED STATES OF AMERICA

TYPOGRAPHY BY SOPHIE ADLER

For *My* Leading Lady, Lily 

Preface

Appreciating the Theater: Cues for Theatergoers examines the popularity of the theater as an art form and as a medium of entertainment throughout the ages. The text surveys the various historical periods during which the theater either flourished or struggled for existence. It notes the impact of dominant personalities on the development of the theater as a social force in the community, and it discusses the effect of political events and social changes upon the thought and works of major playwrights. Additionally, the text analyzes the role of the producer, the playwright, the director, the actor, and the theater technician in mounting the play. *Appreciating the Theater: Cues for Theatergoers* aims to:

1. Provide a background for understanding the origins and history of the theater.
2. Inculcate a respect for the talents and struggles of the playwright and the actor, and their contributions to the development of the theater.
3. Create an awareness of, and an appreciation for, the components of the theater.

To achieve these aims, *Appreciating the Theater* is developed and organized to provide the student with a historical, cultural, and artistic frame of reference for appreciating the art of the theater. Each chapter includes an overview of the period during which the theater developed, cues or guidelines for enjoying the performance and production of a play, and projects to motivate additional study of the theater and its practices.

Setting the Scene, the first section of each chapter, surveys the social, economic, and political background against which the theater developed as an art form, the playwright emerged as an observer of his society, and the actor fought for status in his society. *Cues for Theatergoers,* the second section of each chapter, is directly concerned with the performance and production of the play from the times of the Greeks to the present day. The student is made aware of the various playwriting, performance, and production techniques that have developed throughout the long history of the theater. The aim is to provide the student with an understanding and appreciation of the revival of a classic as well as a production of a contemporary play. *Theater Spotlights,* the concluding section of each chapter, contains projects for additional study of the many facets of the theater that cannot be covered in detail in the text. Additionally, *Appreciating the Theater: Cues for Theatergoers* is organized to simulate the theatergoing experience. The theatergoer enters the architectural environment in which the play is produced in Chapter II. The lights dim and the curtain rises. Attention is focused on the performance of the actor in Chapter III. The words of the playwright are heard in Chapter IV. The craft of the director, the costume designer, the lighting designer, and the set designer is noted. The theatergoer leaves the theater, discusses the production, reads the criticism of the professional reviewer, the critic, in Chapter V. As a general introduction to the theater, *Appreciating the Theater* should aid the student of drama to become a more knowledgeable and appreciative theatergoer.

In conclusion, I wish to express my gratitude for the encouragement of my colleagues at Hofstra University: Professor James Van Wart, Chairman, Department of Drama; Dr. Donald H. Swinney, Professor of Drama; and Dr. Jack Tureen, Chairman, Department of Speech Arts and Sciences. Each gave of his time to read and discuss the manuscript. I appreciate the suggestions made by Dr. H. Charles Kline, Professor of Theater Arts, State University College of Arts and Sciences, Plattsburgh, New York, and Dr. Lewis R. Marcuson, Associate Professor of English, Wilmington College, Wilmington, Ohio. I am indebted to Mr. Gordon Hill, editor, David McKay Company, for his guidance and encouragement throughout the preparation of the manuscript. Finally, I had the services of an excellent and loyal secretary, my wife, who typed and retyped the manuscript with an unwavering belief in its purpose and content. In the same sense that a finished production represents the contributions and cooperation of many hands, this text represents the willingness of many to bring it to fruition.

JULIAN M. KAUFMAN

Contents

I

Theatergoing: an Introduction

Like hungry guests
A sitting audience looks.

GEORGE FARQUHAR, *The Inconstant* Prologue, 1702

A. SETTING THE SCENE

In a sense, primitive man introduced the twentieth-century theatergoer to the theater. Primitive man's theater was the large circle around which he sat, and which he had reserved for performance. His actors were dancers who interpreted life through rhythmic movements set to music. His plays were religious rituals or dramatized events. As a spectator or as a participant, primitive man sought to discover the significance of events, understand nature, and penetrate the powers of the supernatural. Although our theater today is a highly complex commercial venture, and its relationship to religion has been severed, our needs and reasons for theatergoing are not too far removed from those of primitive man and the long queues of theatergoers who came after him.

Greek theatergoers sought first to honor the god Dionysus, and secondly, to appreciate the skill of the playwright. Solon, the chief magistrate of Athens, introduced the recitation of Homer's poems by professional actors to improve the literacy of the populace.

Greek citizens came to view and to understand their legendary and mythological heritage. Later, Pisistratus, who had wrested control of Athens from Solon in 560 B.C., sensed the unifying force of the cult worship of Dionysus, and organized two festivals to honor the god of wine and fertility. The City, or Great Dionysia, Festival was held within the city at the end of March; and the Lenaea Festival was held within the city at the end of January. Performance replaced recitation, the play replaced the dithyramb, and the audience came to see and judge the skill of the playwright and the performer.

Sometime during the middle of the sixth century B.C., Thespis, the first recognized actor, and from whom the name for actors, "thespians" stems, broke the religious character of the performance when he stepped forward and addressed the leader of the chorus. Thus, dialogue was introduced. The idea of the play was born. Thereafter, under the playwriting influence of Aeschylus, Sophocles, and Euripides, the audience came to experience the elements of drama: conflict, action, emotion, surprise, and suspense.

By 499 B.C., a generation of theatergoers had forgotten the religious origin of the festivals. They accepted the celebration in honor of Dionysus as an occasion for theatergoing. Their attention was now focused on the playwright and his interpretation of life. Interest was further whetted by the promise of an award to the best of the competing playwrights. On festival days, business closed its doors, government suspended operations, and all household duties ceased so that the memory of Dionysus could be properly honored by spending an exciting day at the theater.

Religious holidays, military victories, and government-sponsored events afforded the Roman theatergoer more than ample opportunity to attend the theater. The choice of entertainment ranged from athletic events, funeral celebrations, and mimic naval battles to the more conservative fare: farce, comedy, and tragedy. The popular mimi, a form of low burlesque with songs and dances, appealed to the lusty nature of the Roman, and the more sedate and thoughtful pantomime won his respectful attention. The grandeur of Rome was reflected in the approximately six months of periodic holidays he observed. In that time, the Roman theatergoer luxuriated in viewing 101 dramatic performances, 64 chariot races, and 10 gladiatorial contests.

The Church unwittingly introduced its medieval congregation to the dynamics of the theater when it found a need to educate the wayward populace in the meaning of religion. Dramatization began with the Easter service. The congregation was moved by the appearance of the Three Marys at the Tomb of Jesus. When the Angel appeared and lifted the veil to reveal only the cross, thus symbolizing a risen Christ, the congregation became transfixed. A hymn was then sung. Emotions reached fever pitch. In the later development of other Biblical incidents, however, realism, secular life, and special effects were introduced. For example, complicated machinery was installed to hoist the Angel above the altar. Eventually, the Church banned dramatization from its services because theatrical production was defeating the purpose of the Church, namely, the religious education of the people. However, the production of *miracle, mystery, passion,* and *morality* plays continued on the steps of the church and in the marketplace.

The guilds replaced the Church as producers of religious drama. Spectacular parades, featuring pageant wagons or floats that carried segments of a Biblical story, were organized as a community service and presented on the Easter and Christmas holidays. The guilds also used the occasion to advertise their crafts and products. Because the inhabitants of an entire city were involved in the presentation, there emerged six important components involved with any theatrical production—producer, playwright, actor, craftsman, theatergoer, and critic.

The ardent support accorded the Elizabethan theater was rooted in the acceptance of theater as a popular art form. Although there may have been some attempt to imitate royalty—Queen Elizabeth patronized the theater but would not subsidize it, and court members lent their names to protect acting companies—the Elizabethan attended because he truly enjoyed the theater. The Theater, The Rose, The Red Bull, The Fortune, The Globe, The Curtain, and The Swan were places to meet one's friends and indulge in an evening of high adventure—sometimes at the risk of losing one's pocketbook or life. The "groundling," so called because he stood on the ground, paid one penny for the privilege of standing through an entire evening, and an additional penny for the privilege of sitting through the performance. He enjoyed the clowning of Will Kemp, the low comedy of Richard Tarleton, the comic timing of Thomas Pope, and the tragic finesse of Edward Alleyn and Richard Burbage. The Elizabethan theatergoer was stimulated by the language and the intricate plots of William Shakespeare, Thomas Kyd, Christopher Marlowe, Thomas Heywood, and Ben Jonson. The Elizabethan theater reflected the vitality of the age in which it existed. Its actors, managers, and playwrights understood the passion of the audience for earthy humor, puns, ghosts, blood and gore, pageantry, and mistaken identity. The audience repaid the understanding with frequent and enthusiastic attendance.

The most avid theatergoer in seventeenth-century France was Louis XIV. The Sun King, as he is known in history, constantly entertained himself and his court with a variety of theatrical divertissements. The grand ballroom of the Petit-Bourbon Palace at Versailles was converted into a theater for the production of spectacles, operas, musicales, ballets, improvisations, and plays. With his captive audience of ministers of state and petitioning courtiers, Louis XIV set the fashion for theatergoing in France. In Paris, merchants, shopkeepers, professionals, glovemakers, jewelers, and tailors crowded the Hôtel de Bourgogne, Théâtre du Marais—a converted tennis court—and mingled with the upper classes at the Palais Royal, once the palace of Cardinal Richelieu. The spectators sat on benches in the pit, seats on the shelf-like balconies, and frequently upon the stage, where they interfered with the action of the play and the performance of the actor. In the countryside, traveling companies received a hearty welcome. All classes of society, with perhaps the exception of the clergy, supported the theater in seventeenth-century France.

The theatergoer of the Restoration period was a select breed: fop, dandy, man-about-town, member of high society and the King's court. He fervently supported the Restoration theater because actresses were appearing on the English stage for the first time, and, in addition, the theater had been closed for twenty years. Long considered an assembly place for evil and disreputable characters—the Lord Mayor of London and his council had succeeded in driving the theaters beyond the city limits in 1576—the reputation of theater narrowly avoided a mortal blow in 1609 when *The Gull's Handbook* was published. Written by Thomas Dekker, a pamphleteer and playwright (*The Shoemaker's Holiday*), one sensational chapter described the scandalous behavior of theater audiences. Although the references and examples cited pertained mostly to the riffraff who could be found in the theaters nightly, the Puritans believed the handbook to be conclusive evidence that all theaters were dens of iniquity, pandering to a low-class audience.

Despite the fact that James I had extended a measure of respectability to the theater and its actors when he effected the reorganization of two leading acting companies, and despite the fact that Charles I was a theater enthusiast, London theater managers found themselves constantly pressured by the rising tide of Puritanism. It was not surprising, therefore, that one of the first actions of the new parliament, formed after the beheading of Charles I, was the closing of all public theaters in London.

The theaters did not reopen until 1660 when Charles II resumed the throne after a long sojourn in France where he had been granted asylum by Louis XIV. Theater activity, however, was limited to two theaters. The attending audience represented the sophisticated society that surrounded the king. For this very special audience, the playwrights of the Restoration period—George Etherege, William Wycherley, Sir John Vanbrugh, William Congreve, and George Farquhar—wrote the bawdy plays categorized as "Restoration Comedy." The Restoration theatergoer hastened to the theater to identify himself on stage. One play, nevertheless, hit home. William Congreve's *The Way of the World* too closely approximated the manners and morals of the time. It was an instantaneous flop! Today, *The Way of the World* is recognized as a masterpiece of high comic writing.

In the colonies, theatergoers were without professional theater until 1749, when Murray and Kean, two professional actors, arrived in this country. Although the Pennsylvania Quakers and the government of New York were opposed to theater, Murray and Kean managed to play performances of Joseph Addison's *Cato* in Philadelphia and William Shakespeare's *Richard III* in New

York, before proceeding to Williamsburg, Virginia, where a more receptive attitude prevailed.

Three years later, the *Charming Sally* arrived at Yorktown, bearing Lewis Hallam and his company of twelve professional actors who had studied and learned a repertory of twenty plays in London and while en route to the colonies. In subsequent years, Hallam and his company became the mainstay of dramatic presentation for an entertainment-starved theatergoer. The company played the major cities along the coast, hesitating, however, to invade the New England colonies because of the Puritan attitude toward theater.

Shortly after the French and Indian War, an anti-British sentiment became rife in the colonies as a result of the oppressive legislation enacted by Parliament. In 1766, the Sons of Liberty instigated a riot at a performance of *The Twin Lovers* in New York in protest against an all-British cast. To avoid the hostility of the colonial theatergoer, David Douglas, the manager of the Hallam Company, changed the name of the troupe to the American Company. Theatergoers continued to support the American Company until 1774 when the Continental Congress passed a resolution discouraging "every species of extravagance and dissipation, especially horse-racing, and all kinds of gaming, cock-fighting, exhibitions of shews, plays, and other expensive diversions and entertainments."

The British and the American soldier attended the theater, and each participated in the production of plays during the American Revolution. In Boston, a satirical farce, *The Blockade of Boston,* was in rehearsal when a report arrived advising that local patriots were attacking British fortifications on Bunker Hill. It took a few moments for the British cast and spectators to realize the messenger was not a member of the cast! At Valley Forge, General George Washington authorized a soldier performance of *Cato,* hoping the play would help raise the morale of the Continentals. In New York and Philadelphia, the British ran benefit shows for the purpose of "relieving widows and orphans of sailors and soldiers who have fallen in support of the constitutional rights of Great Britain in America." Theatergoing during the American Revolution provided off-duty relaxation for members of both armies.

American theatergoers increased in number at the end of the war. State legislatures repealed existing anti-theater legislation, thus making theater available to those who wished to attend. Royall Tyler initiated the beginning of American comedy with *The Contrast,* a play that espoused the good nature of American character. Citizens of the new nation flocked to see their virtues dramatized on stage. George Washington set a fashion for theatergoing by his frequent presence at the theater in Philadelphia and New York. As President of the United States, he initiated the custom of using the theater as a means of making a public appearance and entertaining guests. Many took to heart the words of Robert Morris who argued against the banning of theater by the state of Pennsylvania —"the state and manners of the people regulate the theater and the theater has a reciprocal effect upon the public taste and manner." Although it would take generations for the American theater to overcome the many expressed prejudices against theatergoing, the enthusiasm of the American theatergoer portended the continuous development of a vigorous and vital theater.

The nineteenth century theatergoer in England, France, Germany, Italy, Russia, and the United States enjoyed a common theater experience: the glow of a star on stage. Although each century had produced some great actors, the nineteenth century was star-blessed. In every major country, a star or stars dominated the stage and the box office. Visitors returning home from abroad publicized the talents of individual performers. In the United States, Stephen Price, a New York theater entrepreneur, sensed the value of importing stars to revitalize an ailing box office. James William Wallack, father of John Lester Wallack, an outstanding American actor–manager, was the first to accept Price's offer. The success of his tour encouraged other stars to venture across the ocean.

In subsequent decades, stars criss-crossed the footlights of theaters around the world. The English star, Fanny Kemble, and her father, Charles Kemble, toured America in 1832. The tour was climaxed by her marriage to Pierce Butler, a Southern plantation owner. Miss Kemble's memoirs concerning the institution of slavery influenced the English Parliament to vote negatively on the question of aid to the Confederacy. Adelaide Ristori, the great Italian tragedienne, visited France and proved a greater actress than the reigning French tragedienne, Rachel. George II, Duke of Saxe-Meiningen, took his renowned company of German actors to Holland, Sweden, Denmark, Poland, England, and Russia. The caliber of their ensemble acting and their production affected staging and production abroad. Tommaso Salvini, the Italian tragedian, came to America where he played Othello in Italian to Edwin Booth's English-speaking Iago! Lillie Langtry, one of the first English society women to go on the stage, so captivated Texas audiences that Sheriff Roy Bean renamed his city in her honor. Theatergoers in the nineteenth century, then, were star conscious. Improvements in transportation and attractive monetary returns encouraged the great stars to travel abroad. Theater managers recognized the importance of the star at the box office. They willingly agreed to pay the high salaries demanded by the actors' agents.

The twentieth-century theatergoer attends the theater for many of the reasons his predecessors did. He attends to view the talents of such established stars as Alfred Lunt and Lynn Fontanne, Richard Burton, Helen Hayes, Sir John Gielgud, Sir Lawrence Olivier, Jessica Tandy, Eva Le Galliene, Shirley Booth, Christopher Plummer, Julie Harris, Maureen Stapleton, Sam Levine, Kim Stanley, and Anne Bancroft. He attends to judge the talents of such rising stars as Ruby Dee, Rosemary Harris, Sidney Poitier, Stacy Keach, Estelle Parsons, Woody Allen, Gloria Foster, Frank Langella, Donald Pleasence, James Earl Jones, Jerry Orbach, and George Grizzard. He attends to revel in the talents of the musical-comedy stars such as Mary Martin, Barbra Streisand, Ethel Merman, John Raitt, Gwen Verdon, Pearl Bailey, Richard Kiley, Barbara Harris, Zero Mostel, and Carol Channing. He wants to hear the scores of the musical comedy composers and lyricists: Irving Berlin, Cole Porter, Richard Rodgers and Oscar Hammerstein II, Frank Loesser, Anthony Newley, Sheldon Harnick and Jerry Bock, Jule Styne, and Burt Bacharach. He attends to behold the ensemble playing of such acting companies as The Actors Studio, The National Repertory Company, The Association of Producing Artists, Inc., American Conservatory Theatre, and the Minnesota Theater Company.

He attends to listen to the words of the playwrights who speak to him: Edward Albee, Tennessee Williams, Peter Weiss, Neil

Simon, Arthur Miller, John Osborne, James Baldwin, Lillian Hellman, Friedrich Durrenmatt, and Harold Pinter. He attends to see a revival of a theater classic: Sophocles' *Oedipus Rex,* Euripides' *The Trojan Women,* Aristophanes' *Lysistrata,* William Shakespeare's *Hamlet,* Molière's *Le Bourgeois Gentilhomme,* Jean Racine's *Phèdre,* Richard Brinsley Sheridan's *The Rivals,* George Bernard Shaw's *Pygmalion,* Oscar Wilde's *The Importance of Being Earnest,* Anton Chekhov's *Uncle Vanya,* Henrik Ibsen's *Peer Gynt,* August Strindberg's *The Dance of Death,* and Eugene O'Neill's *Mourning Becomes Electra.*

He attends because the theater has remained an art form that stimulates his senses, excites his emotions, and reflects the temper of his time.

B. THEATER SPOTLIGHTS

I. ***Theater Terminology:*** Define the following:

angel	"George Spelvin"
box office	"The Method"
claque	Critic
pit	"Theater of the Absurd"
"Annie Oakley"	The *Poetics*
"Dressing the house"	Repertory Company

II. ***Theater Who's Who:*** Identify the following:

Actors Equity Association
American National Theater and Academy
Antoinette Perry Awards
John F. Kennedy Center for the Performing Arts
American Educational Theater Association
National Council on the Arts and Government, Inc.

III. ***Theater Investigation:*** Discuss the following:

1. Indicate in what era, other than the present one, you would have liked to attend the theater. Discuss the reasons for selecting this era of theatergoing.
2. Set up, and discuss the reasons for selection, the criteria an individual should consider before he makes a decision con-

cerning whether or not he should invest in a given theatrical production.

3. There have been complaints, both by the audience and members of the cast, that latecomers are disturbing to the performance. As a theater manager, discuss the measures you would take to eliminate the disturbance.

IV. ***Theater Projects:*** Prepare the following:

1. Prepare a newspaper advertisement and a radio spot announcement of either the opening of a new play by a new playwright, or a revival of a play featuring an established star.
2. A producer has been invited to prepare a symposium for a class of drama students. The topic is "The Entertainment Arts Today." Outline an agenda that would answer the needs and interests of the audience attending the symposium.
3. Prepare a short paper recommending a play that you believe meets the criteria set by the Joseph Pulitzer Prize Committee for Drama.

V. ***Theater Bibliography:*** Read the following:

Cullman, Marguerite. *Occupation: Angel.* New York: Norton Publishing Company, 1963.

Hughes, Glenn. *The Story of the Theater.* New York: Samuel French, 1928.

Oppenheimer, George. *The Passionate Playgoer.* New York: Viking Press, Compass Books Edition, 1962.

Seldes, Gilbert. *The Great Audience.* New York: Viking Press, 1950.

Yurka, Blanche. *Dear Audience.* Englewood Cliffs, N.J.: Prentice Hall, Inc., 1959.

II

Theater in Front of the Curtain

. . . Therefore, I say, let our Gallant (having paid his half Crown, and given the Door-keeper his Ticket) presently advance himself into the middle of the Pit, where having made his Honor to the set of the Company, but especially to the Vizard-Masks, let him pull out his Comb, and manage his flaxen Wig with all the Grace he can . . .

SAM VINCENT, *The Young Gallant's Academy, or, Directions How He Should Behave Himself in All Places and Company,* 1674. Chapter V.

A. SETTING THE SCENE: THREE MODERN THEATER AUDITORIUMS

Our word theater is derived from the Greek word *theatron,* meaning a place of viewing. Throughout the three thousand and more years of theater, the place of viewing has varied in concept and design with regard to audience–actor and auditorium–stage relationship. The Greeks developed a three-unit arrangement that comprised an auditorium, a dancing place or orchestra, and a *skene*-house. The Romans redesigned the Greek theater and produced a single unit by merging the *skene*-house with the auditorium and all but eliminating the orchestra. The Elizabethans erected a playhouse in which an elevated stage projected itself into the audience area. The Restoration designers reduced the projected stage to apron proportions, and placed the play behind the proscenium arch. The theater designers of the nineteenth century maintained the basic Restoration concept, while early twentieth-century architects eliminated the apron in the quest for realism. Today, the place of viewing tends toward the Elizabethan–Greek arrangement; and, in one particular type of theater, the circle arrangement introduced by primitive man is utilized. Consequently, the viewing place for present-day audiences may be one of three types: thrust stage auditoriums, proscenium stage auditoriums, and arena stage auditoriums.

1. Thrust Stage Theaters

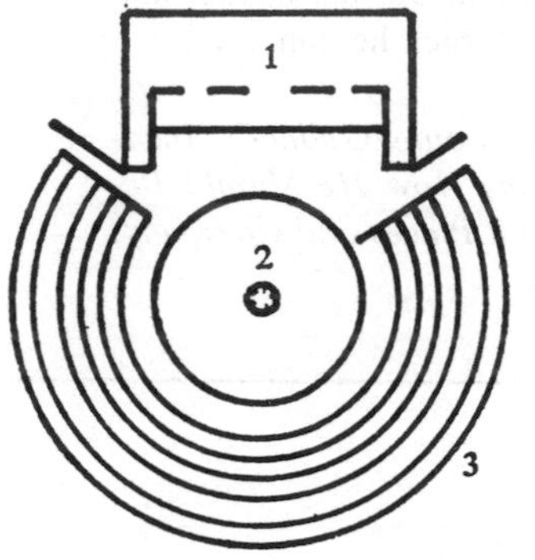

A GREEK THEATER

1. *Skene*
2. *Orkestra*
3. *Auditorium*

Discovered at the end of the eighteenth century, but not completely excavated until many years later, the Theater of Dionysus in Athens is a good example of the three-unit Greek theater in its most developed form. Built of stone on the southern slope of the Acropolis, and in sharp contrast to the wooden theater that served the needs of Aeschylus, Sophocles, and Euripides, the Dionysus Theater is believed to have been completed under the administration of Lycurgus, friend of Demosthenes and protector of the plays of the great writers of tragedy. The semicircular auditorium consisted of 78 tiers, and seated 17,000 people in its fourteen sections which were separated by thirteen vertical aisles. Before the huge auditorium stood the dancing place, or *orkestra.* In all probability the *orkestra* had a *thymele,* or altar, which gave the performance a religious aura. Beyond the *orkestra* stood an elaborate stage building or *skene. Skene* is the Greek word for hut or tent, and from which we derive our word scene. At one point in the development of Greek theater architecture, the *skene* served as a place for the performers to change costumes. In time, the *skene* was moved to its present position. Its size was increased by the addition of wings, or *paraskenia.* Three doors pierced the façade of the *skene,* thus changing its function from a place for costume change to a place for plot action. Although frequently referred to as the area before the *skene,* the façade of the *skene* is called the *proscenium.* The roof of the *skene* was called the *theologeion.* It was generally used as the area from which the gods intervened on behalf of the hero. Two passageways, the *parados,* separated the auditorium from the *skene.*

An Athenian citizen attended a performance of Aeschylus' *Agamemnon* in the Theater of Dionysus with anticipation and interest in the events that were about to unfold before him. As he sat bathed in the warm sunlight, he probably reviewed the plot of the play with his neighbor. Since the plays were usually about mythological and historical heroes and heroines, the Athenian citizen knew what to expect. Familiarity did not affect his interest and rapt attention. As he conversed, his head stretched out to catch a glimpse of the dignitaries and priests of Dionysus who occupied the thronelike chairs that encircled the first row of the auditorium. The center seat was of special interest, because it was canopied and occupied by the Chief Dionysian Priest. Eventually, the eyes of the Athenian shifted to the roof of the *skene.* It is from this point on stage that the play begins.

In time, the actor playing the Watchman appeared. The mask he wore was sufficiently large and exaggerated to enable the spectator to see his features. His padded costume increased his physical size; his elevated shoes, or *cothurnus,* raised his height in proportion to the padded costume and oversized mask. Close up, the Watchman might have appeared to be a monster. From a distance, and in an auditorium that seated 17,000 people, he appeared to be a normal-sized man. As he gazed beyond the roof of the *skene,* the Watchman spoke the lines that set the locale of the play, the time of the action, thus diverting the audience from the fact that a play, which was set at night, was being enacted in broad daylight!

I pray the gods to quit me of my toils,
To close the watch I keep, this livelong year;
For as a watch-dog lying, not at rest,
Propped on one arm, upon the palace-roof
Of Atreus' race, too long, too well I know
The starry conclave of the midnight sky,
Too well, the splendours of the firmament,
The lords of light, whose kingly aspect shows
What time they set or climb the sky in turn—
The year's divisions, bringing frost or fire.
And now, as ever, am I set to mark
When shall stream up the glow of signal-flame,
The bale-fire bright, and tell its Trojan tale—
Troy town is ta'en: such issue holds in hope
She in whose woman's breast beats heart of man.

Thus upon mine unrestful couch I lie,
Bathed with the dews of night, unvisited
By dreams—ah me! for in the place of sleep
Stands Fear as my familiar, and repels
The soft repose that would mine eyelids seal.*

When the signal-flame shot into the air, the Athenian knew that the prologue was near its end, that he could expect the arrival of the Chorus upon the scene. He focused his attention upon the left *parados* that separated the auditorium from the *skene,* in time to see the Chorus of Argive Elders enter in single file, each wearing identical costumes and masks, each leaning on a staff. In marked rhythm, the Chorus makes its way to the *orkestra.* There, the fifteen-man Chorus forms three files of five ranks each.

---

* From *Agamemnon,* trans. by E. D. A. Morshead in Whitney J. Oates and Eugene O'Neill, Jr., eds., *The Complete Greek Drama,* vol. I (New York: Random House, 1938), p. 167. Reprinted by permission of the publisher.

A choral ode opens the first stasimon. It is sung, danced, and chanted by the Chorus. While the Chorus performs, a murmur goes through the audience. The center doors of the *skene* have opened. There stands Clytemnestra, wife of Agamemnon, sister of the beautiful Helen, and mother of Electra, Orestes, and the sacrificed Iphigenia. She lights the altar fires and awaits the conclusion of the first stasimon. Then, she steps forward to exchange dialogue with the leader of the Chorus, and the first episode begins. Thereafter, stasimon alternates with episode as the playwright retells the tragic story of the House of Atreus.

The terrifying events that follow hold the spectator spellbound. He sits in suspense awaiting the moment when Agamemnon will follow the Messenger through the right *parados,* moving one step closer to his doom. The Athenian stares in awe at the gorgeous spectacle of the returning hero, Agamemnon, as he makes his way in his chariot to the steps of the palace, accompanied by the plunder and booty of war. One prize of conquest is Cassandra, the ill-fated daughter of the conquered Hecuba. The emotions of the spectator are stirred by the alternating stasimons and episodes—the singing, chanting, dancing Chorus—the episodes charged with conflict and revenge. The Athenian stifles a desire to cry out a warning that Agamemnon heed the prophetic words of Cassandra whose fate it is to have others cast doubt on her ability to foretell the future. He stiffens as he hears the screams of the helpless Agamemnon caught in his bath, and those of the pathetic Cassandra who accepts her doom. His imagination tells him what has happened behind the palace walls, for the Greeks do not enact scenes of violence in view of the audience. Consequently, the spectator shrinks not from the actual violence, but from the anticipation of the moment when Clytemnestra will open the door and reveal the blood-bathed Agamemnon and Cassandra stretched out upon the *eccyclema,* a rotating device or wagon employed when the playwright felt a need to show what had happened within. The Athenian stares in disbelief at the deed, unconcerned that the playwright had successfully led him through the retelling of a story he knows so well! There is a moment of silence as Clytemnestra joins her lover, Aegisthus, in entering the palace. Then 17,000 pairs of feet applaud the performance by stomping against the stone tiers. The play is over!

The Greek playwright adapted his play to the architectural structure of the theater. The *skene* was identified as a palace through constant word reference in the text, and through a protagonist who stemmed from royalty. All scenes took place outside the palace, thus conforming to the outdoor, open-air characteristic of the Greek theater. The problem of the narrow acting area before the *skene* was solved by bringing the action forward into the *orkestra,* by utilizing the roof of the *skene,* and by a *mechane* that could lower gods from the *paraskenia,* or remove them from the scene. Medea, for example, makes her escape in such a manner. *Periaktoi,* large triangular prisms on which scenes were painted, were placed near the *paraskenia,* and were turned to suggest another locale. *Charon's Steps,* a narrow underground passage that connected the skene with the *orkestra,* and which was appropriately named for the ferryman who conveyed the dead across the river Styx, was used for the appearance of ghosts. The Greek playwright, in short, was not handicapped by the architectural structure of the theater, but wisely incorporated it in the writing and production of his play. Subsequent playwrights, such as Shakespeare, Christopher Marlowe, Ben Jonson, and John Ford, to cite a few, followed the technique of the Greek playwright, each adapting his play to the physical structure of the theater.

The Romans initiated the concept of the single-unit theater plant. Content at first to merely remodel the existing Greek theaters, they soon developed an architectural unit that was distinctly Roman in style. The engineering genius displayed, the radical changes effected, and the extravagances engaged in for the purpose of impressing the populace can be demonstrated in three theaters built in Rome.

In 55 B.C., Pompey built Rome's first theater. It was made of stone and was erected on level ground. It seated 40,000 people, rose three stories high, and incorporated changes made in the Greek theater. For example, the *skene* building was joined to the auditorium, thus eliminating the *parodi;* the *orkestra* was reduced in size, thereby permitting additional seating area; and performances

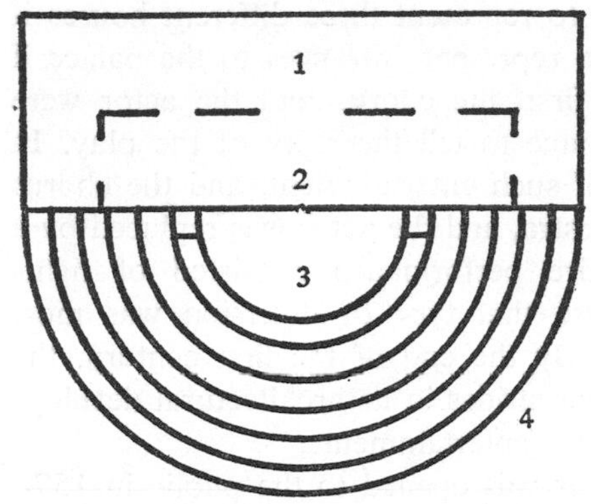

A ROMAN THEATER

1. *Skene*
2. *Stage*
3. *Orchestra*
4. *Auditorium*

were staged on a raised platform before a highly decorative *skene* building. To overcome the antipathy of the Romans for anything Grecian, Pompey declared his theater to be a temple to Venus Victrix. A small shrine dedicated to the goddess was placed over the last row of the auditorium, so that spectators approaching their seats moved in the direction of the shrine. Four years later, a temporary theater was erected by Aemilius Scaurus, a magistrate who served on a board in charge of public buildings. The façade of the *skene* consisted of three levels: one was made of marble, another of glass, and a third of gilded wood. More than 300 columns decorated the façade, and it is said that 3,000 statues filled the niches between the columns. Sometime during the first century B.C., Scribonius Curio erected a theater to commemorate his father's death. It was unique in design and operation because it consisted of two auditoriums, back to back. At the end of the performance of plays, the auditoriums were swung so that each faced the other. The audience was then entertained with a program of athletic events!

In all Roman theaters, boxes were situated at either side of the *orkestra* and were reserved for presiding officials. Senators sat in the first fourteen rows, and the remaining seats were occupied by the common people. There may or may not have been a curtain to protect the *skene's* elaborate façade or to drop into a slot at the beginning of the performance. On stage, the actors used the three doors that pierced the *skene* to represent three different houses if the play was a comedy, or to represent entrances to the palace if the play was a tragedy. At first, the chorus and the actor were prominently placed on the stage to tell the story of the play. In time, the audience wearied of such entertainment, and the chorus was replaced by a small orchestra, and the actor was replaced by a dancer. Eventually, the entire performance consisted of light-hearted entertainment because that type of diversion was most pleasing to the theatergoers. By the end of the first century, the Roman theater had made great strides in its architectural development, but not in the quality of the entertainment.

The first Elizabethan theater was opened to the public in 1576 when James Burbage, a carpenter turned actor, built The Theater on the outskirts of London in an attempt to thwart the hostile actions of city authorities who were opposed to theatrical performances. Although there is no record of the size or construction of The Theater, it is believed that it was built of wood and was circular. Twenty years later, James Burbage dismantled The Theater because he could not negotiate a lease renewal for the property

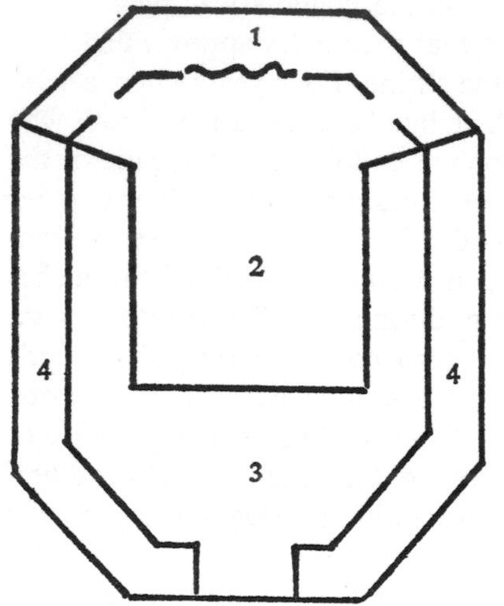

AN ELIZABETHAN THEATER

1. *Inner-stage*
2. *Outer-stage*
3. *Pit or Yard*
4. *Auditorium*

on which it stood. The materials were carted away to a new site, where The Globe was constructed.

Our knowledge of the architecture of the Elizabethan theater is based upon a diary, a sketch, and a building contract. The diary was kept by a competitor of James Burbage, Philip Henslowe, who operated The Rose, The Hope, and The Fortune. The sketch was drawn in 1596 by Johannes DeWitt, a Dutch traveler who attended The Swan (another theater of the period); he was so awed by the magnificence of the structure that he sketched the auditorium. The contract was written for the construction of The Fortune, Henslowe's answer to Richard Burbage's Globe. The many references in the contract to duplicating the architectural features of The Globe reveal the keen rivalry that existed between the two men. It would seem, however, that Burbage had a decided advantage: he had a gifted playwright, William Shakespeare, to create roles for him.

The Elizabethan theater was an open-air theater, approximately three stories high. Physically, the theater plant sometimes resembled a square (The Fortune), sometimes a circle (The Rose), and sometimes an octagon (The Globe). Inside, the auditorium revealed the influence of the audience–stage arrangement found in the performance of plays in the courtyard of an inn. At the opposite end of the entrance to the theater, a wide elevated permanent stage projected well into the ground-floor area. Trap doors in this outer stage made it possible for actors to seemingly emerge from nowhere. An inner stage was located to the rear of the outer stage and could be separated from it by a curtain. To the right and left of the inner stage there was a doorway. The chamber, with its overhanging balcony, was located on the second level above the inner stage and was separated from the balcony by a curtain. Windows flanked either side of the chamber. A third room topped the chamber and was used by the musicians. A "hut" over the musicians' room was used for the storage and operation of stage machinery. A flagpole extended from the "hut." On performance day, a flag was flown to notify the audience. The audience either sat in one of the three galleries that faced three sides of the stage, or stood on the paved ground around the stage. Thatching roofed the upper gallery and the stage. In 1613, the first Globe burned to the ground during a performance of *Henry VIII* when a cannon was fired and accidently ignited the thatched roof. In time, tile replaced thatching as a safety precaution.

Architectural design was of no consequence to the groundling as he observed with intensity the horror that flooded the stage in Act IV of *Macbeth.* Shakespeare describes the first scene as "A cavern. In the middle, a boiling cauldron." A clap of thunder starts the scene. The three Witches appear, probably from one of the many traps on the outer stage. As they move about the cauldron which has been placed on stage in view of the audience, and over another trap in preparation for its sinking later, the Witches begin their chant:

FIRST WITCH:
Thrice the brinded cat hath mewed.

SECOND WITCH:
Thrice and once the hedge-pig whined.

THIRD WITCH:
Harpier cries; " 'Tis time, 'tis time."

FIRST WITCH:
Round about the cauldron go;
In the poisoned entrails throw.
Toad, that under cold stone
Days and nights has thirty-one
Sweltered venom sleeping got,
Boil thou first i' the charmed pot.

ALL:
Double, double, toil and trouble;
Fire burn, and cauldron bubble.

As they continue their incantations and work themselves into a state of ecstatic frenzy that concludes with "Music and a song: 'Black Spirits,' " Macbeth enters. Although the playwright does not say from where he enters, perhaps a logical point might be the balcony above the inner stage, thereby giving the effect of his being in a high place looking down upon the Witches.

MACBETH:

How now, you secret, black, and midnight hags!
What is't you do?

Their reply causes Macbeth to ask for a demonstration of their powers. A clap of thunder is heard and the First Apparition, "An Armed Head," appears from one of the traps. A second clap of thunder is heard as the apparition descends. The Second Apparition, "A Bloody Child," appears from the trap. A third clap of thunder follows the descent of the Second Apparition. A Third Apparition, "A Child Crowned with a tree in his hand," appears. After it has warned:

THIRD APPARITION:

Macbeth shall never vanquished be until
Great Birnam Wood to high Dunsinane Hill
Shall come against him.

the apparition disappears whence it came.

Scoffing at what he has learned, but nevertheless anxious to know more, Macbeth challenges the Witches further:

MACBETH:

. . . Tell me, if your art
Can tell so much, shall Banquo's issue ever
Reign in this kingdom?

ALL:

Seek to know no more.

MACBETH:

I will be satisfied. Deny me this,
And an eternal curse fall on you! Let me know.
Why sinks this cauldron? And what noise is this?

A sound of hautboys (oboes) is heard. The cauldron sinks beneath the trap. The Witches stand about the trap as if to conjure up something within it.

ALL:

Show his eyes, and grieve his heart;
Come like shadows, so depart!

Slowly from the trap comes "A show of Eight Kings, the last with a glass in his hand; Banquo's Ghost following." The audience sees the ghastly face of each ghost as it arises from the trap and moves about the stage, finding its place where it may, then turns and faces Macbeth, who cries out:

MACBETH:
Thou art too like the spirit of Banquo; down!
Thy crown does sear mine eyeballs. And thy hair
Thou other gold-bound brow, is like the first.
A third is like the former. Filthy hags!
Why do you show me this? A fourth! Start, eyes!
What, will the line stretch out to the crack of doom?
Another yet! A seventh! I'll see no more.
And yet the eighth appears, who bears a glass
Which shows me many more; and some I see
That two-fold balls and treble sceptres carry.
Horrible sight! Now, I see, 'tis true;
For the blood-boltered Banquo smiles upon me,
And points at them for his.
What, is this so?

As he poses his question, the ghosts vanish—perhaps through other trap doors in the outer stage, or through the doors that flank the inner stage. The triumphant Witches assure him that it is so and begin a dance to cheer Macbeth. Suddenly, the music stops. The Witches disappear, perhaps through the trap from which the ghosts appeared. A stunned Macbeth is left alone on the balcony. Then Lennox breaks the silence with news that Macduff has fled to England. The scene ends with Macbeth's decision:

MACBETH:
. . . The Castle of Macduff I will surprise;
Seize upon Fife; give to the edge o' the sword
His wife, his babes, and all unfortunate souls
That trace him in his line . . .

The next scene begins immediately. The curtain separating the inner from the outer stage parts. A simply furnished room is seen. A chair and a stool is sufficient. The door to the inner stage opens and "Enter Lady Macduff, her Son, and Ross." What ensues is a charming scene that reveals their feelings toward Macduff, both as husband and father. In direct contrast to the preceding scene, this scene is a quiet one, sentimental, domestic; yet, overcast with doom, because the audience knows what the characters do not, that their remaining life span is but minutes long. A messenger enters and breaks the tranquility with a warning that "some danger does approach you nearly." He departs before Lady Macduff can comprehend his words, before she can devise a plan of escape. The murderers are upon her before she is able to realize that "I am in this earthly world." They stab Macduff's son. They are in pursuit of her as she runs crying, "Murder!" A quick curtain shuts off the inner stage.

The scene is now "England: before the King's palace." Malcolm and Macduff enter from one of the doorways that flank the inner stage. They move forward onto the outer stage to bemoan the fate of their country and the tyranny of Macbeth. When Macduff discovers the fate that has befallen his family, he joins Malcolm in his determination to overthrow Macbeth. They both depart to enlist the aid of the King of England.

A groundling viewing a performance of *Macbeth* accepted the many uses of the stage without question. He was not disturbed by the fact that the outer stage might represent a park near the palace, a banquet hall in the palace, or a country near Birnam Wood. It mattered not that the inner stage was one moment an anteroom in Macbeth's castle, or the next, a sitting room in Macduff's castle. The groundling cared little that the overhanging balcony might be utilized first as the passageway to Banquo's room, and then as a castle wall from which Macbeth spied the approaching Macduff. The groundling accepted each playing area for what the playwright represented it to be, as long as nothing interfered with the action of the play. His imagination supplied the details. He accepted the Elizabethan theater for what it was: a multiple arrangement of playing areas that facilitated the staging of a play with many scenes.

Theater architecture as developed by the Greeks and the Elizabethans virtually set the play in the lap of the audience. This arrangement created an intimate relationship between actor and audience in that the audience was drawn into the play, and the actor was stimulated to respond accordingly. This actor–audience arrangement has been revived in the construction of many theaters built in the last decade.

2. Proscenium Stage Theaters

Although the Romans devised the single architectural theater unit, the architect of the Renaissance is credited with the proscenium stage as we know it today. The stage evolved from a combination of interest in reproducing classical theatrical architecture and from a growing interest in perspective painting. The Renaissance architect was motivated to experiment in theater architecture and perspective scene design by the recovery of a ten-volume manuscript, *De Architectura,* written by Marcus Vitruvius Pollio, architect and engineer to Emperor Augustus. The description of the Greek scenic device, the *periaktoi,* which Pollio had recorded in this manuscript, inspired Sebastiano Serlio to create three perspective scene designs that he considered appropriate background for the performance of tragedy, comedy, and the satyr-play as well. Andrea Palladio, another Renaissance architect influenced by Vitruvius, incorporated features of the Roman theater in his plans for the Teatro Olimpico at Vincenza. Unfortunately, Palladio did not live to see his theater materialize. The theater was completed by Vincenso Scamozzi, another prominent Renaissance architect, who later designed a theater with a single large vista at Sabionetta. Today, nearly 400 years later, the Teatro Olimpico is an indoor theater with a semi-elliptical auditorium. The arrangement of its thirteen rows of orchestra seats resembles the steps in a Roman amphitheater. A colonnade rims the last row and supports a balcony. The *scaena frons,* as the Romans called the *skene* façade, reveals the interest in Roman theater architecture and perspective design. Vistas depicting street scenes extend beyond the large central door, the doors that flank it, and the doors on either side of the wide stage. The vistas are the work of Scamozzi. The *scaena frons* of the Teatro Olimpico is in Roman style, extremely ornamental. The theater seats about 3,000 spectators.

It is the Farnese Theater at Parma, however, whose stage represents the final transition in the evolution of the proscenium arch stage. Erected in 1608, the Farnese Theater is an indoor type with a ballroom arrangement of seats on either side and a stage at one end. The stage is elevated and curtained. There is no decorative façade with doors piercing it. There is only space for the actors to perform and space for scene designers to fill with scenic background. When the curtain parts, there is the illusion of seeing a frame with a picture behind it. In their attempt to combine the principles of perspective painting with the architecture of the classical theater, the Renaissance architects evolved a picture that was framed by the proscenium arch and could be seen in depth. The Farnese Theater at Parma has been termed our first modern theater because of this illusion. The theater still stands, although it was severely damaged during World War II.

Inigo Jones, architect and designer, became intrigued with the concept of perspective painting while traveling in Italy. Upon his return to England, he applied this concept to designs he executed for court productions. In collaboration with Ben Jonson, Inigo Jones created many masques for King James. A masque was a musical interlude that featured masked entertainers—frequently royal players. These elaborate masques afforded Jones the opportunity to apply his talent to producing the type of scene designs that were so popular on the Continent. One masque set a precedent for the use of a temporary proscenium arch: two statues held a globe behind which the performance occurred. Other masques contained revolving scenery, moving set pieces, and changes of scene. Inigo Jones also used a curtain to signal the beginning and end of a performance, much as the Romans had done. More important, he devised a system whereby it was possible to move painted flats in grooves, thus extending or limiting the depth of the stage when the flats were brought together. The groove system had been introduced at the Farnese Theater with which Jones was acquainted. Eventually, scenery for the masques became so elaborate that Ben Jonson broke with Jones because he felt that Jones's creative efforts overshadowed the theme of the masque. In 1643, one year after the theaters in London were officially closed by the Puritans, Inigo Jones was dismissed because of his loyalty to the crown. Although he died before the theaters were reopened and before a new theater architecture replaced the "wooden O" of Shakespeare's day, Inigo Jones's scenic innovations, and his knowledge of Renaissance theater architecture, influenced scenic production in, and the architecture of, the Restoration theater.

In England, the architecture of the open-air Elizabethan theater continued to dominate the architecture of new theaters well into the seventeenth century. Although there were indoor private theaters, notably The Blackfriars, they were few in number and were supported only by those who could afford the high price of admission, three pennies. However, after Charles II ascended the throne in 1660, new theaters were planned to house the two companies licensed by the monarch. The theater at Lincoln's Inn Fields was built in 1662 to house a company of actors headed by Sir William D'Avenant. The theater was commonly referred to as The Duke's Theater because it was attached to, and provided entertainment for, the Duke of York. Thomas Betterton, one of England's great actors, headed the roster of the company. Later, he directed Mrs. Anne Bracegirdle, a Restoration actress, in plays written by William Congreve. The other playhouse, the Theater Royal, was erected in 1663 to house a company of actors headed by Thomas Killigrew. Sometimes referred to as The Drury Lane because of its location, the Theater Royal provided entertainment for King Charles II, also known as "The Merry Monarch," and his court. Nell Gwyn, a favorite of the pleasure-seeking monarch, was a member of the acting company. The architecture of both theaters followed that of the Farnese Theater with modifications that reflected the architectural thinking of English designers. In later years, Sir Christopher Wren, the noted English architect, designed new theaters for both acting companies.

The typical Restoration theater was an indoor one that seated approximately 1,200 spectators. Created for the theatergoing sovereign and a fun-loving aristocratic society, the theater was elaborately decorated and intimate in its environment. Candlelight cast a soft glow over an audience whose everyday antics bore a resemblance to the behavior being portrayed on stage. Above the orchestra, or pit, two tiers of box seats and a gallery curved around the sides and rear of the auditorium, and extended from one end of the stage to the other. Viewed from the stage, the auditorium appeared to be horseshoe-shaped because of the curvature of the tiers and gallery. One box was reserved for the royal family when its members attended the theater; the gallery was occupied by the common citizens. The gallery was referred to as "paradise" because of its proximity to "heaven." A proscenium arch separated the auditorium from the stage, which was elevated. The proscenium opening was curtained. In front of the curtain, an acting area called the apron was all that remained of the stage that once extended into the ground floor or yard of the Elizabethan theater. Two doors at either end of the apron permitted the actors to enter or leave the acting area in front of the curtain. In effect, the architect had reduced the depth of the Elizabethan outer stage and had increased the width, depth, and height of the inner stage of the same theater.

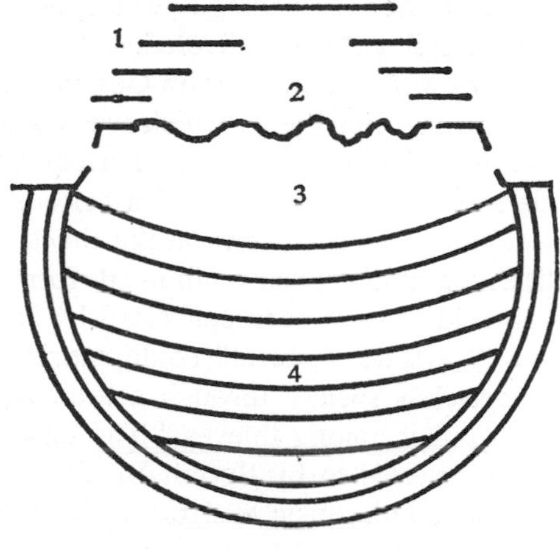

A RESTORATION THEATER

1. *Wing and Border Set* 2. *Stage* 3. *Apron* 4. *Auditorium*

The Restoration theater employed a popular method of the day to set the scene and effect a change. The method was introduced in the masques designed by Inigo Jones, and used what was termed a wing and border set. Pairs of flats, cloth-covered wooden frames painted in perspective, were aligned on either side of the stage. The flats extended from the wings onto the stage. Sufficient space was provided between each flat to permit a member of the company to enter or leave the stage. Each flat extended a few inches beyond the one in front of it so that the width of the set receded as the eye traveled to the backdrop, which closed off the scene. The flats were placed in grooves that sometimes ran the full width of the proscenium opening. Oil and soap were used to grease the grooves so that the flats could move freely and easily. Grooved shutters were also used to stretch across the stage so that a scene could be changed, although flats were sometimes drawn together for the same purpose. Suspended chandeliers containing candles illuminated the stage whether the scene was set in a forest, a street, or a tavern. Candles were mounted on the back of each flat to provide additional illumination. Apparently, fire inspection was not the order of the day! The stage was raked and frequently covered with a ground cloth. The curtain was raised after the prologue was spoken and did not descend until after the epilogue was delivered.

The Beggar's Opera was written by John Gay in 1728. It opened at the theater at Lincoln's Inn Fields which was owned and operated by John Rich, who had originated the harlequinade, a pantomime that featured entertainment both of a serious and comical nature. A political and social comment on the times, *The Beggar's Opera* also satirized a popular entertainment form of the day, opera. Its theme is said to have been suggested by Jonathan Swift, who sensed that a "Newgate Pastoral" could satirize the manners and morals of upper-class society through a dramatization of the old adage, "There's honor among thieves." The universality of the theme of this play is attested to by Bertolt Brecht's restatement in the *Three Penny Opera* with music by Kurt Weill; the motion picture version with Sammy Davis, Jr., and the recent presentation of the original version on television. *The Beggar's Opera* offers an opportunity to examine how such a play might be staged in a theater that employed staging and scenic techniques that began in the Restoration theater and that remained standard techniques until the advent of the box set, introduced in the mid-nineteenth century.

John Rich's theater in Lincoln's Inn Fields was jammed for the occasion—the sixty-second and final performance of *The Beggar's Opera.* The opening performance had been an instantaneous success. The enthusiastic reception continued unabated, and the play set a record number of performances in an age when the demand for new entertainment caused a quick turnover in productions. As the audience argued and chatted, it observed the candle-snuffer tend the chandeliers. The attention of the audience shifted to the stage as the Beggar entered from the proscenium door right and the Player entered from the proscenium door left. They met at center stage and came forward on the apron to address the theatergoer:

BEGGAR:

> If Poverty be a Title to Poetry, I am sure No-Body can dispute mine. I own myself of the Company of Beggars; and I make one at their Weekly Festivals at St. Giles. I have a small Yearly Salary for my Catches, and am welcome to a Dinner there whenever I please, which is more than most Poets can say.

PLAYER:

> As we live by the Muses, 'tis but Gratitude in us to encourage Poetical Merit where-ever we find it. The Muses, contrary to all other Ladies, pay no Distinction to Dress, and never Partially mistake the Pertness of Embroidery for Wit, nor the Modesty of Want for Dulness. Be the Author who he will, we push his Play as far as it will go. So (though you are in Want) I wish you Success heartily.

BEGGAR:

> This Piece I own was originally writ for the celebrating the Marriage of James Chanter and Moll Lay, two most excellent Ballad-Singers. I have introduc'd the Similes that are in all your celebrated Operas: The Swallow, the Moth, the Bee, the Ship, the Flower, etc. Besides, I have a Prison Scene which the Ladies always reckon charmingly pathetick. As to the Parts, I have observed such a nice Impartiality to our two Ladies, that it is impossible for either of them to take Offence. I hope I may be forgiven, that I have not made my Opera throughout unnatural, like those in vogue; for I have no recitative: Excepting this, as I have consented to have neither Prologue nor Epilogue, it must be allow'd an Opera in all its forms . . .

The Beggar's wit and language amuses the audience, for was there ever a Beggar who spoke so knowingly and eloquently?

Others, partial to the writings of English playwrights, applaud his caustic references to the conventions of opera. All wait for the overture to begin, for the play will start immediately thereafter. Finally, the curtain rises, revealing Peachum, sitting at a table with a large book of accounts. The side flats and those that back the shallow playing area are painted in perspective and identify the locale as Peachum's home. After a few moments of perusing his book, Peachum stands up and comes forward on the apron to sing the opening air:

PEACHUM:
(*singing*)
Through all the Employments of Life
  Each neighbor abuses his Brother;
Whore and Rogue they call Husband and Wife;
  All Professions be-rogue one another.
The Priest calls the Lawyer a Cheat,
  The Lawyer be-knaves the Divine;
And the Statesman, because he's so great,
  Thinks his Trade as honest as mine.

(*speaking*)
A Lawyer is an honest Employment, so is mine. Like me too he acts in a double Capacity, both against Rogues and for 'em; for 'tis but fitting that we should protect and encourage Cheats, since we live by them.

Act I consists of thirteen scenes that alternate dialogue with solos and duets sung by Peachum, Mrs. Peachum, Filch, Polly, and Macheath. Only part of the stage behind the proscenium is used to represent Peachum's house. There are never more than three people on stage at one time during Act I; it is not until Act II that the stage is filled with Macheath's Gang and Women of the Town. Thus, the locale of Act II, A Tavern Near Newgate, can be prepared behind the drawn flats that represent Peachum's home. Moreover there is the apron that extends beyond the proscenium, affording an excellent spot from which to project a song. It is the logical place for Polly and Macheath to exchange sentiments when Macheath enters at the conclusion of Act I:

MACHEATH:
Were I laid on Greenland's Coast
And in my Arms embrac'd my lass;
Warm amidst eternal Frost,
Too soon the Half Year's night would pass.

POLLY:
Were I sold on Indian Soil,
Soon as the burning Day was clos'd,
I could mock the sultry Toil,
When on my Charmer's Breast repos'd.

MACHEATH:
And I would love you all the Day,

POLLY:
Every Night would kiss and play,

MACHEATH:
If with me you'd fondly stray

POLLY:
Over the Hills and far away.

The audience applauds and perhaps the actors sing an encore. Then Polly warns Macheath of her father's dastardly plans and bids him to be on his way. Once again the pair sing a duet before each departs through the proscenium doors, one exiting left, and the other right.

Simultaneously, as they exit, the flats representing Peachum's home are withdrawn into the wings. We find ourselves at a tavern near Newgate. While Macheath's gang moves forward to take the stage, the tavern flats are inserted into the grooves and are pushed into place on stage. The table at which we found Peachum at the beginning of Act I remains to serve as a table in the tavern. Seated around the table are Jenny Twitcher, Crook-finger'd Jack, Wat Dreary, Robin of Bagshot, Nimming Ned, Henry Padington, Ben Budge, and Matt of the Mint, each philosophizing about the inequities of the law as it applies to thievery, each extolling the nobility that exists among the members of the fraternal order of cutthroats. Matt of the Mint summarizes their view:

> We retrench the Superfluities of Mankind. The World is avaritious, and I hate Avarice. A covetous fellow, like a Jackdaw, steals what he was never made to enjoy, for the sake of hiding it. These are the Robbers of Mankind, for Money was made for the Free-hearted and Generous, and where is the injury of taking from another, what he hath not the Heart to make use of?

The audience applauds Matt's sentiments, oblivious to the fact that this bit of moralizing is coming from the mouth of a highwayman! The gang then breaks into song as they get ready to depart for the day's pickings:

> Fill ev'ry Glass, for Wine inspires us,
> And fires us
> With Courage, Love, and Joy.
>
> Women and Wine should Life employ.
> Is there ought else on Earth desirous?

As the song reaches its conclusion, Macheath enters from the proscenium door left. He questions the gang members concerning their faith in his word and in his ability as a leader. When they have proved themselves to be "Men of Honor," he informs them that they are to continue without him until he has had an opportunity to adjust a situation that exists between Peachum and himself. The gang agrees to obey his instructions, promising to meet with Macheath later in the evening. Wearily, Macheath sits at the table. For a moment, the gang is seemingly without spirit. However, Matt the Mint rallies and raises his voice in song, and thus revives their interest in their duties:

> Let us take the Road.
> Hark! I hear the sound of Coaches!
> The hour of Attack approaches,
> To your Arms brave Boys, and load.
> See the Ball I hold!
> Let the Chymists toil like Asses,
> Our fire their fire surpasses,
> And turns all our Lead to Gold.

(The Gang, rang'd in the Front of the Stage, load their Pistols, and stick them under their Girdles; then go off singing the first Part in Chorus.)

Macheath, alone on stage, reflects upon his predicament. He rises and comes forward. He expresses his love of the fairer sex, and the difficulty he has in being true to Polly alone, in song:

If the Heart of a Man is deprest with Cares,
The Mist is dispell'd when a Woman appears;
Like the Notes of a Fiddle, she sweetly, sweetly
Raises the Spirits, and Charms our Ears.
  Roses and Lillies her Cheeks disclose,
  But her ripe Lips are more sweet than those.
    Press her,
    Caress her
    With Blisses,
    Her Kisses
Dissolve us in Pleasure, and soft Repose.

Suddenly, the stage is swarming with the Women of the Town: Mrs. Coaxer, Dolly Trull, Mrs. Vixen, Betty Doxy, Jenny Diver, Mrs. Slammekin, Suky Tawdry, and Molly Brazen. All have come to soothe the dejected Macheath in his hour of need. A musician is among them. Macheath orders ". . . the French Tune, that Mrs. Slammekin was so fond of." (The music begins and there is a "Dance a la ronde in the French Manner; near the End of it this Song and Chorus":)

Youth's the Season made for Joys,
  Love is then our Duty,
She alone who that employs,
  Well deserves her Beauty.
    Let's be gay,
    While we may,
  Beauty's a Flower, despised in decay.
Youth's the Season made for Joys.

Let us drink and sport today,
  Ours is not to-morrow.

Love with Youth flies swift away,
  Age is nought but Sorrow.
    Dance and sing,
    Time's on the Wing,
Life never knows the return of Spring.

CHORUS:
Let us drink, etc.

The audience taps its feet in rhythm to the music as it watches Macheath and the Women of the Town dance on stage. The atmosphere in the theater takes on a party-like air as the audience identifies with the fun-loving, charming Macheath. In fact, the spectators are so taken with the dance, they are completely unaware that the shutters have been drawn across the scene, thus closing out the tavern proper.

But wait! Something strange is happening on stage. What are Jenny and Suky doing? Macheath, take heed of foul play! Unfortunately, however, the high-spirited Macheath is enjoying the antics of the Women of the Town too much to notice that Jenny has removed one of his pistols and, Suky, the other. He does not see Peachum and the Constables hiding within each of the proscenium doors right and left. He does not know that now, at this very moment, as Jenny and Suky are caressing him, each is signaling to Peachum and the Constables to rush in and seize him. Suddenly, they are there! The party is over! Macheath is taken! Guarded by Peachum and the Constables, Macheath walks upstage after he sings his bitter farewell to the Ladies. The shutters, painted to represent Newgate, part to permit Macheath to enter. The illusion is that of the Constables escorting Macheath to the prison where the next scene takes place. The Women of the Town remain on stage to badger the two informers into giving them a share of the money they have received for turning in Macheath. They "Exeunt with great Ceremony" after Jenny promises a "Bowl of Punch or a Treat." The shutters then part and the audience sees Macheath handed over to Lockit, keeper of prisoners at Newgate, the setting for the remainder of Act II. What fate awaits Macheath, the rogue, highwayman, and lover? Will the virtuous Polly get her man? Or will the scheming Lucy triumph over virtue? Will Peachum's plan be undone? Will justice triumph in the end? All these problems are resolved in Act III!

This hypothetical staging of *The Beggar's Opera* illustrates how the stage was utilized in the Restoration theater and subsequent proscenium stages that duplicated its architectural design. The apron was the main acting area. Scenes that began behind the curtained area invariably moved forward where the illumination was better and where the actor could project his voice with better results. Here the actor was able to take the audience into his confidence, and here scenes with many characters were staged. The proscenium doors provided logical exits and entrances, although the constant movement from right to left, left to right, became repetitious and dull. The acting area behind the curtain was of secondary importance, for, while the wing-border-backdrop arrangement set the locale and gave the stage dimension, the action always moved forward to the apron. An exception occurred when the playwright wanted to suggest movement to another interior within the same building. Then the scene would be played against shutters that divided the acting area behind the curtain. At a given point in the scene, the shutters would separate and be withdrawn into the wings. The characters would then move upstage, thereby creating the illusion that they were passing from one interior to another. Playwrights wrote their plays to fit these features of the Restoration proscenium stage. The use of specific scenery resulted in the elimination of reference to locale in the dialogue; and the relative realism of the scene painted in perspective resulted in the writing of dialogue that was less poetic and more related to the environment of the plot. In short, the seed that produced the picture-frame, peep-hole proscenium stage we are familiar with today was sown in the sixteenth- and seventeenth-century theater.

3. ARENA STAGE THEATERS

The development of the arena stage theater stems from an interest in reviving the actor–play–audience relationship that was characteristic of the Greek and Elizabethan theaters, and an earlier rebellion against the realistic principles established by André Antoine in France, Constantin Stanislavski in Russia, and David

Belasco in the United States. The rebellion began in Europe early in the twentieth century. In Germany, Max Reinhardt remodeled the Circus Schumann to resemble the Greek theater for his production of Sophocles' *Oedipus Rex.* A semicircular stage jutted into the audience; huge black screens formed the palace in the background. Actors entered down the aisles of the orchestra. By bringing the actor–play–audience together in this manner, the audience became an integral part of the performance—as if it were part of the Chorus approaching the palace of Oedipus. In another production, *The Miracle,* the entire theater was converted into a cathedral. Processions of actors moved up and down the aisles. The audience was caught up in the religious fervor of the atmosphere and the performance. In France, Jacques Copeau opened the Théâtre du Vieux-Colombier in 1913. The proscenium arch, curtain, and footlight arrangement was abandoned. Instead, the auditorium and the stage appeared to be one architectural unit, an effect created by steps that led from the orchestra level to platform areas that became the stage proper. In Russia, Vsevolod Meyerhold and Nikolai Okhlopkov effected other changes. Meyerhold removed the stage curtain, lighted the auditorium and exposed the stage lights, and placed his actors on abstractly designed platforms against a background that consisted of the stage wall. Okhlopkov carried the action of the play into the center of the audience, frequently on ramps that led to runways around the audience. He advocated a flexible auditorium and stage, one that permitted the audience to move in any direction the action of the play might lead them. Although the rebellion did not lead to immediate changes in architecture, it did create an awareness that dissatisfaction with the existing proscenium stage theater was stimulating new concepts of theatrical production.

B. CUES FOR THEATERGOERS

1. THE THRUST STAGE THEATER

The Festival Theater, Stratford, Ontario, Canada, is an example of a thrust stage auditorium. Unlike the commercial theaters built earlier in the twentieth century, the Festival Theater has no proscenium opening and no curtain separating the actor from the audience. Instead, a structure resembling the façade of three adjoining houses fronting a five-sided courtyard replaces the conventional proscenium arch and proscenium opening. The pentagonal

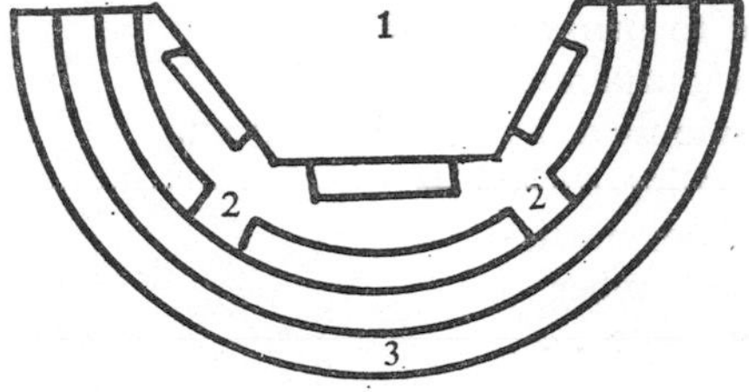

A THRUST THEATER

1. *Stage*
2. *Passageway*
3. *Auditorium*

courtyard with extensions on either side stretches into the orchestra seating area. The "courtyard" is the main acting area and consists of six levels that rise from the orchestra floor. From the upper main level, stairways connect with open doorways right and left. At center, a third doorway is seen beneath a balcony that is supported by five columns. Overhead, a fourth doorway pierces the structure and leads onto the balcony. Stairways extend from the balcony to levels that connect with the doorways right and left, and thence to the main acting area. Canopies project from above each doorway and across the entire structure, thus creating a house-like effect. A semicircular seating arrangement wraps the audience around three sides of the stage. Vaulted passageways extend from the stage into and beneath the orchestra, and are used by the actors for exits and entrances. The theater seats approximately 2,200 theatergoers. The stage was created by Tanya Moiseiwitsch in 1953, in collaboration with Sir Tyrone Guthrie. The Festival Theater cost approximately two million dollars to construct.

On such a stage the performance of the many-scened Elizabethan play is an effective one. For example, suppose the play is *Richard III* by Shakespeare. Imagine, then, that you are within a thrust stage theater. The house lights dim to darkness.

A spotlight circles the misshapen Richard standing center stage. He begins his famed soliloquy:

Now is the winter of our discontent
Made glorious summer by this sun of York;
And all the clouds that lowered upon our house
In the deep bosom of the ocean buried.
Now are our brows bound with victorious wreaths;
Our bruised arms hung up for monuments;
Our stern alarums changed to merry meetings,
Our dreadful marches to delightful measures.
Grim-visaged war hath smooth'd his wrinkled front,
And now,—instead of mounting barbed steeds
To fright the souls of fearful adversaries,
He capers nimbly in a lady's chamber
To the lascivious pleasing of a lute . . .

As Richard begins to bemoan his ugliness—"Cheated of feature by dissembling nature"—and to outline the "plots have I laid, inductions dangerous," the stage is illuminated to prepare for the entrance of Clarence, Brakenbury, and guards. The entrance is made from the right vaulted passageway and halted by Richard:

Brother, good day. What means this armed guard,
That waits upon your grace?

We learn that Clarence does not know why he has been taken prisoner, except that the King—

. . . says a wizard told him that by G,
His issue disinherited should be;
And, for my name of George begins with G,
It follows in his thought that I am he.

The "wizard," no doubt, is Richard, for his title, Duke of Gloucester, begins with "G." The moment ends with Clarence, Brakenbury, and guards exiting through the doorway left as if entering the Tower. As Richard bids Clarence a villainous farewell at the foot of the stairway:

Simple, plain Clarence!—I do love thee so
That I will shortly send thy soul to heaven,

Lord Hastings enters from the vaulted passageway, left. He strides up the levels leading to the main stage and crosses toward the doorway beneath the balcony. His exit is broken by Richard who inquires about his destination.

We learn that Hastings, who has recently been freed from prison, has come to call upon the ailing King who is "sickly, weak, and melancholy." Richard pretends concern and promises that he will join Hastings, who then exits beneath the balcony. Alone on the stage as he was when the scene started, Richard confides his thoughts:

> He cannot live, I hope; and must not die
> Till George be pack'd with posthorse up to Heaven.
> I'll in, to urge his hatred more to Clarence,
> With lies well steel'd with weighty arguments;
> And, if I fail not in my deep intent,
> Clarence hath not another day to live:
> Which done, God take King Edward to his mercy,
> And leave the world for me to bustle in!

As Richard follows Hastings into the palace, the stage lights dim and somber tolling bells can be heard.

Scene 2, London, another street, is about to begin. A slow procession emerges from the doorway right. It spreads itself across the stage, moving diagonally in the direction of the vaulted passageway left. It consists of the corpse of King Henry VI, Gentlemen with halberds to guard it, and Lady Anne, the mourner. When the corpse has reached center stage, Lady Anne, standing on the level before the right doorway, speaks:

> Set down, set down your honorable load,—
> If honor may be shrouded in a hearse,—
> Whilst I awhile obsequiously lament
> The untimely fall of virtuous Lancaster.—
> Poor key-cold figure of a holy King!
> Pale ashes of the House of Lancaster!
> Thou bloodless remnant of that royal blood!
> Be it lawful that I invocate thy ghost,
> To hear the lamentations of poor Anne,

Wife to thy Edward, to thy slaughtered son,
Stabb'd by the selfsame hand that made these Wounds!

As she continues her lament, Richard appears on the balcony and observes. When Anne countermands her order to continue the woeful journey, so that the bearers may rest, and that she may continue her lament, Richard speaks and makes his presence known. He moves down the stairway to join Anne. What ensues is a most unusual courting of a fair maiden by a villainous swain, as Richard fends off Anne's insults and defilements, and turns her emnity into amity. After he is assured that a friendlier and more receptive Anne will greet him when next they meet, Richard permits the procession to continue. When the procession has cleared the stage, Richard turns to the audience and confesses :

Was ever a woman in this humor woo'd?
Was ever a woman in this humor won?
I'll have her; but I will not keep her long.
What!—I, that kill'd her husband and his father,
To take her in her heart's extremest hate;
With curses in her mouth, tears in her eyes,
The bleeding witness of her hatred by;
Having God, her conscience, and these bars against me
And I no friends to back my suit withal,
But the plain Devil and dissembling looks,
And yet to win her,—all the world to nothing!

After Richard completes his confession of further villainy, he exits in the direction of the procession. Because Richard had earlier ordered the procession to attend him at Whitefriars, the audience accepts the direction of his exit as the way to the monastery. Meanwhile, on stage, serving-men with burning torches take their place at the various doorways in preparation for transforming the stage from the street locale of Scene 2 to Scene 3, The Palace. Queen Elizabeth enters, and we can tell by the attention paid her by Lord Rivers and Lord Grey that we are in the presence of royalty. The play continues.

A theatergoer attending a performance in a thrust stage theater can expect to find architectural features of the Restoration, Elizabethan, Roman, and Greek theaters. Like the Restoration theater, the thrust stage theater is an indoor-type. Like the Elizabethan theater, the thrust stage theater projects its performance area into the audience. Like the Roman theater, the thrust stage theater is a single unit. Like the Greek theater, the auditorium of the thrust stage theater is semicircular, surrounding the stage on three sides. However, unlike the Restoration theater, the thrust stage theater does not utilize scenery, although there may be some selective pieces to dress the stage. Unlike the Elizabethan, Roman, and Greek theaters, there is no permanent proscenium façade (the Festival Theater is an exception in this respect). In short, our thrust stage theaters combine the architectural features of many earlier theaters in the attempt to return the play and the actor to the audience.

The plays generally seen in a thrust stage theater predate those written during and after the Restoration period. The reasons for this are many. Pre-Restoration plays were written for stages such as the thrust stage. Playwrights incorporated the locale and time of the play into the dialogue. Universality of theme and greatness of language lend themselves to space. Worldliness and nobility of character expand and fill the space of the thrust stage. Rich fabrics and imaginatively designed costumes compensate for the lack of scenery. Pageantry needs space and is an integral part of almost all the pre-Restoration plays. The thrust stage is particularly useful in the flexible staging of the play with many scenes that do not depend upon the establishment of locale, but rather on fluidity of movement. Consequently, the theatergoer attending a performance in the thrust stage theater can expect to see a pre-Restoration classic on stage. When he does view a play that was written after the Restoration, the theatergoer will notice that the thrust stage has lost its beauty because of the need for furniture, a need for some scenic background, and a need for a degree of realism that seems wrong for a theater that is dependent upon an unencumbered performance area to be theatrically effective.

In recent years, the architectural principles of the thrust stage have been incorporated into designs for new theaters throughout the country. For example, The Tyrone Guthrie Theater, Minneapolis, Minnesota, has a thrust stage. The Vivian Beaumont Theater, Lincoln Center, New York City, has a thrust stage that can be removed for plays that require proscenium staging. A new thrust stage theater has been opened recently in Atlanta, Georgia, and one is planned for Houston, Texas. New generations of theatergoers in most sections of the United States will be able to experience the excitement of performance that was experienced by the Greek and Elizabethan theatergoer.

2. THE PROSCENIUM STAGE THEATER

The Lyceum Theater, New York City's second oldest proscenium stage theater, opened its doors to the public on November 2, 1903. Its initial attraction, *The Proud Prince,* starring E. H. Sothern and Cecelia Loftus, was not a new play and had, in fact, been transferred from the Herald Square Theater. However, it was an appropriate selection, because it marked the long and amicable

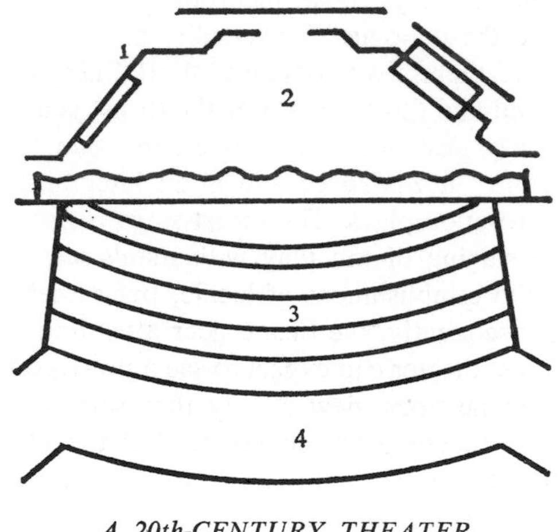

A 20th-CENTURY THEATER

1. *Set Outline* 2. *Stage* 3. *Orchestra* 4. *Balcony*

working relationship between E. H. Sothern and Daniel Frohman, the manager of the new theater. Their professional association had begun in 1886 when Mr. Sothern announced that he was available for any manager during the summer months. Although Sothern was under contract to tour in *One of Our Girls* later in the season, Frohman agreed to manage Sothern in the interim, and he produced a script that appealed to Sothern. When the script, *The Highest Bidder,* proved to be a successful attraction, the actor sought release from his touring contract. His manager, Helen Dauvray, agreed to dissolve the contract if Frohman would pay three thosuand dollars for the release. Frohman refused, but Sothern paid the money himself, confident that his future lay in association with Daniel Frohman. Thereafter, the manager successfully presented the actor in many productions at the old Lyceum Theater on Fourth Avenue. Now, on this occasion, Daniel Frohman repaid Sothern's confidence in his managerial ability by opening his new theater with *The Proud Prince.* Accordingly, the audience came not to see a new play, but a new theater, and to honor the friendship that existed between the two men.

The new theater delighted and impressed the fashionable audience that arrived in hansom cabs, and perhaps in an automobile or two! The gray limestone and marble façade that fronted on West 45th Street was highly decorative and in the style of the proscenium façade of the Roman theater. Adorned columns, carefully spaced and interspersed with three full-length windows, enhanced the height of the building. Above the graceful marquee, and before each window, statues of Poetry, Drama, and Music posed on balustrades to create the illusion that the windows were entrances to a balcony. Below the marquee, three vestibules opened into the main foyer where two marble staircases led to the first balcony. Two lunettes, one of Mrs. Sarah Siddons and the other of David Garrick, attracted the attention of the audience. Each had been painted by James Wall Finn, decorator consultant to the architects, and an artist whose talent could be seen in the home of Stanford White, the ceiling of the ballroom at Sherry's, and the furbishings of the St. Regis Hotel.

The auditorium won great praise because of its decorative color scheme, its improved sight-lines, and its comfortable seats. Autumnal colors—yellow, brown, and red—relaxed the spectator as he sat in the dark yellow, cordovan leather covered seats. The extended width of the auditorium, and the relatively shallow depth, brought the stage closer to the audience. The arrangement of longer but fewer rows improved the sight-lines; even the box seats offered an unobstructed view of the stage. Overhead, above the proscenium arch, Pallas Athena, Goddess of Wisdom, and her two muses, Music and Drama, looked down upon the audience that occupied the 995 seats proportionately allotted to the orchestra, balcony, and second balcony. No chandelier or cluster of lights hung from the ceiling. Rather, an arrangement of carefully concealed electric lights cast a rosy glow upon the audience, and especially so during a scene change. This innovation represented the epitome of concern for the comfort of the audience, because there were many theatergoers, especially women, who felt uncomfortable when the theater was darkened during a scene change.

While the audience waited for the performance to begin, other facts came to mind. For example, everyone knew that the offices of Daniel Frohman were located on the top floor of the 45th Street side (the building extended through to 46th Street), that it was furnished with Chippendale, that Frohman's library was a reproduction of David Belasco's, that portraits of great actors graced the walls, that a secret window concealed in the ceiling of the auditorium enabled Frohman to observe the activities on stage from his office, that he could, in fact, telephone backstage and give instructions to the stage manager! From newspaper articles covering the opening, the audience knew that the stage was 89 feet wide, the proscenium opening 35 feet, the proscenium height 30 feet, that the stage extended 77 feet to an opening on 46th Street, that the main stage contained elevators and that it dropped 30 feet so that an auxiliary stage could be fitted over it, thus facilitating the performance of a play with many scenes. Other data included the details of the ten-story annex that connected with the stage proper, and that faced 46th Street. The annex provided accommodations for 200 actors, a mechanical plant that housed a carpenter shop capable of employing 25 carpenters, a studio paint shop large enough to paint four drops simultaneously, and a costume room that could utilize the services of 50 seamtresses, cutters, and costume makers. The audience marveled at the architectural feat of Messrs. Hart and Tallant, for they had managed to incorporate, into one single unit, all the necessities for producing a play.

The theatergoer attending a performance in a proscenium stage theater can expect to see a representation of life framed by the proscenium arch. Fifty-two years after it opened its doors, the Lyceum Theater premiered *A Hatful of Rain* by Michael V. Gazzo. The extent of the realistic stage picture seen by the theatergoer is apparent in the set description written by the playwright:

> A tenement apartment on New York's Lower East Side. To our left we see a small kitchen, and to our right a combination living room-bedroom. There are two doors in the kitchen—one leading to the hallway, left, and the other, in the rear wall, leading to a bedroom. Looking through the living-room windows, we see the worn brick of the building next door and—beyond the fire-escape railing, which is just outside—distant window lights that outline a suspension bridge, marred only by the occasional suggestion of rooftops with jutting black chimneys.
>
> It is only because of what is seen from these windows that we can place the apartment in the Lower East Side. Within the apartment itself there is everywhere the suggestion of a ceaseless effort to transform the bedraggled rooms into rooms of comfort and taste. All the woodwork—formerly coated with twenty coats of paint—has been scraped, cleaned, stained, and varnished. The windows have been refurbished; cases have been built beneath them, and they are spotlessly clean, as are the shades and draw curtains. Though the sink-and-tub combination is outdated in design, plywood has been used to cover up the intricacies of old-fashioned piping. Between the kitchen and bedroom, a partition of shelving has been built, and on each shelf are flowerpots, some of glass, others of copper, containing green plants. There is a sense of life.
>
> In the kitchen, we see a cupboard, its paint removed, a table and four chairs. The chairs are old—picked up from one of the antique shops along Third Avenue. The table is solid and of heavy wood, something that might have been picked up from a farmer along a Jersey road.
>
> In the living room, we see an armchair in a corner and a bed against the side wall. There is an unusual and startling use of color in the room; the bedspread is particularly lively, and all the objects in the room are colorful. Homemade bookcases made of wood planks and bricks line another wall.
>
> The hallway, off the kitchen, is clearly in contrast to the apart-

ment. Its walls are a drab brown and, off it we see a suggestion of a stairway, leading to the roof, the railing of painted iron. Overhead there is a dim light, covered with a dusty and cracked skylight.

When the curtain rises, we hear the sound of rain. In the kitchen area, at the table, are Johnny and his Father. The meal is almost at an end.*

A Hatful of Rain is one of the few successful attempts to portray the problem of narcotics addiction on stage. As played by Shelley Winters, Ben Gazzara, Anthony Franciosa, and Frank Silvera, the characters awaken the audience to the plight of the hero whose present and future are threatened by his forty-dollar-a-day habit. The set designed by Mordecai Gorelik skillfully showed the cramped kitchen-living room-bedroom apartment, the pathetic attempts by the wife to make the apartment more cheerful, and the elements of melodrama that underscore the play.

Architecturally, the proscenium stage theater has changed little since its inception during the Restoration period. The proscenium arch still separates the auditorium from the stage and the theatergoer from the actor. Any changes that have occurred have been directed toward auditorium decor, audience comfort, scene design, and play production. Theaters which are of the same period as the Lyceum are ornate, whereas new proscenium stage theaters are contemporary in decor. The number of balconies has been reduced to one, and the box seat is no more. Sight-lines have been improved by widening the auditorium and bowing the balcony. Comfortable seats have replaced benches; electricity has replaced gas to brighten the auditorium and light the performance. Air-conditioning, a fairly recent innovation, now prolongs the run of a play through the summer season. On stage, scene design has moved from the wing-and-border arrangement to the box set with its variations. Backstage, electronic devices and modern stage equipment make possible the staging of the most complicated play or musical comedy. Nevertheless, the aesthetic principle of the proscenium stage theater still applies: a representation of life framed

* From *A Hatful of Rain,* by Michael V. Gazzo. Copyright © 1956 by Michael V. Gazzo. Reprinted by permission of Random House, Inc.

by the proscenium arch that separates the theatergoer from the actor.

3. THE ARENA STAGE THEATER

The Penthouse Theater, Seattle, Washington, is an example of the arena stage theater. Located on the campus of the University of Washington, the theater is a one-story building, both elliptical and rectangular in architectural design. The auditorium is located within a central unit. A wide circular foyer surrounds the auditorium and separates it from rectangular wings that contain dressing rooms, storage and furniture rooms, and a kitchen. One hundred seventy-two theatergoers sit in three rows of seats that surround the elliptically shaped sunken stage. The raised seating area is broken into four sections by ramps that are utilized by the actors for exits and entrances. The ramps lead to rooms where the actors await their cues. A dome-shaped ceiling is punctured by forty holes from which the stage is illuminated; a glass-encased lighting control booth is located in one wall of the auditorium so that cues can be synchronized with the performance on stage. The

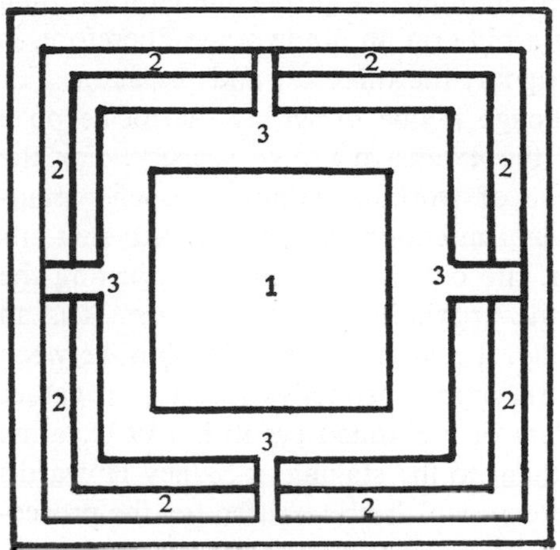

AN ARENA THEATER

1. *Stage*
2. *Auditorium*
3. *Passageways*

theater was the first of its kind to be built in the United States for the express purpose of staging plays in-the-round. The Penthouse Theater has been in operation since 1940, and its name stems from the use of a penthouse in a local hotel for experiments in arena staging conducted by the late Professor Glenn Hughes.

The arena theater is a space stage theater. There is no architectural façade, such as we find in the Greek and Elizabethan theaters, to help set the scene, or against which the play can be performed. There is no proscenium arch, such as we find in the Restoration and twentieth-century theaters, to separate the audience from the actor or to give illusion to the stage picture. There is no curtain. There are no footlights. There is only flat horizontal space to accommodate plays which were written for proscenium rather than for arena staging. Mounting a play on an arena stage, therefore, is a challenge to the scene designer, the director, and the actor. For the scene designer, the challenge is one of setting the locale on a stage that is not meant for the extensive use of scenery. For the director, the challenge is one of working within an open rectangular area, and one of focusing attention for an audience that sits on four sides. For the actor, the challenge is one of adjusting the size of his performance to the proximity of the audience. It is an exciting theater, consequently, because the relationship between stage and audience exemplifies man's instinctive reaction to gather around an unexpected incident or a planned event. Let us examine these challenges and apply them to the staging of Sidney Howard's play *The Late Christopher Bean,* which was written for the proscenium arch stage.

This three-act play takes place in the office–dining room of Dr. Haggett, a Yankee country doctor. The furniture includes an old-fashioned roll-top desk, a swivel chair for the Doctor, a chair for patients, a centrally placed armchair, and a dining-room table with four chairs. A door up center serves as the main entrance from outside. A stairway leads off the foyer to the upper part of the house, and a doorway leads to the kitchen off left. Part of the humor and suspense in the play is derived from not always knowing who is about to arrive, and from the family spying on Abby, who spends most of her time in the kitchen when she is not on stage. When the play begins, there is evidence that the office–living–dining room has been freshly painted and papered. The home–work environment is important to the play, because it represents part of the conflict between Doctor and Mrs. Haggett: The Doctor is happy to be where he is, and Mrs. Haggett would be happier elsewhere—up Boston way! The meager, unstylish furnishings reveal the time of the play, the Great Depression, and the frugality of the Yankee character.

In adapting the play to the arena stage, the scene designer concentrates on factors other than scenery to establish the locale, and the character and financial status of the Haggett family. The stage floor offers a starting point. An appropriate covering, a tattered, well-worn rug, establishes the scene. Furniture of the period, low in height and light in bulk, serves to set the time. The placement of the furniture in corners of the stage, or in front of an exit that is not being used by the actors (only three exits need to be used for the play; one leading to the kitchen, one to other parts of the house, and one to the outside), ensures an unobstructed view for the audience. Carefully selected props, realistic in size and limited in number, dress the set, thus establishing the locale without cluttering the scene. A chandelier representative of the period gives a final sense of office–living quarters. In short, the scene designer working on the arena stage utilizes arrangement and selectivity to achieve artistic effect and dimension.

The director's problem is to stage the play so that it can be adequately seen from all sides. For example, the scene between Abby and Tallant must be staged to permit the entire audience to sense the expression on the faces of both actors despite the fact that, at any given moment, one quarter of the audience sees only the back of the actor. A scene between more than two people offers an even greater problem in staging, for some obstruction by one of the actors is inevitable and difficult to overcome. The handling of large groups is particularly hard, because the playing space is reduced as additional characters appear on the scene. Although there are a number of two-character scenes in *The Late Christopher* Bean, there are also times when groups fill the stage. A good example is the final scene when the entire cast of nine participates in an auction sequence set around two trunks that have been brought on stage in preparation for Abby's departure. The director must evince a degree of ingenuity in staging the play in-the-round, because he must maintain the aesthetic effect of a space stage without cluttering it and, in addition, he must move his actors about the stage so that each side of the audience sees the play from the same visual perspective.

The actor, too, must make a professional adjustment when he appears on the arena stage. Proximity to the audience enables him to see their reactions to his performance and to the play. Therefore, although audience communication is more direct and intimate, and this may, in turn, spur him to greater performance, there is always the possibility that negative response may inhibit his performance. Consequently, the actor must discipline himself to look through the sea of faces and be impervious to the negative. This close relationship between the actor and the audience gives credence to the life-like quality of the character. The reduction of aesthetic distance—the distance that makes it possible for the audience to reflect upon the character for what he is—raises the problem of performance size. To what degree can the actors play the farcical moments in *The Late Christopher Bean* without destroying the credibility of the situation? To what extent can Dr. Haggett's comical greediness be exaggerated without affecting the empathy that the audience feels for him? To what degree can the actor modify his performance to meet the problem of audience proximity, and at the same time adequately project the character he is portraying? Arena acting, therefore, is an exercise in control and projection—control in the sense of maintaining a life-size characterization, and projection in the sense of supplying the character with the energy and vitality that make him larger than life.

Although arena stage theaters are comparatively few in number, the quality of production and performance on some of them has earned acclaim for this very theatrical form of stage architecture. In New York City, the Circle-in-the-Square, under the management of Theodore Mann, has been responsible for exceptional performances of *Summer and Smoke* by Tennessee Williams, *Our Town* by Thornton Wilder, *The Iceman Cometh* by Eugene O'Neill, and *The Balcony* by Jean Genêt. As a result of the accolades bestowed upon productions at the Alley Theater in Houston, Texas, under the aegis of Miss Nina Vance, the founder and permanent director, the theater has been the recipient of a Ford Foundation grant for the construction of both an arena and thrust stage theater. In Washington, D.C., Miss Zelda Fichlander has achieved the ultimate in both community support and theater plant: a successful box office has made possible the building of a permanent arena stage theater. It was the vision and steadfast purpose of the late Margo Jones, however, that provided the impetus to break with proscenium stage techniques and to return the play to the audience. Her enthusiasm for the form, her skill as a director, and her introduction of three major plays, *Summer and Smoke* by Tennessee Williams, *Inherit the Wind* by Jerome Lawrence and Robert E. Lee, and *The Dark at the Top of the Stairs* by William Inge, drew the attention of the professionals to the arena stage theater. Miss Jones details her experiences with her arena theater in Dallas, Texas, in her book *Theater-in-the-Round*.

C. THEATER SPOTLIGHTS

I. *Theater Terminology:* Define the following:

cyclorama	tormentors	abstract set
backdrop	wings	constructivism
teasers	skeleton setting	flies

II. *Theater Who's Who:* Identify the following:

Adolphe Appia	Jo Mielziner
Edward Gordon Craig	Jean Rosenthal
Steele MacKaye	Donald Oenslager
Robert Edmond Jones	The Théâtre Libre
Lee Simonson	Madam Eliza Vestris

III. *Theater Investigation:* Discuss the following:

1. Explain the difference in viewing a play in a thrust stage theater, a proscenium stage theater, and an arena stage theater.

2. Indicate the reasons why scenery may or may not affect the enjoyment of a play. Cite specific play examples to defend your point of view.
3. Discuss how the *orkestra* and the *skene* in the Greek theater might be used for the staging of Act III of *Our Town* by Thornton Wilder.
4. Read *The Girl of the Golden West* by David Belasco. Note the set descriptions carefully. What would be the obstacles to producing this play on a thrust stage?
5. State the reasons why *The Rivalry* by Norman Corwin lends itself to mounting on an arena stage.

IV. *Theater Projects:* Prepare the following:

1. Prepare a short paper comparing the architecture and production techniques of the Chinese and Japanese theaters with those of the Greek and Elizabethan theaters.
2. Select a scene from Sophocles' *Antigone,* one in which Antigone exchanges dialogue with the chorus. Stage the scene as it would be performed on a thrust stage, a proscenium stage, or an arena stage.
3. Construct a model set for one of the following:
   a. Performance of *The Creation of Man,* York Cardmaker's Play, on a medieval pageant wagon.
   b. Performance of *Master Pierre Patelin* on a platform stage in the court of an inn.
   c. Performance of *Street Scene* on a proscenium stage.
   d. Performance of *Home of the Brave* on an arena stage.

V. *Theater Bibliography:* Read the following:

Boyle, Walden P. *Central and Flexible Staging.* Berkeley and Los Angeles: University of California Press, 1956.

Brown, Martin E. *Religious Drama.* New York: Meridian Books, 1958.

Ganong, Joan. *Backstage at Stratford.* Toronto, Canada: Longmans Canada, Ltd., 1962.

Gorelik, Mordecai. *New Theaters for Old.* New York: Samuel French, 1947.

Guthrie, Tyrone. *A New Theater.* New York: McGraw-Hill Book Company, 1964.

Hughes, Glenn. *The Penthouse Theater*. Seattle, Washington: University of Washington Press, 1958.

Jones, Margo. *Theater-in-the-Round*. New York: Rinehart and Co., Inc., 1951.

III

Theater on Stage: The Player

The play is done; the curtain drops,
Slow falling, to the prompter's bell;
A moment yet the actor stops,
And looks around, to say farewell.
It is an irksome word and task;
And when he's laughed and said his say,
He shows, as he removes the mask,
A face that's anything but gay.

WILLIAM MAKEPEACE THACKERAY, *Doctor Birch and His Young Friends; Epilogue,* Stanza 1.

A. SETTING THE SCENE: THE ACTOR YESTERDAY

The player has performed many roles in the fall and rise of the acting profession. Professionally, the player has been a priest, a slave, a rogue, a vagabond, and an honored citizen. Artistically, he has been a rank amateur, a conscientious craftsman, and an established star. Socially, the player has been a member of the nobility, a king's favorite, and a disreputable outcast. Financially, he has been a government employee, an itinerant player, a pauper, and a millionaire—as well as an investor, a gambler, and a loser. Patriotically, the player has been a soldier, a legislator, an ambassador—

and a conspirator. In the long, turbulent history of his profession, the player has been all of these because his public has been slow to accept the acting profession as an honorable one, inconsistent in its support of the theater, and limited in numbers who have been exposed to the joys of theatergoing.

1. The Greek Actor: Priest and Honored Citizen

The concept and craft of the actor was born when Thespis of Icaria stepped forth from the chorus and took upon himself the impersonation of the various deities in the dithyramb he performed. Thus, the choric quality of the dithyramb was broken, and the play form was foreshadowed in the exchange of dialogue with the chorus leader. No one knows exactly when Thespis innovated the change, but this was the nature of the performance he presented when he came to Athens in the middle of the sixth century B.C. The reaction of the government was not entirely favorable. Solon, Archon of Athens, viewed the performance with misgivings because he believed that Thespis's impersonation was a form of deceit that might well encourage others to emulate the art of *hypokrisis* and thus dupe the populace. It was not until 534 B.C., when Pisistratus invited him to help inaugurate the City Dionysia Festival with a performance by his troupe, that Thespis received a measure of recognition. On that occasion, Thespis was acknowledged victor of a contest for the best presentation of a tragedy rather than for an acting performance. It would be another eighty-five years before an actor would receive the same consideration and honor as that accorded the playwright.

A second step forward in the evolution of the acting profession occurred in 495 B.C. when Aeschylus introduced a second player on stage. Sophocles further attested to the importance of the skill and craft of the actor when he assigned his roles to another player because his own voice lacked vocal power; and he introduced a third player when his contribution to the play form necessitated the presence of three characters on stage simultaneously. Euripides focused attention upon the performer when he decreased the importance of the chorus and when he endowed his characters with recognizable human traits. The development of comedy also contributed to the emerging importance of the actor when a fourth, and frequently a fifth, actor was brought on stage to join the three principal actors in a scene.

The government's strict supervision of the City Dionysia and Lenaea Festivals also contributed to the growing popularity of the actor and his profession. Initially, the playwright cast his plays, generally assigning all roles to himself. This feat of performance was made possible by the introduction of the mask by Thespis, and by the structure of the play, which permitted quick changes offstage. Then, when Aeschylus introduced a second actor, the government became involved with the hiring and reimbursing of actors, because it agreed to underwrite the salary of the second actor (all other expenses were assumed by the *choregus,* the forerunner of our present-day producer, a wealthy citizen who deemed it an honor and a privilege to participate in the festival by providing financial assistance). This agreement apparently set the precedent for paying the salaries of the three principal actors, and for eventually assigning, by lot, one of the three competing actors to each of the competing playwrights. When it became obvious that the selection of a winning play might be affected by the skill and popularity of the leading player, the government decreed that each playwright was to have the benefit of each of the competing players so that the work of each playwright could be judged fairly. The popularity of the actor at this time, about the middle of the fourth century B.C., was probably the result of government initiation and sponsorship of an acting contest between tragic actors in 449 B.C., and one between comic actors seven years later.

Athenian playgoers expected the player to exhibit skill in the use of his voice while sustaining a long role that kept him on stage constantly. The player was expected, by the very nature of the playwriting and the age in which he lived, to demonstrate vocally that he could speak, chant, and sing the role written by the playwright. Consequently, he spent many hours practicing the oral techniques that the Greeks associated with the good speaker; namely, faultless diction, expert timing, emphasis of word and phrase, effective pausing, and appropriate inflection. Frequently, he refrained from excessive eating, drinking, and sexual relations in the belief that such earthly pleasures would have an adverse effect upon his voice. The actor used an inordinate amount of energy to project his voice to 17,000 or more spectators, although the acoustics were very good. It was imperative that he be heard clearly and that his voice reveal the nuance of meaning in his delivery. Let him fail, and he was hissed and booed from the stage!

Despite the fact that his costume was an obstacle to graceful movement, the audience was additionally critical of how the actor moved on stage. On his head and over his face, each of the principal players wore the mask with its protruding *onkos* to give him height and add to his stature. Under the long flowing *chiton,* the actor's breast and stomach were padded to increase his size. On his feet, he wore the platformed *cothurnus* which, with the *onkos,* gave him additional height. Fortunately, the action was relatively simple and the dancing highly stylized. Yet, let him fall, or even stumble, and he chanced the fate of an Aeschines, who was denigrated by the audience for one such clumsy moment, and who was never permitted to forget the incident by Demosthenes.

Athenian theatergoers did not question the convention of three actors playing the principal speaking parts. The chances are the audience accepted the convention as a matter of play structure and, later, as a demonstration of skill on the part of the actor. The audience expected that the first actor, the protagonist, would be assigned the leading role and that all other roles would be divided between the second actor, the deuteragonist, and the third actor, the tritagonist. If there had been such an item as a printed program for the theatergoer to peruse, the assignment of roles in Sophocles' play *Oedipus Rex* might have read as in the table on page 58.

In its 1967 season, the Minnesota Theater Company revived *The Oresteia* by Aeschylus. Using a free adaptation titled *The House of Atreus* by John Lewin, the Minnesota Theater Company succeeded in providing today's theatergoer with an excellent example of how the play might have been performed for a Greek audience. All the leading female roles were portrayed by male actors: Mr. Douglas Campbell, for example, played Clytemnestra and the Goddess Athena; Mr. Robert Gammel played Cassandra and Electra; and Mr. Philip Kerr played a Priestess of Apollo. The actors wore masks that covered all the head and face except the

Dramatis Personae	EPISODES 1	2	3	4	5	6	7
Oedipus Rex	P	P	P	P	P	P	P
Priest	D						
Creon	T		T				T
Tiresias		D					
Jocasta			D	D	D		
Messenger						T	
Herdsman						D	
Second Messenger							D
Antigone and Ismene							M*

KEY: P = Protagonist, the first actor
D = Deuteragonist, the second actor
T = Tritagonist, the third actor
* = Non-speaking parts identified as mutes and played by other members of the cast

mouth. The actor's height was increased by the *cothurnus* he wore on his feet. Each actor was well-padded, so that the image he presented to the audience was larger than life. A chorus sang and spoke the lines in unison. Sir Tyrone Guthrie's direction emphasized the ritualistic movement associated with the performance of Greek tragedy. The total effect was stunning, forcing the theatergoer to become involved and mesmerized by the horrifying events that unfolded before him.

Douglas Campbell was superb in the roles of Clytemnestra and Athena. His initial entrance was awe-inspiring because Mr. Campbell firmly established his credibility as Clytemnestra without resorting to feminine gestures and movements. Rather, Mr. Campbell's movements and gestures were those we associate with royalty. Mr. Campbell's Clytemnestra strode upon the stage gracefully, the actor holding Clymestra's flowing gown before him so that he could move with ease. Clymnestra's head was held high as Mr. Campbell within the mask peered majestically above the chorus members who had gathered in front of Agamemnon's palace. Gestures were few and simple; yet sweeping, dignified, and definitive in purpose and meaning. The scene completed, Mr. Campbell as Clytemnestra turned and literally floated into the palace. Not a word was spoken because Clytemnestra does not speak in this scene. Mr. Campbell's voice had not been heard—but that was of no consequence, so compelling had been his initial appearance as Clytemnestra.

Mr. Campbell made no attempt to reproduce a feminine voice for the roles of Clytemnestra and the goddess Athena. Rather, Mr. Campbell applied his vocal skills and his tenor-like voice to cry out the anguish of Clytemnestra and to sing the poetic dialogue written by the playwright. As Athena, Mr. Campbell was vocally wise, witty, and coldly logical as he sustained the long final scene encased in the statue of the seated Athena. With only his hands free for gestures and his head free for limited movements, Mr. Campbell was as much the Goddess as he was the Queen of the House of Atreus. One quickly sensed in Mr. Campbell's creative effort the talent and skills needed to perform the mighty heroes and heroines as conceived by the early Greek playwrights.

In view of the demands made upon the skill of the tragic actor in performing a role, it is reasonable to assume that the Athenian playgoer demanded the same high standard of performance from the comic protagonist. In addition to demonstrating his skill in enacting a long role, or in a variety of roles that required him to sing, dance, and debate, the comic actor was expected to display his skill in the quick delivery of lines, the adept telling of jokes, and the participation in humorous horseplay with which the action of the play generally abounded. To meet the physical requirements of the part, the comic actor was well-padded, fore and aft, thus giving his figure a squat, horizontal appearance. An almost bubble-shaped mask that identified his sex, age, profession or type, covered his head and his face. Over his flesh-colored tights, the comic actor wore an abbreviated *chiton* that emphasized the attached symbol of Dionysus, a red leather phallus. Quick of tongue, nimble on foot, ever in motion, the comic actor used considerable energy in meeting the demands of a fast-paced prformance.

The comic protagonist was generally accompanied through the merry proceedings by the deuteragonist, a "second banana" in this instance, and by the tritagonist, likewise a comedian who played the minor comic parts. In time, a fourth, and sometimes a fifth, comic actor appeared in a scene to multiply the laughter and to complicate the humorous situation. How these four actors may have been assigned parts in *The Frogs* by Aristophanes is illustrated in the following chart:

Dramatis Personae	EPISODES 1	2	3	4	5	6	7	8	9	10	11	12	13
The God Dionysus	P	P	P	P	P	P	P	P	P		P	P	P
Xanthias	D	D	D		D	D	D	D	D	D			
Aeschylus											D	D	D
Euripides											T	T	T
Heracles	T												
Corpse		A*											
Charon			T	T									
Aeacus						T			T	T			
Maidservant							A*						
Landlady								T					
Planthane								A*					
Pluto													A*

KEY: P = Protagonist, the first actor
D = Deuteragonist, the second actor
T = Tritagonist, the third actor
* = Minor parts performed by a fourth actor

The Greek actor was deemed an honored citizen in Greek society. He was considered a priest of Dionysus because of his early association with the rites of commemorating and honoring the birth and death of the god of fertility. The great philosophers of the times speculated about the source of the talents of the actor. Socrates thought his ability sprang from a natural talent for speaking and performing. Plato opined that a divine spark rested within the actor. Aristotle tended to agree with Socrates, and added that the natural gifts of the actor were enhanced by study and practice. Respect and esteem for Aeschylus and Sophocles probably had a positive effect on the attitude of the populace toward the acting profession. Each playwright had been an actor as well. Each had contributed to the importance of the actor in the course of developing the play form. Admiration for the skill of the performer and the nature of his performance also enhanced his reputation. Everyday behavior was complimented as being similar to that of the performance of a particular actor. Greek citizens were impressed with the fact that players associated with heads of state and fulfilled assignments as messengers and ambassadors. Two popular tragic actors of the day, Aristodemus and Neoptolemus, were said to have been involved with negotiations with Phillip of Macedonia to end the war. However, the decree issued by the Amphictyonic Council perhaps best exemplifies the respect and esteem conferred upon the actor at the close of the third century:

> It has been resolved by the Amphictyonic Council that security of person and property, and exemption from arrest during peace and war, be ensured to the artists of Dionysus at Athens; . . . that they enjoy that exemption from military service, and that personal security which have been previously been granted to them by the whole Greek nation; that the artists of Dionysus be exempt from military service, in order that they may hold the appointed celebrations in honor of the gods at the proper seasons, and be released from other business, and consecrated to the service of the gods; that it be unlawful to arrest or seize an artist of Dionysus in time of war or peace; that if an artist be arrested in violation of these conditions, the person who arrests him, and the city in which the violation of the law occurs, be brought before the Amphictyonic Council; that the immunity from service and personal security which are granted by the Amphictyonic Council to the artists of Dionysus at Athens be perpetual; that the secretaries cause a copy of this decree to be engraved on a stone pillar and erected in the temple, and another sealed copy of the same be sent to Athens, in order to show the Athenians that the Amphictyonic Council are deeply concerned in the observance of religious duties at Athens, and are ready to accede to the requests of the artists of Dionysus,

and to ratify their present privileges, and confer such other benefits upon them as may be possible.*

"The Craftsmen or Artists of Dionysus," a guild consisting of actors, dancers, musicians, and chorus trainers, was organized in 277 B.C. to meet the demands for performers throughout the Greek world, and to protect the rights of performers as they traveled from one city-state to another. No longer was the actor referred to as a *hypokrites,* an appellation that stemmed from the deceit inherent in acting noted by Solon. Now the public recognized the actor as an artist, a term preferred by the actor. The recognition, however, was short-lived, because within another century, when the grand manner of tragic acting lost favor with the public, and when the Romans conquered Greece, the reputation of the actor and his profession took a mightly plunge—almost comparable to the fall of Greece itself. Nearly 2,000 years were to pass before the actor and his profession would again be accorded the position once enjoyed in Greek civilization.

2. The Roman Actor: A Little Less Than Slave

In 146 B.C., Rome, triumphant in her domination of the Mediterranean, conquered a war-weary and impoverished Greece. The ego of the Greek actor, captive or otherwise, was undoubtedly shattered by the event, for, as he was to discover, the status of the actor in Roman society was in stark contrast to the status of the actor in Greek society. Unlike the Greek theater which had its roots in a religion, the Roman theater had its roots in the personal pleasure of participating in simple native entertainments, and in the pleasure of being entertained. Performers and performances were added attractions that gave a religious festival a holiday aura, and detracted from the religious purpose of the occasion. Theater, therefore, was viewed as a form of organized entertainment, not as an institution that sprang from religious worship of a deity.

---

* From Arthur E. Haigh, *The Attic Theater* (Oxford, England: Clarendon Press, 1907). Reprinted by permission of the publisher.

Frequently, the entertainment consisted of a performance by a company of slave actors headed by a freedman who did not hesitate to harass, flog, and vilify the actor if his performance displeased the audience, or if his performance in any way caused the company to be adversely criticized. As a performer, the actor was considered to be in the same category as the juggler, the singer, the dancer, and the musician—nothing more than a novelty, a momentary diversion, an entertainer. His membership in companies that specialized in the popular mimes, a low entertainment that featured obscene language, lewd subject matter, and nude female performers, placed him at the bottom rung of the social ladder in Rome. His skill in performing the lascivious, amorous, and sensuous pantomimes of the day identified his character with the lusty nature of man, rather than with the image of the ideal Roman—hearty, vigorous, stalwart, and virile. His selection of a profession that provided a sporadic livelihood and that attracted persons of ill-repute branded him a ne'er-do-well. Additionally, despite the fact that the government had relaxed its ban against the construction of permanent theater plants, and despite the fact that the government saw the wisdom of employing the skill of the actor in its "bread and circuses" policy designed to calm and distract a restless populace, the actor was denied civil rights, could not attain civic honors, and was expressly forbidden to marry government officials or their progeny. No honored citizen, and little less than a slave, the Roman actor and the Greek actor taken captive, were, ironically, admired, praised, and appreciated for their talents, but despised for their chosen profession.

Nevertheless, two actors, Quintus Roscius Gallus (126–62 B.C.) and Claudius Aesopus (?–54 B.C.) managed to overcome this denigrating opinion of the acting profession and to win the approbation of both the populace and officials. Born a slave, Roscius became one of the all-time great comedians. Performing at a time when over-acting was a common practice, Roscius tempered his acting with many refinements associated with the Greeks. His diction was excellent, and his movements and gestures were related to the character that he played. Cicero expressed his admiration for the actor and acknowledged that he studied Roscius to improve his ability as an orator. In one instance, the famed orator and statesman defended Roscius in a law suit that involved the ownership of a slave-actor, Panurgus, whom Roscius had successfully trained and launched on a lucrative acting career. Sulla, Roman general and dictator, was so moved by the actor that he gave him a ring, thereby elevating Roscius to equestrian, or senatorial rank in Roman society. In the eyes of the public, Roscius could do no wrong. A cancelled performance was accepted without question or criticism because of his reputation, both personal and professional. When he died in 62 B.C., Roscius left a fortune and a reputation that through the centuries has become synonymous with great acting. Talented comedians are frequently referred to as "another Roscius."

Claudius Aesopus, a native Greek and a contemporary of Roscius, was the great tragic actor of the time. An emotional performer of great range, his simple rendition of lines brought tears to the eyes of the listener. Realism characterized his performance and, on one occasion, resulted in the death of a slave-actor while Aesopus was playing the role of Atreus. A spendthrift, his off-stage reputation was seemingly not as favorable as that of Roscius. In spite of his squandering, he died a wealthy man, and, before his death, he established a school for the training of tragic actors just as Roscius had established a school for the training of comic actors.

Neither the brilliance of a Roscius and an Aesopus, nor the skill of a Demetrius and a Stratocles who followed, however, could obliterate the stigma of disrepute stamped upon the acting profession. As the golden days of Rome began to fade, and as the populace became disgruntled with government policy, the actor and his profession became too closely connected with the frantic attempts to substitute entertainment for economic and political reform, and too closely identified with the behavior of a decadent society. Spectacles that once served to distract and amuse the public by offering actual crucifixions on stage now began to horrify the viewers; neither did they solve the economic problems that plagued Rome. Nero's preoccupation with elaborate and expensive pantomimes that featured diaphanously costumed male and female performers further damned the profession. A royal scandal erupted when Nero ordered the death of the talented pantomimist Paris, because of an alleged affair with the Empress. Word spread of erotic performances at banquets and private parties, thus confirming the belief that actors were an immoral breed. Mimes that mocked the Christians angered the Church, and the Church announced that any person who became an actor would be denied acceptance into the faith. In the declining years of the Roman Empire, the acting profession fared badly. Sometime during the sixth century A.D., approximately 1,000 years after Thespis won his first victory at Athens, a nadir was reached. Organized entertainment ceased. The actor packed his bags, took to the road, scrounged for a livelihood, and drifted into oblivion in the centuries that followed.

3. The Medieval Actor: The Minstrel and the Zealous Amateur

From the sixth to the tenth centuries, when feudalism was the way of life and when the Church extended its influence throughout Europe, the minstrel, or jongleur, kept the acting profession alive. The peasants in isolated hamlets welcomed the minstrel because he brought with him a touch of gaiety to an otherwise dreary and monotonous existence. The feudal lords housed and fed the minstrel because he provided entertainment and because his scraps of gossip and information were a link with the outside world. The Church ostracized the minstrel because he was what he was—an itinerant member of a profession held in contempt. Personally charming and vocally talented, the minstrel lived by his wits and maintained himself on the few pennies he begged as he traveled the countryside, singing and reciting stories to the accompaniment of a musical instrument.

The minstrel appears in the person of Autolycus in *The Winter's Tale* by Shakespeare. The playwright introduces Autolycus in true minstrel fashion in Act IV, Scene 3. In a monologue that combines song and speech, Autolycus identifies himself:

When daffodils begin to peer,
  With heigh! the doxy over the dale,
Why, then comes in the sweet o' the year,
  For the red blood reigns in the winter's pale.

> The white sheet bleaching on the hedge,
> With heigh! the sweet birds, oh, how they sing!
> Doth set my pugging tooth on edge,
> For a quart of ale is a dish for a king.
>
> The lark, that tirra-lyra chants,
> With heigh! with heigh! the thrush and the jay,
> Are summer songs for me and my aunts,
> While we lie tumbling in the hay.
>
> I have served Prince Florizel and in my time wore three-pile, but now I am out of service:
>
> But shall I go mourn for that, my dear?
> The pale moon shines by night.
> And when I wander here and there,
> I then do most go right.
>
> If tinkers may have leave to live,
> And bear the sow-skin budget,
> Then my account I well may give,
> And in the stocks avouch it.
>
> My traffic is sheets. When the kite builds, look to lesser linen. My father named me Autolycus, who being, as I am, littered under Mercury, was likewise a snapper-up of unconsidered trifles. With die and drab I purchased this comparison, and my revenge is the silly cheat. Gallows and knocks are too powerful on the highway. Beating and hanging are terrors to me. For the life to come, I sleep out the thought of it. A prize! A prize!

The prize is a purse that Autolycus filches from the Clown by pretending he has been downed by a highwayman. The simple-minded Clown accepts Autolycus's explanation and he agrees the assailant must have been "Autolycus" who "haunts wakes, fairs, and bearbaiting" without suspecting that he is speaking to the rogue himself. It is a humorous scene that employs the talents of the minstrel to entertain the audience and the activities of the rogue to create a comic situation on stage.

In Scene 4 of the same act, the technique of the minstrel in selling a song is used to develop the character of Autolycus, to reveal the naiveté of the Clown and the Shepherdesses, and to maintain the pastoral charm that permeates *The Winter's Tale.* First, Autolycus entices the Clown and the Sherpherdesses, Mopsa and Dorcas, with a song:

> Lawn as white as driven snow,
> Cypress black as e'er was crow,
> Gloves as sweet as damask roses,
> Masks for faces and for noses,
> Bugle bracelet, necklace amber,
> Perfume for a lady's chamber,
> Golden quoifs and stomachers
> For my lads to give their dears,
> Pins and poking sticks of steel,
> What maids lack from head to heel.
> Come buy of me, come, come buy, come buy,
> Buy lads, or else your lasses cry.
> Come buy.

When his listeners cannot agree upon a purchase, Autolycus cons the Clown, Mopsa, and Dorcas into considering the purchase of a ballad or two. To Mopsa's request for "a ballad in print o'life," Autolycus offers one that tells of the miseries suffered by a usurer's wife and one of a woman who "was turned into a cold fish for she would not exchange flesh with one that loved her." The trio settle for a merry ballad, a three-part song, that is sung by Autolycus, Mopsa, and Dorcas to the tune of "Two maids wooing a man":

AUTOLYCUS:
> Get you hence, for I must go
> Where it fits not you to know.
>
> D: Whither? M: Oh, Whither? D: Whither?

MOPSA:
> It becomes thy oath full well,
> Thou to me thy secrets tell.
>
> D: Me too, let me go thither.

MOPSA:
Or thou goest to the grange or mill.

DORCAS:
If to either, thou dost ill.

A: Neither. D: What, neither? A: Neither.

DORCAS:
Thou hast sworn my love to be.

MOPSA:
Thou has sworn it more to me.
Then whither goest? Say, whither?

Because a life-like situation underlies each scene, it is reasonable to assume that the Elizabethan comedian played the situation with a degree of realism that enabled the audience to recognize the situation and to identify the Clown and Autolycus with everyday people and happenings. Pickpockets, thieves, and knaves did roam the countryside and did operate in the cities. Ballad singers did hawk their wares in the villages and the marketplaces. The innocent were no match for the rogues who made their living by duping others. However, in the hands of two gifted comedians adept at playing the foil and the knave, the realistic situation is lightly treated through song and comic by-play. Gentle satire emphasizes the gullibility of the Clown and the Shepherdesses and also gives dimension to the character of Autolycus. In all probability, the Elizabethan actor played the situation and the trait of each character as written by the playwright. The minstrel reached the height of his popularity during the thirteenth century. The invention of the printing press diminished the importance of the minstrel as a source of information, and his popularity waned. It is likely that, in order to overcome this adversity, the minstrels banded together with their brethren and formed acting companies that began to appear professionally early in the sixteenth century.

However, until the time when the professional actor would again dominate the stage, the amateur actor wore the mantle of Thespis. The prominence of the amateur during the medieval period resulted from the use of dramatization by the Church as a means of educating an ignorant and illiterate populace in the precepts of the Christian religion. Initially, the actors were members of the clergy—priests, nuns, and choir boys who enacted simple tropes, independently sung lines of dialogue that accompanied a religious service. The first of these, the *Quem Quaeritis,* required the antiphonal singing of four lines that were inserted to precede the Mass as a means of dramatizing the resurrection of Christ. Four members of the clergy, one impersonating the Angel, and the others, the Marys, sang the four questions. The innovation was so successful and inspiring that a similar and equally successful experiment was made with the Christmas service. Once again the actors were members of the clergy. Eventually, the altar of the Church became the playing area for other Scriptural dramatizations, which received elaborate staging. Even though the Church had banned the actor from entering the faith, the laity was pressed into performing the actor's art when the dramatis personae increased in number. Townspeople crowded the cathedrals at holiday time to see the religious dramas performed by their friends and neighbors. Ultimately, everyday occurrences found their way into the performance of the religious episodes, and the vernacular permeated the dialogue which had heretofore been spoken in Latin. Detailed characterizations made the acting more dramatic and earthy, thus obscuring the religious purpose of the occasion. When the crowds became too large to be accommodated within the church, and when Church officials sensed that the original intent had been lost in theatrical production, the presentation of religious drama was moved out of doors, first to the steps of the church, then to the marketplace. Shortly thereafter, a papal edict forbade members of the clergy to perform before the public. Enthusiastically, the amateur actor, who was enjoying favor with the public, seized the opportunity to perform all the roles. From the thirteenth to the sixteenth centuries, the devotion of the amateur actor to the performance and production of religious drama helped revive interest in the return of a professional theater.

The community took over the production of religious drama when the Church withdrew. In France, Germany, and Switzerland, town corporations and specially organized societies assumed the responsibility for presentation. In England, the trade guild shouldered the obligation. Each guild accepted the episode assigned by the town council with pride and fervor, for generally, the assignment provided the guild members with an opportunity to display their skill as artisans. Thus, the shipwrights were charged with the construction of Noah's Ark; the bakers with The Last Supper; the goldsmiths with the gifts of the Wise Men. The actors were guild members or townspeople who were selected after auditioning for a role. Occasionally, professional actors augmented the amateur cast. The actors were paid from funds provided by the town council and from funds raised by levying a tax on guild members for this purpose. Generally, the rate of compensation depended upon the dignity and length of the role. Sometimes Noah received more remuneration than God. In other instances, the actor playing God was the highest paid performer. Lost souls received minimum salary, and Judas was sometimes rewarded for the pain he endured. The actors were pledged to attend all rehearsals, to remain in place during the performance, to refrain from drinking, and to eat only that which was provided. The guild and the town council also demanded that the actors be letter perfect in memorization of roles. The recalcitrant player was penalized for any infringement.

The acting evinced all the characteristics of the unskilled but energetic amateur performer. What he lacked in finesse, he compensated for in spontaneity, vitality, and zeal. He declaimed his lines, ranted and roared, gesticulated wildly and, in general, portrayed himself with gusto. We can easily imagine what an apprentice or journeyman guild member might have done with the part of the Young Man in *The Woman Taken in Adultery* to prove himself with his peers and to establish himself favorably with a master craftsman. The playlet is concerned with adultery and the determination of the Pharisee, Accuser, and the Scribe to prove Jesus a hypocrite. To make their point, they raid the home of a suspected prostitute. The play is a moral one, but the moment is comic:

SCRIBE:

Break up the door and go we in;
Set to the shoulder with all thy might.
We shall take them even in their sin;
Their own trespass shall them indict.

Here a young man runs out in his doublet with shoes untied and holding up his breeches with his hand.

ACCUSER:
Stop that harlot, some earthly wight
That in adultery here is found.

YOUNG MAN:
If any man stop me this night,
I shall give him a deadly wound.

If any man my way doth stop,
Ere we depart dead shall he be;
I shall this dagger put in his crop;
I shall him kill ere he shall me.

PHARISEE:
May Great God's curse go with thee!
With such a shrew will I not mell.

YOUNG MAN:
That same blessing I give you three,
And bequeath you all to the devil of hell.

To audience
In faith, I was so sore afraid
Of yon three shrews, that sooth to say,
My breech be not yet well untied;
I had such haste to run away.
I shall never catch me in such a fray;
I am full glad that I am gone.
Adieu, adieu, in twenty devils' way!
And God's curse have ye every one.*

We may assume that the young actor brought personal experience to understanding the situation, and that guild "man-talk" whetted his imagination in enacting the part, for it was the responsibility of the guild to train and coach the actors. Similarly, we may assume that a master craftsman, playing the lead role in

* Reprinted by permission of The World Publishing Co. from *Religious Drama II,* edited by E. Martin Browne, pp. 161–162. Copyright © 1958 by The World Publishing Co.

Herod and the Kings, which was performed at Coventry by the Shearmen and the Tailors, injected the same degree of temper, impatience, and authority when instructing his apprentices:

HEROD:

Another way? Out! Out! Out!
Hath those false traitors done me this deed?
I stamp! I stare! I look about!
Might I them take I should them burn at a glede.
I rend! I roar! And now run I wood!
Ah, that these villain traitors hath marred thus my mood!
They shall be hanged if I come them to.

*Herod rages in the pageant and in the street also**

Every now and then the "feel" for a part overwhelmed an actor and caused him undue pain in the search for realism. It is said that one actor almost hung himself while playing the part of Judas, and that another fainted from exhaustion while being crucified.

Shakespeare used the guild actor as the prototype for the amateur actors who play an important part in the plot of his play *A Midsummer Night's Dream.* Disguised as Athenian workmen so as not to offend the audience, many of whom were guild members, the amateur players are brought on stage early in Act I as those "thought fit, through all Athens, to play in our interlude before the Duke and Duchess on his wedding day at night." At once we find ourselves in the company of Quince, a carpenter; Snug, a joiner; Bottom, a weaver; Flute, a bellows-mender; Snout, a tinker; and Starveling, a tailor. At once we sense the reluctance, the stage-fright, and the enthusiasm that must have attended the casting of guild members in roles for which they may or may not have been suited. Flute shies away from playing Thisby because "I have a beard coming." Snug worries that he cannot play the lion's part unless it is written, "for I am slow of study." Only Bottom is

---

* Reprinted by permission of The World Publishing Co. from *Religious Drama II,* edited by E. Martin Browne, p. 144. Copyright © 1958 by The World Publishing Co.

ready to have his talents tested, commenting when he is assigned the role of Pyramus, the lover, that:

> That will ask some tears in the true performing of it. If I do it, let the audience look to their eyes; I will move storms; I will condole in some measure. To the rest. Yet my chief humor is for a tyrant. I could play Ercles rarely, or a part to tear a cat in, to make all split.
>
> The raging rocks
> And Shivering shocks
> Shall break the locks,
> Of prison gates.
>
> And Phibbus' car
> Shall shine from far,
> And make and mar
> The foolish fates.
>
> This was lofty! Now name the rest of the players. This is Ercles' vein, a tyrant's vein. A lover is more condoling.

In Act III, Scene 1, the workmen meet to rehearse the play. However, before the rehearsal can commence, script and production problems are called to the attention of the company members. Bottom fears that Pyramus's suicide will frighten the ladies. This reminds Snout that the presence of the lion is apt to have the same effect. All agree that a prologue is needed to explain that "Pyramus is not killed indeed. And, for the more better assurance, tell them that I Pyramus am not Pyramus, but Bottom the weaver. This will put them out of fear." Continuing, Bottom, ever ready to grab the limelight, proposes that the actor playing the role of the lion:

> Must name his name, and half his face must be seen through the lion's neck. And he himself must speak through, saying thus, or to the same defect—"Ladies"—or "Fair Ladies—I would wish you"—or "I would request you"—or "I would entreat you—not to fear, not to tremble. My life for yours. If you think I come hither as a lion, it were a pity of my life. No, I am no such thing, I am a man as other men are." And there indeed let him name his name, and tell them plainly he is Snug the joiner."

In the matter of producing moonlight and a wall, the company decides that two of its members must represent these objects on stage. In exasperation at all the quibbling and at Bottom's assumption of the duties of the director, Quince orders the rehearsal to begin. It ends almost as soon as it begins when Bottom, sent off stage to make his entrance, enters wearing an ass's head as the result of Puck's mischievousness. The company flees in panic, leaving the stage to Bottom, who interprets their action as an attempt to unnerve him. Suddenly, reality becomes fantasy. Titania, now under Oberon's spell, awakens and, upon seeing Bottom, proclaims her love for him. At her direction, Bottom is led to her bower.

When Bottom is released from Puck's spell in Act IV, Scene 2, he returns to Quince's home where he issues orders to the company to ready themselves for the performance:

> . . . Get your apparel together, good strings to your beards, new ribbons to your pumps. Meet presently at the palace. Every man look o'er his part, for the short and the long is, our play is preferred. In any case, let Thisby have clean linen, and let not him that plays the lion pare his nails, for they shall hang out for the lion's claws. And, most dear actors, eat no onions nor garlic, for we are to utter sweet breath, and I do not doubt but to hear them say it a sweet comedy. No more words. Away! Go, away!

The presentation of *The most lamentable comedy, and most cruel death of Pyramus and Thisby* is also the most lamentable and cruelest exposé of amateur actors and amateur productions.

An Elizabethan comedian cast in the role of an Athenian workman would undoubtedly have brought his special comic talents to playing the part. For example, if Richard Tarleton, the first of the great Elizabethan comedians, had been assigned the role of Bottom, Tarleton probably would have found some moment to display his ability to extemporize upon any given subject. A likely moment for such ad-libbing and jesting occurs in Act III, Scene 1, when the workmen meet to rehearse the play. Shakespeare had great admiration for Tarleton's wit and talents, and the playwright might very well have permitted the actor to digress from the script. Many people believe that Hamlet's remembrance of Yorick in the Gravedigger's scene is Shakespeare's tribute to the acting talents of Richard Tarleton. Had the role of Bottom fallen into the hands of another great Elizabethan comedian, Will Kemp, the audience in all probability would have viewed a nimble-footed Bottom. Kemp was widely known for his footwork, once having won a wager that he could dance his way from London to Norwich! Lacking any special comic talents such as those possessed by Tarleton and Kemp, an Elizabethan comedian could always draw upon his experience in reading for a role, rehearsing a play, and performing before royalty to project the trials and tribulations endured by the Athenian workmen in preparing their play for presentation at court. Although the Elizabethan actor, comic or tragic, is not known to have had a method for creating and playing a role—he was much too busy learning new parts and switching daily from one play to another to delve into what motivated a character—it is reasonable to suppose that in playing the roles of the Athenian workmen, the Elizabethan comedian brought a great deal of personal knowledge about the theater to the acting of Quince, Bottom, Snug, Snout, Starveling, and Flute—for what are the roles other than actors playing actors, albeit amateur ones?

As the power of the guild began to decline, as towns grew into cities, and as the omnipotence of the Church began to be questioned, the popularity of religious drama was adversely affected. The time was ripe for the professional actor and the professional acting company to reclaim their audience.

4. THE RETURN OF THE PROFESSIONAL: ENGLAND

In Act II, Scene 2, of Shakespeare's *Hamlet,* Rosencrantz informs the young Prince that he has invited a troupe of traveling actors to the court for the purpose of amusing the melancholy Dane. The invitation recalls the facts concerning the development and status of the professional acting companies that operated in London at the start of the seventeenth century. A century earlier, the professional companies had been nothing more than troupes of wandering actors who were hounded from one village to another because of their profession. Their status in society was similar to that of the rogue and the vagabond; namely, outcasts. Their only hope for survival and protection from abuse and arrest lay in the patronage of a member of the nobility. When they were fortunate enough to secure a royal supporter, they were obliged to wear the livery of the house to which they were attached, and they were expected to remain on call for the moment the master wanted to be entertained. Royal support, however, did not guarantee freedom of performance beyond the castle walls. When the actors became restless for a new audience and chanced an opportunity to perform in a nearby village without the consent or knowledge of their master, local officials invariably took the actors into custody and an appeal would have to be made to the master to intervene. Despite the fact that two English monarchs, Richard III and Henry VII, had set a precedent for accepting acting as a reputable profession by including a troupe of actors as members of the royal household, and although a considerable number of members of the nobility had followed the example of royalty in maintaining troupes, local officials continued to harass the fifteenth-century acting company.

However, the status of the actor and his profession gradually improved during the reign of Queen Elizabeth the First. The Queen marked her ascension to the throne with a proclamation that charged the nobility and local officials with keeping a watchful eye on the activities of professional acting companies. Members of the nobility who supported acting troupes were asked to prevent their troupe of actors from playing without a license and without giving proper notice to local officials. Local officials were charged with curbing the performing of plays whose themes had religious and political overtones. In part, the Queen's proclamation followed the policy set by her predecessor, Queen Mary, who, in 1556, had issued an official decree forbidding acting companies from touring because it was believed that the companies were fomenting treason through their plays. Fortunately, Queen Elizabeth's policy toward the acting profession altered as her right to the throne became more secure politically, and as England moved steadily forward to becoming a dominant world power.

In 1572, a royal decree gave the acting profession legal status by requiring all actors to obtain a license from either a nobleman or a justice of the peace. In 1574, the Crown removed this responsibility from the local justices and the noblemen and placed it with the Master of Revels, a court official whose office had been established by Henry VIII. The Master of Revels was also empowered to examine all plays intended for production by the acting companies. In that same year, the Earl of Leicester's Men, having met the requirement of first obtaining royal patronage, applied for and was granted a license under the new statute. Two years later, James Burbage, who headed the Earl of Leicester's Men, to avoid further conflict with London officials, built London's first commercial playhouse, The Theater, on the outskirts of the city. Thereafter, the acting companies seem to have been caught up in the struggle for power between the local authorities and the central government. Happily for the acting profession, the Queen, who was generally at odds with local authorities, allied herself with the players, thus strengthening her position of leadership.

In 1597, a further revision in the granting of licenses occurred. At that time, the Privy Council announced the licensing of only two acting companies who would receive the patronage of the Queen. One, the Lord Admiral's Men, was led by Philip Henslowe; the other, the Lord Chamberlain's Men, was led by James Burbage. When James I ascended the throne in 1603, another change was effected. The Lord Chamberlain's Men were officially recognized as the King's Men and the Lord Admiral's Men as the Duke's Men. In summary, acting companies at the time of the premiere of *Hamlet* in 1602 had come a long way since the day they resembled the footsore, body-weary, mind-weary, shabbily-dressed, stomach-hungry troupe of actors who arrive at Elsinore to unwittingly perform the play that catches the conscience of a king.

The patron of an acting company did not contribute to the financial needs of the company. He contributed only the prestige of his name which was necessary to obtain a license for performing, and the power of his position when the company encountered difficulty with the local authorities. The cost of operating the theater plant, building or renting a theater, paying salaries to actors and hired help, and mounting a production was defrayed by the company itself. Continuing operation of the company depended upon a successful box office. The business structure of the company followed corporate organization, and the classification of personnel resembled the organization of the craft guild. At the head was the housekeeper, or producer, who made the initial monetary investment needed to rent or build a theater and to employ a company of ten to twenty actors. The housekeeper was paid from the box-office sale of the more expensive seats, which were located in the gallery. The actors shared the proceeds from the sale of general admission tickets. In the period before royalties, the playwright sold his play to the company, and the company retained the play as its property. Apprentice actors were assigned to a master actor to whom the apprentice paid a fee that included board, room, and training. When a master actor left the company, the apprentice, if he were ready, assumed the roles for which he had been trained by the departing actor. Young boys were recruited to play the roles of female parts. Musicians, stage managers, and money-takers were hired on a wage basis. In all respects, a first-rate professional acting company was a highly structured business enterprise with each permanent member owning a share, or shares, in the company.

To illustrate the nature of Elizabethan acting, we have only to examine Hamlet's advice to the players in Act III, Scene 2.

HAMLET:

> Speak the speech, I pray you, as I pronounced it to you, trippingly on the tongue. But if you mouth it, as many of our players do, I had as lief the town crier spoke my lines. Nor do not saw the air too much with your hand, thus, but use all gently. For in the very torrent, tempest, and, as I may say, whirlwind of passion, you must acquire and beget a temperance that may give it smoothness. Oh, it offends me to the soul to hear a robustious periwig-pated fellow tear a passion to tatters, to very rags, to split the ears of the groundlings, who for the most part are capable of nothing but inexplicable dumb shows and noise. I would have such a fellow whipped for o'erdoing Termagant—it out-Herods Herod. Pray you, avoid it.

1st Player:
I warrant your Honor.

Hamlet:
Be not too tame, neither, but let your own discretion be your tutor. Suit the action to the word, the word to the action, with this special observance, that you o'erstep not the modesty of nature. For anything so overdone is from the purpose of playing, whose end, both at the first and now, was and is to hold as 'twere the mirror up to Nature —to show Virtue her own feature, scorn her own image, and the very age and body of the time his form and pressure. Now this overdone or come tardy off, though it make the unskillful laugh, cannot but make the judicious grieve, the censure of the which one must in your allowance o'erweigh a whole theater of others. Oh, there be players that I have seen play, and heard others praise—and that highly, not to speak it profanely—that neither having the accent of Christians nor the gait of Christian, pagan, nor man, have so strutted and bellowed that I have thought some of Nature's journeymen had made men, and not made them well, they imitated humanity so abominably.

The role of Hamlet was written for Richard Burbage. Shakespeare also created the roles of Richard III, Othello, and King Lear for Burbage, thus providing us with an idea of Burbage's range as an actor. From the substance of the advice to the players, we can conclude that Richard Burbage must have held the "mirror up to nature" in creating the roles Shakespeare wrote for him. Richard Burbage's rival was Edward Alleyn, another great actor of the period. He had at one time been a member of the Earl of Leicester's Men when James Burbage managed the troupe. Edward Alleyn was a partner and son-in-law of Philip Henslowe. Alleyn's acting range may be conjectured from his playing of the lead roles in *Doctor Faustus* and *The Jew of Malta* by Christopher Marlowe, and the role of Hieronimo in *The Spanish Tragedy* by Thomas Kyd. When he died in 1625, Alleyn left an endowment for the support of a school for poor children at Dulwich. Today, the College and School of God's Gifts is known as Dulwich College.

5. THE RETURN OF THE PROFESSIONAL: FRANCE

The status of the professional theater in France at the end of the sixteenth century was less than that of the professional theater in England and Italy. In England, James and Richard Burbage, William Shakespeare, Philip Henslowe, and Edward Alleyn had succeeded in establishing a professional theater that had the patronage and legal protection of the central government, but not its financial support. In Italy, the Renaissance had inspired architects to experiment with scene design and theater architecture, playwrights to imitate Aeschylus, Sophocles, and Euripides, and actors to develop a popular theater, the *commedia dell'arte*. In France, however, the professional actors were hindered by many obstacles. The Church remained adamant in its position concerning the acting profession, and was steadfast in refusing actors the last rites and burial in consecrated ground. The production of religious drama was controlled by amateur societies organized for that purpose. One, the *Confrèrie de la Passion,* held a monopoly on theater production in the city of Paris well into the seventeenth century. Royal interest and patronage had only begun to manifest itself when the sixteenth century drew to a close. Moreover, the nation was embroiled in a series of civil and religious wars that militated against the establishment of a professional theater. It was during the reign of Louis XIII (1610–1644) that specific events occurred which portended the national theater that was to flower when Louis XIV ascended the throne.

From 1578, when the *Confrèrie de la Passion* started to withdraw from play production and to lease the Hôtel de Bourgogne to professional acting companies, until 1625 when Cardinal Richelieu became chief minister to King Louis XIII, the acting companies were only intermittently successful in stimulating theater attendance and in overcoming the resistance of the *Confrèrie* to the establishment of a permanent company in Paris. Despite the fact that the comic talents of Gros-Guillaume, Gaultier-Garguille, and Turlupin, the tragic acting of Montdory, the plays of Alexandre Hardy, the introduction of professional actresses, and the unceasing efforts of Valleran le Conte added up to an irresistible force that focused attention on an emerging French theater, little was achieved in sustaining public support and royal patronage. The fortunes of the French theater took an upward turn in 1629 when the reign of Louis XIII was brought under control by the administration of Cardinal Richelieu. In that year, the huge success of Pierre Corneille's first play, *Mélite,* encouraged the company led by Montdory to remain in the capital city and to make a fight for professional existence. In 1632, the two leading companies, Les Comédiens du Roi and The Prince of Orange's Troupe, decided to propagandize their profession by presenting dramatizations that would improve the image of the actor.

Meanwhile, Cardinal Richelieu had evinced an interest in, and a concern for, raising the cultural level of the French populace. In 1629, the Cardinal instituted a policy designed to improve French art and literature. At his suggestion, the French Academy was established in 1635. His interest in the theater led him to study playwriting, and to encourage Montdory, then the leading tragic actor in France, to establish a second theater that would break the monopoly on play production in Paris. The Théâtre du Marais was converted from a tennis court in 1634. Prior to its opening, however, King Louis XIII, in a moment of pique at the Cardinal, transferred six of Montdory's leading actors to the troupe the King patronized at the Hôtel de Bourgogne.

In 1641, Cardinal Richelieu, dissatisfied with the platform stage and the mansion settings that crowded the acting area in the Théâtre du Marais and the Hôtel de Bourgogne, furnished his palace with a proscenium arch theater that later became the home for Molière and his troupe. In the same year, the King issued an edict announcing the pensioning of Les Comédiens du Roi, and requesting that the populace regard the acting profession with respect. King Louis XIV ascended the throne in 1644. The French professional actor found an ally in the King, one whose enthusiasm and indulgence led to the founding of the French National Theater.

The organization and the operation of the French professional acting company was similar to that of the Elizabethan acting company. Company officers kept records of the productions, payment of salaries to actors and hired help, and arranged for production of new works. The company members, usually ten to fifteen in number, were each granted a share or a fraction of a share according to his professional standing in the company. Three to four performances were played each week. After the costs of each performance were deducted from the box-office receipts, the profits were divided among the shareholders. Consequently, the actor's salary depended upon the success at the box office, although an additional sum was received from monies contributed by the King. The playwright received an outright sum for his play or was awarded shares after a predetermined number of performances (or a testing of the play at the box office!). The play was read to the actors who discussed casting the roles. Because the playwright generally wrote with certain company members in mind for specific parts, and because actors realized that certain parts were the specialty of a particular actor, there was little bickering about how the play was cast—at least, not publicly or before the company. The play was usually staged by the playwright. Although women played the female roles, an exception was made in the casting of elderly and unattractive female characters. Then male actors who specialized in such roles were cast in the parts. Actresses were billed either by their surname or their husband's name. The actors, however, assumed stage names. For example, Molière was legally Jean-Baptiste Poquelin; Montfleury, Zacharie Jacob; and Turlupin, Henri Legrand.

Seventeenth-century French actors adhered to the principles of oratory practiced by the Greek actors, but which had long since developed into bombastic declamation that touched an audience more through sound and fury than through concept. Despite his reputation as the first great French actor of tragedy, Montdory was a ranter, who moved his audience through elocution, trickery, and noise. Bellerose is thought to have become so involved with the beautiful sounds of his own voice that he frequently did not project the meaning of what he was speaking. Montfleury, the fat tragedian whom Molière satirizes in *L'Improptu de Versailles,* was driven from the stage by the temperamental Cyrano de Bergerac when he became infuriated with the actor's bombastic declamation. In contrast to these declaimers, Floridor (Josias de Soulas) was hailed for his quiet manner and his sincere vocal quality in playing the lead roles in *Horace* and *Cinna* by Pierre Corneille. Floridor succeeded Montdory at the Hôtel de Bourgogne when Montdory, stricken with paralysis of the tongue, was forced to retire from the stage. Toward the end of the century, Michel Baron, once a protégé of Molière's, electrified audiences with his natural acting style. However, in 1691, at the height of his popularity, Baron retired. Nearly thirty years later, Baron ended his retirement to play opposite Adrienne Lecouvreur, a young French actress whose style was similar to Baron's—simple, natural, human, and emotionally touching. At the age of sixty-seven, Baron was hailed as the greatest French actor of his time.

Declamation and bombast did not characterize the performance of the comedians. The great farceurs, Gros-Gaullaume (Robert Guérin), Gaultier-Garguille (Hugues Guéru), and Turlupin (Henri Legrand), played their *commedia*-like roles with the gusto and earthiness that farce demands. Molière, the greatest of all French comedians, played with a decisive wit that cut to the quick of the character's being, a charm that identified the *commedia* roots of the character, and a naturalness that gave the character reality. In *L'Impromptu de Versailles,* Molière advises his actors to draw upon their knowledge of others in playing their roles:

> . . . Endeavour then all of you, to take the Character of your Parts right, and to imagine that you are what you represent. (To Du Croisy) You play the Poet, and you ought to fill yourself with that Character, to mark the Pedant Air which he preserves even in the Conversation of the *Beau Monde;* that sententious Tone of Voice, and that Exactness of Pronunciation which lays a Stress on all the Syllables, and does not let one Letter escape of the strictest Orthography. (To Brecourt) As for you, you play a Courtier, as you have already done in *The School for Wives Criticis'd;* that is you must assume a sedate Air, a natural Tone of Voice, and make the fewest Gestures possible. (To LaGrange) As for you, I have nothing to say to you. (To Mrs. Bejart) You represent one of those Women who, provided they don't make love, think that everything else is permitted 'em; those Women who are always fiercely intrenched in their Prudery, look upon every body with Contempt, and think all the good Qualities that others possess are nothing in comparison of a wretched Honour which no body regards. Have

this Character always before your Eyes, that you may make the Grimaces of it right . . .*

Molière died in 1673 while playing a performance of *Le Malade Imaginaire.* King Louis XIV ordered that his company of actors be combined with the actors at the Théâtre du Marais. Seven years later, the King decreed another consolidation. The actors of the Hôtel de Bourgogne were ordered to join the Molière troupe to form the Comédie-Française, frequently referred to as the "House of Molière." At the conclusion of the seventeenth century, the French actor had achieved all that he had struggled for a century earlier—status in society, professional recognition, financial security—everything—except recognition of his profession by the Church.

6. Commedia Dell'Arte All'Improviso: The Actor Is King

While the English professional actor sought the protection of royalty in England and the French professional actor sought to break the monopoly held by the *Confrèrie* in Paris, there developed in Italy a brand of theater termed the *commedia dell'arte all'improviso,* or professional improvised comedy. It is not certain just when the troupes of Italian professional comedians began to appear, but the middle of the sixteenth century is generally accepted as the date when the troupes achieved prominence in the Italian theater. Their origin, too, is uncertain. Some hold that the *commedia* stemmed from the Greek mime, the *fabulae atallanae* of Rome, and the plots, masks, and stock characters that characterized Greek and Roman comedy. In any event, the traveling comedians were different and novel.

The *commedia dell'arte* differed from the standard presentation of a written script spoken and performed by actors in that *commedia* actors performed a scenario that permitted them to improvise situations and dialogue. They specialized in performing recognizable types, and a mask helped to identify the type. Before

---

* From *Sources of Theatrical History* by A. M. Nagler. Dover Publication, Inc., New York. Reprinted through permission of the publisher.

the performance took place, the company manager, *il corago,* met with the actors to review the scenario. Then the scenario was placed off stage so that the actor could keep up with the action on stage and check his cue for entrance. A simple and an agreed-upon plot held the action together. The charm and delight of the *commedia dell'arte* lay in the spontaneous performance of the actor and his special skill in portraying types that may be categorized as old men, young lovers, scheming servants, and the militia.

The "old men" category included the Dottore and Pantalone. The Dottore was a learned man—a lawyer, a philosopher, and so on—who had earned his degree at the University of Bologna. The Dottore was too immersed in the wisdom gained from books to realize when he was being duped. He cited proverbs, clichés, authorities, and Latin phrases to prove his point and to solve all problems. Dressed in a long black academic robe and wearing the cap that marked him an educated man, the Dottore personified all that was foolish and vain about the man who had spent his life between book covers. His everyday counterpart was Pantalone, a retired businessman from Verona, or from any of the large commercial Italian cities. His first passion was money. His second passion was his young wife. Invariably, he was a cuckold whose obsession for money blinded him to the romantic escapades his wife indulged in. Pantalone generally wore a mask that featured a hooked nose and a beard. He derived his name from the pantaloons he wore.

Usually, the plot of the scenario involved a pair of young lovers who attempted to outwit the schemes of the Dottore and Pantalone. The *innamorato* was the young man who fell in love, out of love, fought for love, moped for love of the *innamorata,* his female counterpart, who responded with love, yearned for love, wept for love, and gave all her love to the *innamorato*. The *innamorato* was always handsome, stalwart, and verile. The *innamorata* was always beautiful, winsome, and virtuous. Both the *innamorato* and the *innamorata* wore costumes appropriate for young lovers, but neither wore a mask. Isabelle Andreini, the leading lady of the Gelosi troupe, epitomized the ideal *innamorata.* So unique was her beauty, talent, and voice, that she became identified with the role and was considered the first outstanding actress in Europe. Her death in 1604 caused the dissolution of the Gelosi troupe.

The *zanne* were the scheming servants who provided much of the intrigue that complicated the simple plots and the spontaneous humor that set the audience rolling with laughter. The *zanni* was identified by a specific name, by his degree of intelligence—bright or half-witted—and by his traditional costume and mask, which immediately cued the audience as to what to expect from his behavior. Arlecchino, later our Harlequin, promised action and trouble. He wore a brightly colored costume and a black mask that permitted the actor to stare at the audience through narrow slits. The spectators identified Brighella as one to watch closely. Sly and crafty, Brighella was always ready to indulge in some bit of humorous mischief that caused frustration and indignation. He always carried a dagger which he would quickly draw to comically taunt his victim. His companion in "humorous" crime was Scapino, bold in deeds, but out-of-view in actions. Pulcinella and Pedrolino were more easy-going, not quite as bright or as witty as the others, yet fun-loving and harmless. The *fontesca* was a female companion of the *innamorata.* When she appeared as the companion of Arlecchino, she was identified as a *soubrette.* Her presence meant twice as much intrigue and, consequently, twice as much fun.

The Capitano completes the types portrayed by the *commedia* actors. At first, the Capitano was modeled after the Italian soldier. Later, his characteristics were changed to satirize Italy's rival, Spain. On his head, the Capitano always wore a plumed hat. His tight clothes emphasized his corpulent waist. A sword dangled from the wrong side of his body. His mask included an over-sized nose and a good-sized mustache, which he constantly twirled. Conceited and petty, boastful and proud, the Capitano eloquently recited deeds he had never accomplished, victories he had never experienced, and friendships he had never known. A coward and a braggart at heart, the Capitano played the hero to the hilt.

Set speeches and comic business enabled the actor to reveal his special comic skills and to expand the script outline. The *chiusetti* permitted the actor to bring a stretch of dialogue to a conclusion through a memorized couplet, epigram, or pithy saying spoken at the appropriate moment. The *repertorio* of each actor included memorized soliloquies, riddles, witticisms, and tirades that the actor would spew forth at the proper moment. The *lazzi* allowed for special comic business that gave the actor an opportunity to demonstrate the comic artistry for which he had become known. One *commedia* actor specialized in footwork so deft in its execution that he could box another actor's ears with his toes. Another *commedia* performer always managed to work his acrobatic skill into the action. The theatergoer awaited that moment when the comedian would perform his special *lazzi* with the same degree of expectancy that we await Jack Benny staring at us helplessly; Groucho Marx flicking his cigar ash, rolling his eyes, and chasing the elderly matron; Charles Chaplin tipping his derby, twirling his cane, and sidling around a corner on one foot. When we see such *lazzi* as this—an example of another kind occurs in *Voice of the Turtle* by John Van Druten when the young man uses a monkey wrench to pry open a zipper on the heroine's dress—then we are viewing a facet of *commedia dell'arte all'improviso.*

Troupes of *commedia* actors enchanted theatergoers throughout Europe for nearly 150 years. The Italian comedians amused the populace with performances in the marketplaces of cities in France, Italy, Austria, and Spain. The troupes delighted royalty with performances at court. The *commedia* even managed to charm high Church officials, although not enough to persuade the Church to rescind its position on the acting profession. As the eighteenth century began, the popularity of the *commedia* started to wane. The reasons for the decline are similar to those that have constantly confronted and haunted acting companies throughout the centuries: lack of interest and support by a new generation of theatergoers, competition with other producing organizations, and changes in acting styles and techniques. In France, for example, the Comédie Italienne found it difficult to compete with the popular Comédie-Française. In Italy, Carlos Goldoni stripped the *commedia* of its improvisational techniques when his plays replaced the loosely constructed scenario. In his attempt to erase the ills that afflicted the Italian theater and in his efforts to get his actors to perform in a more natural manner, Goldoni eliminated the mask, humanized the stock characters, and urged his actors to use gestures and movements appropriate to the character and the situation. However, all this was to no avail, and by the conclusion of the eighteenth century, the *commedia* was only a romantic memory of the days when the actor was king, and the theatergoer a loyal subject who rewarded the comic skill of the king with spontaneous laughter and enthusiastic applause.

7. The Restoration Actor: Devil's Disciple and Society's Darling

It was inevitable that the London theaters would be closed when the Puritans became the ruling political power in England. The Puritans believed the theaters were cesspools that hatched plagues and pestilence. The Puritans saw The Fortune, The Globe, The Red Bull, The Cockpit, and other London theaters as gathering places for the wicked and the licentious. The plays were deemed evil gospels designed to arouse base emotions and to distract man from leading a godly life. The Puritans viewed the actor as an instrument of the devil, a lost soul who had strayed from the pursuit of a respectable and meaningful profession. The closing of the London theaters ended a long campaign by the Puritans to exorcise the playhouse and the player from English society. Similarly, an ordinance passed by Parliament in 1642 banning the performance of plays ended the conflict that had existed between civil authorities and the Crown over control of the activities of the acting profession. The conflict had begun a century earlier when professional acting companies sought the patronage and protection of royalty and when the acting companies attempted to expand their professional activities beyond the confines of the royal court. The intensity of the struggle flamed as the Crown counteracted local laws with royal decrees that benefited the actor and denied jurisidictional control to civil authorities. Undoubtedly the Crown intervened on behalf of the actor primarily to establish itself as the ruling authority in all matters. Now the tables were turned. Parliament, in line with its policy of challenging Charles I in all matters, also questioned the right of the king to control the activities of the acting profession.

London actors ignored the ordinance of 1642 and continued to perform their plays. Naively, they probably assumed that Charles would come to their defense if Parliament attempted to enforce the ordinance. However, as the breach between the King and Parliament widened, and as the conflict between the Roundheads and the Cavaliers gained momentum, the actors were forced to recognize that Parliament was determined to destroy all theatrical endeavors. In 1643, soldiers, acting on orders of Parliament, raided The Fortune during a performance. The actors were required to forfeit their costumes as punishment for disobeying the ordinance. In 1644, the actors found themselves with one less playhouse in which to practice their art when The Globe was demolished so that a tenement could be built on the site. In 1647, a second ordinance attempted to suppress all public plays and playhouses by threatening the actor with imprisonment if he persisted in performing in public. In 1648, Parliament, irritated by the number of illegal performances, struck at the economic existence of the actor. A new ordinance not only reiterated imprisonment as punishment if the actor performed in public, but, in addition, the law ordered the demolition of playhouses, the seizure of box-office receipts, and the penalizing of spectators found in the theater! In 1649, Charles I, the actor's protector and benefactor, was beheaded. In that same year, soldiers wrecked the interiors of The Cockpit, The Salisbury Court, and The Fortune theaters. In 1650, the status of the actor reached a nadir when a petition to Parliament pleading for mercy and consideration fell on deaf ears.

When Oliver Cromwell died in 1658, Parliament negotiated for the return of Prince Charles to England. Charles II ascended the throne in the spring of 1660. The "illegitimate" theater which was in operation at the time was given "legitimate" status when Charles II officially reopened the London theaters. In issuing his decree, however, Charles II granted theater patents to Thomas Killigrew and William D'Avenant only. Thus Killigrew and D'Avenant enjoyed a monopoly and actors were forced to seek employment with the two men. Thomas Killigrew chose the older actors and formed the King's Company. The younger but less experienced actors joined William D'Avenant and formed the Duke's Company. Both companies started production in the fall of 1660; the

King's Company in a theater converted from a tennis court, and the Duke's Company in the Salisbury Court theater. In 1661, D'Avenant opened the Lincoln's Inn Field theater, which had formerly been a tennis court and which now boasted a proscenium arch stage, the first of its kind in London. In 1663, Thomas Killigrew moved his company to the newly constructed Theater Royal in Drury Lane. Unlike his predecessors who had limited their theatergoing to productions at court, Charles attended public performances.

The organization of the Restoration theater company differed from the organization of earlier English theater companies in that the patentee and his associates determined the artistic policy of the company and the distribution and ownership of shares in the company. The associates of the patentee included actors and playwrights whose talents swelled box-office receipts, and acquaintances to whom the patentee sold a share or two if he needed money to finance the productions of the company. Thus, the average Restoration actor was a paid performer, hired by the patentee for a given period of time at a stipulated salary. Actors received higher salaries than actresses who were just beginning to appear on the English stage as a result of a royal decree ordering that all female roles be played by women. The patentee required the Restoration actor to perform six days each week and to be a quick study in order to meet the daily change of program demanded by an audience that was hungry for entertainment. Later, in response to pressure, the patentee guaranteed his leading actors one or more benefit performances during the season as an additional form of compensation other than owning shares in the company. On such occasions, the patentee turned over the net box-office receipts to the actor. A forerunner of our modern-day producer, the patentee dominated the activities of the Restoration theater company.

A Restoration theatergoer attended a performance of a tragedy written by a Restoration playwright, such as *The Conquest of Granada* by John Dryden, or *The Tragedy of Mustapha* by The Earl of Orrery, or *Empress of Morocco* by Settle, with one intention of observing the antics of the audience and another intention of observing the performance of the actors. Restoration playhouses were gossip centers where intrigues were hatched to set Restoration society spinning. Here gallants flirted with court ladies who wore vizards to conceal their identity. Here beaux pursued the actresses to their dressing rooms. Here fop vied with fop in creating and disclosing the tittle-tattle of the day. Here courtiers arranged for liaisons with courtesans. Here Charles II cast a speculative eye upon an actress on stage (Nell Gwyn, perhaps) while his current favorite occupied a seat next to him and his ex-favorite a seat in a box above him! Apparently, the clime in the theater was not conducive to watching a performance of a tragedy on stage. However, when the theatergoer did turn his eyes toward the stage, his attention and interest was fleeting because of what he saw and heard. The actors declaimed and intoned the words of the playwright much as their predecessors had before the days of the Commonwealth and the Restoration. The heroic couplet had replaced blank verse in an attempt to imitate the polite tragedy written by the French playwrights, and the actors had fallen into the trap of chanting the rhymed verse. The manner of acting was elegantly stylized in movement and gesture as well as artificial in feeling. Passionate moments and emotionally charged speeches were ranted by the actor. It was little wonder, then, that the Restoration theatergoer quickly directed his attention toward the audience, where the comedy being played by the theatergoers was performed with greater finesse than was the play being performed on stage. The Restoration period was definitely not a time for tragedy!

The Restoration actor was probably more at ease playing comedy than he was playing tragedy. The artificial comedy of manners created by George Etherege (*Love in a Tub,* 1664, and *She Would If She Could,* 1668), John Dryden (*Marriage a la Mode,* 1672), William Wycherley (*The Country Wife,* 1675), Sir John Vanbrugh (*The Relapse,* 1696), William Congreve (*The Way of the World,* 1700), and George Farquhar (*The Beaux Stratagem,* 1707) mirrored Restoration society from the days of Charles II to the reign of Queen Anne. The Restoration actor was part of that society and knew its follies and foibles well. The actor had only to recognize the relationship between the detached viewpoint of Restoration society and the comic viewpoint of the playwright to perform the play with a sense of innocent wickedness. The actor had only to recall the gestures, facial expressions, and body movements of his social acquaintances to breathe life into the characters created by the playwright. The actor had only to recollect the vocal nuances of gossip to project the sly innuendos that colored the dialogue of the play. The actor had only to remember the intrigues on which Restoration society thrived to grasp the intricate plot woven by the playwright. Finally, the Restoration actor had only to look at himself and his society to perform that which was decadent but not without elegance, that which was bawdy but not without wit, and that which was immoral but not without morals.

However, if the performer was Thomas Betterton, the Restoration theatergoer did fix his attention on the stage. Thomas Betterton was one of the young actors selected by Sir William D'Avenant to join the Duke's Company in 1661. Seven years later, when D'Avenant died, Betterton became the actor–manager of the Company. In 1682, the Duke's Company and the King's Company were merged and became the United Company, thus giving Betterton an opportunity to portray all the Shakespearean heroes. Ten years later, the actor was granted a license to form a second company because the machinations of Christopher Rich, who had bought out the patentee of the United Company, prohibited Betterton and his associates from enjoying their rights as company members. Thomas Betterton's career in the theater spanned fifty years, during which time he earned the accolades of such reigning monarchs as Charles II, James II, William and Mary, and Queen Anne. He also won the plaudits of Samuel Pepys, the Restoration journalist, Sir Richard Steele, co-editor of *The Tatler,* and Colley Cibber, the actor–playwright–manager who was named Poet Laureate in 1730. Unlike many of the actors of his day, Betterton's performances were free from rant and exaggeration. His dignified manner, his imaginative characterizations, and his judicious use of voice, body, and gesture made him the leading actor of the Restoration theater. Colley Cibber provides us with some idea of Betterton's acting skill when performing the role of Hamlet:

> You have seen a Hamlet perhaps, who, on the first appearance of his father's spirit, has thrown himself into all the straining vo-

ciferation requisite to express rage and fury, and the house has thundered with applause; though the misguided actor was all the while (as Shakespeare terms it) tearing a passion into rags. I am the more bold to offer you this particular instance, because the late Mr. Addison, while I sat by him, to see this scene acted, made the same observation, asking me with some surprise, if I though Hamlet should be in so violent a passion with the Ghost, which though it might have astonished, it had not provoked him? for you may observe that in this beautiful speech the passion never rises beyond an almost breathless astonishment, or an impatience, limited by filial reverence, to enquire into the suspected wrongs that may have raised him from his peaceful tomb! and a desire to know what a spirit so seemingly distressed, might wish or enjoin a sorrowful son to execute towards his future quiet in the grave? This was the light into which Betterton threw the scene; which he opened with a pause of mute amazement! then rising slowly to a solemn, trembling voice, he made the Ghost equally terrible to the spectator as to himself! and in the descriptive part of the natural emotions which the ghastly vision gave him, the boldness of his expostulation was still governed by decency, manly, but not braving; his voice never rising into that seeming outrage, or wild defiance of what he naturally revered. But alas! to perserve this medium, between mouthing, and meaning too little, to keep the attention more pleasingly awake, by a tempered spirit, then by mere vehemence of voice, is of all the masterstrokes of an actor the most difficult to teach. In this none yet have equalled Betterton . . .*

When performing tragedy, Betterton played opposite Elizabeth Barry. Mrs. Barry had begun her acting career in a most disastrous manner: she was discharged from her company because of poor diction and improper use of voice. Now, after years of diligently working on her speech deficiencies, Elizabeth Barry reigned as London's queen of tragedy. Her acting style matched that of Betterton in awakening terror and pity in the heart of the theatergoer. When performing comedy, Thomas Betterton played opposite Anne Bracegirdle. A gifted singer and dancer, Anne Bracegirdle

---

* From the book *An Apology for the Life of Colley Cibber* by Colley Cibber. Everyman's Library. Reprinted by permission of E. P. Dutton & Co., Inc. and J. M. Dent and Sons, Ltd. London, England.

inspired William Congreve to write many of his plays for her. A versatile actor capable of playing both comedy and tragedy, Betterton commanded the attention of the theatergoer when he appeared on stage with either of his two leading ladies.

The economic, social, and professional status of the seventeenth-century English actor rose and fell with the political upheavals of the time. At the beginning of the century, theaters thrived under the patronage and protection of Elizabeth I and, later, James I. The King's Company and the Duke's Company enjoyed the prestige of playing before the court, and each company was supported at the box office by a segment of the public. Actors shared in the profits of the company, and the leading actors retired or died wealthy men. The economic status of the actor was at its lowest point during the period of the Commonwealth. A systematic purging of the theater left the actors without sufficient employment to keep body and soul together. A reversal of this nadir occurred when Prince Charles ascended the throne. The demand for entertainment created a need for actors, and a good actor had little difficulty finding employment. Although he was not generally granted a share in the profits of the company, unless he was an obvious asset at the box office, the actor was adequately compensated for his performances and he was guaranteed additional compensation through benefit performances. However, the English actor was not as economically secure as the French actor, who, at the end of the seventeenth century, could look forward to a pension upon retirement. The social acceptance of the actor varied with each segment of English society. Royalty, for example, accepted the actor as a liveried servant subject to its call and need for entertainment. In turn, royalty guaranteed the actor the right to perform in public and he was subject to arrest only upon the order of the Lord Chamberlain. Fashionable society, Restoration society in particular, accepted the actor as a talented artist, a wit, and a sophisticate similar to themselves. The Church accepted the actor into the faith, although the actor frequently antagonized the clergy by performing in plays that satirized the Church. The general public supported the actor at the box office, in spite of his unsavory reputation. In contrast, the Puritans despised the actor and deemed him a social outcast. All segments of society, whether or not they patronized the theater, probably agreed that the acting profession was not a respectable one. Professionally, the actor made little progress in improving his skills and techniques during the century. Although the changing political scene may have been a deterrent to learning new skills and methods of performance and characterization, the chances are the actor was hampered by an apprentice system that taught a new actor old tricks. Still, there were, as there usually are in every century, those actors who rose above the commonplace to develop a style that was true to the nature of the character they portrayed. These gifted actors elevated the status of the profession from that which supplied entertainment and diversion to that which became an art in the portrayal of human nature. Each portended a day when actors would use their skills and talents in holding the mirror up to nature. Although the economic, social, and professional status of the actor may not have notably advanced during the seventeenth century, the actor and his profession had managed to survive the political changes and, at the beginning of the eighteenth century, each was ready to meet the challenge of a new generation.

8. The Rise of the Star

The eighteenth century ushered in an Age of Great Actors that lasted for nearly two centuries. In England, Anne Oldfield, Barton Booth, Catherine Clive, Peg Woffington, Charles Macklin, and Sarah Siddons won the plaudits of eighteenth-century theatergoers. A century later, English audiences thrilled to the talents of Edmund Kean, William Charles Macready, the Bancrofts, Ellen Terry, and Henry Irving. In France, Adrienne Lecouvreur, Mlle. Dumesnil, and Mlle. Clairon excited eighteenth-century French theatergoers in much the same manner that Rachel, Gabrielle Rejane, and Sara Bernhardt commanded the attention of nineteenth-century audiences. In Germany, Carolina Neuber, Conrad Ekhof, and Friedrich Schröder promoted interest in the theater; and in Italy, nineteenth-century playgoers looked with favor and pride upon the extraordinary talents of Adelaide Ristori, Tommaso Salvini, and the great Eleanora Duse. In the United States, devotees of the theater rushed to see the influx of English actors who toured the new nation at the start of the nineteenth century. Later, American theatergoers transferred their affections and loyalty to their native sons and daughters: Edwin Forrest, Charlotte Cushman, Joseph Jefferson, Edwin Booth, Ada Rehan, William Gillette, Clara Morris, and Minnie Maddern Fiske. An abundance of acting talent characterized the eighteenth- and nineteenth-century theater, thus giving credence to the theory that an age of great acting generally follows an age of great playwriting.

Although an actor's talent and his personality were undoubtedly responsible for his popularity at the box office, other factors contributed to his eminence during the Age of Great Actors. Audiences were attracted to the theater because playwrights began to fashion plays that reflected the problems of everyday living. In 1731, George Lillo's *The London Merchant; or, The History of George Barnwell* shifted the emphasis of English tragedy from a concern with the fate of kings and queens to a concern with the tragic errors committed by members of the mercantile society. In Germany, *Miss Sara Sampson,* a domestic version of the Medea story by Gotthold Ephraim Lessing, had a similar effect on German drama. In France, Alexandre Dumas *fils* sentimentally related the trials and tribulations of a Parisian cocotte in *La Dame aux Camélias.* In the United States, Bronson Howard caught the tempo of American contemporary life in *The Henrietta.* In short, because the theater presented insights into daily living, eighteenth- and nineteenth-century theatergoers embraced it as its own. Thus, theater, which had once depended upon the patronage and protection of royalty for its existence, was now supported by a wealthy middle-class society. Finally, the attitude of the public toward the actor and his profession took a positive turn as the actor gave evidence of living an exemplary life, improving standards of performance and production, and acquiring wealth because of his business acumen. Consequently, Anne Oldfield, Barton Booth, David Garrick, and Henry Irving were honored with burial in Westminster Abbey; François Joseph Talma was hailed as a hero of the French Revolution; Edwin Booth was accorded an ovation when he came out of the voluntary retirement which had been induced by his brother's dastardly act; and Henry Irving was knighted by Queen Victoria. Only the Church remained obdurate in its condemnation of the actor and his profession. Passing time and a growing change in the sentiment of the Church, however, would eventually surmount this one obstacle that militated against achieving the full measure of respectability accorded to the other professions.

a. David Garrick

On October 19, 1741, London audiences trekked to the theater in Goodman's Fields to hear a concert in two parts, and to observe a performance of *Richard III.* Earlier, Henry Giffard, manager of the theater, had announced that the part of Richard would be played by "a Gentleman (who has never appeared on any Stage)." Although the announcement proved effective in arousing the curiosity of the theatergoer and attracting him to Giffard's out-of-the-way theater, the truth of the announcement was open to question. The "Gentleman" was not without acting experience. A year earlier, he had played a number of small roles in a production of *The Mock Doctor* by Henry Fielding, the novelist. In addition, he had written a play, *Lethe; or Aesop in the Shades,* which had been produced at Drury Lane. He was a personal friend of Charles Macklin who had recently captivated London with his interpretation of Shylock. He was more than a casual acquaintance of Peg Woffington, the popular commedienne who specialized in "breeches parts." He was known to a number of professional London actors who frequented a coffee house near his place of business, a wine shop. Perhaps he preferred anonymity on this particular occasion because of his pride lest he fail, or because he was still uncertain about foregoing the respectable life he led as a wine merchant. Perhaps the "Gentleman" cloaked himself in mystery because he possessed a good sense of theater. Whatever the reason, the "Gentleman," David Garrick, mesmerized his audience with his interpretation of Richard III.

James Quin and Charles Macklin were leading actors in the London theater at the time David Garrick gave his memorable performance in *Richard III*. Each of these established actors differed in acting style; Quin exemplifying a declamatory style that focused attention upon the poetry of the playwright, and Macklin exemplifying a naturalistic style that focused attention upon the nature of the character. A hot-tempered man off stage, James Quin was an awkward actor who spoke without emotion and gesticulated without meaning. Considered an especially good Falstaff, Quin was an indifferent tragedian who hewed to traditional stage business and characterization in performing a role. After observing Garrick play Richard, a role which he often essayed, Quin remarked: "If this young fellow is right, we have all been wrong."

In contrast, Charles Macklin borrowed from nature to project the character he was performing. Irish born, Macklin had difficulty finding employment early in his career because of his radical departure from the traditional style of the times. Then in 1741, a few months before Garrick appeared as Richard, Macklin portrayed a Shylock that caused Alexander Pope to exclaim: "There is the Jew that Shakespeare drew." Shakespeare's words rolled from Macklin's lips as thoughts from Shylock's mind; gestures and expressions were motivated by Shylock's behavior and actions. Now, through Macklin's interpretation, Shylock emerged as a character ironically caught in a web of circumstances he had partly created, rather than as the low comic figure heretofore depicted by other actors. Once again the role became a challenge for great actors rather than an assignment for the company comedian. A proponent of naturalistic acting, Charles Macklin was avant-garde in urging his student-actors "to know the passion and humor of each character" when studying a role. He also advised his student-actors to free their speech of rant and bombast, suggesting that lines first be learned and spoken as one would in life, then elevated when spoken on stage. In the early 1770s, Macklin seized an opportunity to bring naturalism to the London stage by performing Macbeth in Scottish attire. Thus, Macklin introduced period costuming to the English theater, although he could not persuade his leading lady to follow his example. Macklin's life spanned nearly a century, a good part of which was spent in the theater.

However, it was David Garrick, actor, playwright, director, and theater manager, who popularized the trend toward acting that was more realistic, if not entirely naturalistic. Like Charles Macklin, both a friend and a foe with whom he discussed the art of acting, David Garrick broke with the declamatory style of the day by speaking in a conversational manner that was considerably heightened through emphasis, pause, and timing. Garrick's Richard fascinated theatergoers because Garrick concentrated on the speech rhythms of Richard's thinking rather than on the cadence of the playwright's poetry. Consequently, Richard emerged as a human and frightened monster because he spoke like other men in London society. Despite his short stature and heavy-set body, Garrick was a well coordinated actor whose graceful movements and appropriate gestures had a hypnotic effect upon audiences. In complete control of facial expressions, Garrick astounded viewers with his ability to project the thoughts and feelings of the character he was portraying. Theatergoers were transfixed by the shades of meaning Garrick conveyed through the unique use of his eyes. An observer of human nature and human affairs, Garrick studied and adopted the behavior of a prototype in creating a role. His King Lear was based on his study of a man gone mad; his Abel Drugger in *The Alchemist* by Ben Jonson was a classic study of London low-life. Finally, Garrick was endowed with a creative imagination that enabled him to create fresh and original characterizations each time he undertook a new role. He had no peers among his contemporaries. Gifted in playing both comedy and tragedy, Garrick was challenged in acknowledged greatness only by the memory of those who had witnessed the performances of other great English actors. Eventually, however, he was recognized as a worthy colleague of Richard Burbage, Edward Alleyn, and Thomas Betterton, who had preceded him.

In September 1763, an overworked David Garrick and his wife left London for an extended vacation on the Continent. The previous season had been a difficult one. During the 1762–1763 season, Garrick had managed to rid the playing area of seated spectators who constantly interfered with the performance. The actors rebelled against the new policy because on a benefit night, they derived a good source of income from these privileged spectators. To appease the actors, Garrick increased the seating capacity of the theater so that their income would not be appreciably affected. The spectators, too, would not accept the new policy gracefully and frequently showed their irritation by disrupting performances. A weary Garrick hoped that a leave of absence would revitalize him. The Garricks remained on the Continent for nearly two years, during which time they were entertained by high society and feted by members of the acting profession in each of the major European cities visited. French actors recalled the celebrated actor's visit when, in 1769, they read a pamphlet titled, *"Garrick, ou les Acteurs Anglais; Ouvrage contenant des réflexions sur l'art dramatique, sur l'art de la représentation et le jeu des acteurs; avec des notes historiques et critiques sur les différents théâtres de Londres et de Paris; traduit de L'Anglais, 1769."*

Antonio Fabio Sticotti was the author of the pamphlet that had been translated from one titled *The Actor: a Treatise on the Art of Playing*. The latter had been written in 1750 by John Hill, an Englishman, and had been revised by the author in 1755. What Sticotti may or may not have realized was that John Hill had based his pamphlet on a French work, *Le Comédien,* written by Pierre Remond de Sainte-Albine in 1747! Like *Le Comédien* and the Hill translation, Sticotti's pamphlet concerned itself with the art, the qualifications, and the sensibility of the actor. The pamphlet espoused the need for the emotional involvement of the actor in preparing and performing a role. The arguments advanced by Sainte-Albine and his translators were opposed by Denis Diderot in his *Le Paradoxe sur le Comédien* (*The Paradox of Acting*). In contrast to Sainte-Albine, Hill, and Sticotti, Diderot held that the actor "must have in himself an unmoved and disinterested onlooker—and no sensibility." Diderot, who admired Garrick's demonstrated ability to produce any number of facial expressions without feeling any emotion whatsoever, believed that, unless the actor remained detached from the emotional nature of the role he was playing and which he had created from a close observation of human nature, the actor could not "play the same part twice running with the same spirit and success." Written nearly 200 years ago, *Le Paradox* is as provocative today as it was when

Diderot wrote it. Actors, critics, and drama teachers still ponder and debate whether the actor should present the character, that is, imitate the nature of the character in performance, or whether the actor should represent the character, that is, live the nature of the character in performance.

David Garrick retired in 1776. In his nearly thirty years as actor–manager of the Drury Lane Theater, Garrick brought about many changes in acting and play production. As an actor, Garrick routed an artificial manner of acting from the stage through a personal acting style that, though calculated and controlled, gave the illusion of reality. As a director, he insisted that his actors be punctual for rehearsal and that a seriousness of purpose accompany the rehearsal period. Moreover, he urged his actors to listen to one another on stage and to speak in a manner that was natural. As an adapter, Garrick popularized the works of Shakespeare, although his adaptations frequently did the Bard an injustice: Juliet wakened before Romeo could commit suicide, Macbeth's death was prolonged by a speech of repentance, Queen Gertrude confessed her guilt and was removed from the scene in a state of insanity. As a playwright, Garrick contributed to the many farces and comedies that amused theatergoers of the period. As a producer, Garrick hired the best actors available, mounted plays written by new playwrights, and influenced the development of scene design in England by hiring Jacques de Louthebourg, a talented scene artist. In the course of his spectacular career, David Garrick created approximately a hundred different roles and appeared 2,251 times before an audience. When he died in 1779, David Garrick was accorded an honor given few men in his profession—he was buried in Westminster Abbey.

b. François Joseph Talma

On November 4, 1789, approximately four months after French citizens had stormed the Bastille, theatergoers crowded the Comédie-Française to witness a new play that was to be performed by a relatively unknown actor. The play, *Charles IX,* was written by Marie Joseph de Chénier, a revolutionary who aimed to draw an analogy between the intolerance of Charles IX and the autocracy of Louis XVI. The title role was performed by François Joseph Talma, a "pensionnaire du roi," who had accepted the role when it was rejected by Saint-Fal who feared the reaction of the audience to the political overtones of the play. In all probability, Talma agreed to accept the role because of his friendship with Chénier and because Talma's rank in the company limited him to playing third parts only. In a recent book, *Talma, A Biography of an Actor,* the author, Herbert F. Collins, describes the performance of the actor and the impact of his interpretation of Charles IX upon the audience:

> . . . This night proved a turning point in Talma's career. He had studied that nervous poltroon of a King to the very last detail. His make-up reproduced the mongolian eyes, the thin-lipped, tightly drawn mouth of the tyrant with such success that David told him he looked like a portrait taken down from the walls of the Louvre.
>
> His costume was historically accurate in every particular. Add to this, his sensitive playing. His emotional outbursts, running the whole gamut from childish petulance to frenzied horror, brought to the mannered acting of his day, with its monotonous chanting and stereotyped gestures, a new conception based on nature and truth, in fact a new life. Like our own Kean, yet to arrive, he showed he could command the lightning-flash to dispel the foggy gloom that all too often enveloped contemporary tragic acting. And what panache was his! He could preen, he could strut in that decadent Valois Court. He could arouse horror, inspire terror and hold an audience frozen in the hollow of his hand. From his lips Chénier's pedestrian verse rang out like a tocsin. All who saw his performance realized that something vital, something new had come to the French stage.
>
> Not only did this man enthrall them with his voice, he gripped them with his by-play, with his silence, with his least movements . . . The parterre went mad with enthusiasm. This Charles IX, tyrant, hypocrite, weakling, held them as in a vice. The play was a prodigious success; for Talma a personal triumph . . .*

---

* From Herbert F. Collins, *Talma: A Biography of an Actor* (New York: Hill and Wang, 1964), p. 52. Reprinted by permission of Hill and Wang, Inc., and Faber and Faber, Ltd., London.

Born in France, François Joseph Talma spent his boyhood and adolescence in London, where he mastered the English language. It was during those years, too, that he became acquainted with the works of Shakespeare by observing the performances of John Kemble and Charles Macklin. At the age of twenty-one, Talma was enrolled in the École de Medicine in Paris by his father, who hoped that Talma would become a dentist! However, because the rigorous training tired him and the practical experience depressed him, Talma turned toward the theater. In 1786, he was accepted at the École Royale de Déclamation, which trained actors for admission to the Comédie-Française. A year later he began a series of debuts that led to an appointment with the Comédie-Française as a "pensionnaire du roi," a junior company member restricted to playing third parts. From the date of his appointment, December 1787, until his performance as Charles IX, Talma played a number of minor roles that barely tested his acting talents. However, it was in the course of performing one of these small parts that Talma initiated a costume reform overdue in the French theater. As Proculus in Voltaire's *Brutus,* Talma appeared on stage realistically garbed in Roman attire. Although his attention to costume accuracy amused his fellow actors who wore contemporary dress, including an eighteenth-century wig out of deference to the King, the audience enthusiastically applauded Talma's efforts. Thereafter, actors of the Comédie-Française paid more attention to their costumes. Talma's success as Charles IX marked the beginning of a career that spanned nearly forty years, during which time the Comédie-Française experienced many changes as the result of the political turmoil that beset the nation.

As a member of the Comédie-Française, Talma was committed to performing the classics, comedy and tragedy, or those new plays that adhered to classical play elements: elevated themes, heroic characters, poetic dialogue, and the unities of time, place, and action. In the course of his career, Talma essayed the leading roles in the tragedies written by Pierre Corneille, Jean Racine, and Voltaire. He also originated roles in plays written by the contemporary playwrights: Marie Joseph de Chénier, Antoine de Lafosse, Pierre Lafon, Étienne de Jouy, and Jean François Ducis, whose distorted adaptations of Shakespeare's plays provided Talma with an opportunity to play Hamlet and Macbeth (as an adapter, the Great Garrick did a similar disservice to Shakespeare). The great actor rarely played comedy because tragedy was his forte; however, at the age of sixty, Talma triumphed in the role of Danville in *L'École des Vieillards* by Casimir Delavigne. As an actor of the Comédie-Française, Talma was committed to performing classical roles in a manner that stressed vocal excellence, dignity, and quietude. Talma, however, was not satisfied with anything less than a truthful representation of the character on stage. He immersed himself in the emotions of the character while on stage, and he allowed inspiration to help him create an effective moment while performing. Although he agreed that the actor benefited from training in voice and diction and body movements, Talma believed that sensibility—"that faculty of exaltation which agitates an actor, takes possession of his senses, shakes even his very soul, and enables him to enter into the most tragic situations, and the most terrible of the passions, as if they were his very own"—was of paramount importance in projecting a characterization. A classical actor who took nature as his model, Talma on stage portended Romanticism in the French theater.

Talma died in 1826, a scant few years before Victor Hugo's *Hérnani* precipitated a battle between the Classicists and the Romanticists. The "Frenchman's David Garrick" was buried at Père-Lachaise without religious ceremony.

c. *Edwin Booth*

At the time of his death in 1893, Edwin Booth was America's leading tragedian and the acknowledged dean of his profession. He had earned his accolades the hard way. As a child, Booth acccompanied his father, the great but eccentric Junius Brutus Booth, on tours that took the pair to theaters far from their residence in Baltimore. Booth was of a tender age when he nightly escorted his father to their lodging where he ministered to the needs of the failing actor. Once, when his father became too ill to perform, Booth was pressed into playing Richard III to fulfill his father's obligations. In 1852, Junius Brutus Booth died and Edwin was freed from being his father's dresser, companion, guardian, and understudy. Knowing no other profession and deeply influenced by his years of traveling with his father, Booth was determined to have a theatrical career. For the next five years, the young actor traveled the western, southern, and New England theater circuits, playing comedy, farce, melodrama, and tragedy, utilizing every acting experience as an insight to the demands of his profession. A successful engagement in Boston in 1857 encouraged him to try his talent in New York. His performance of Richard III won plaudits from the press and the public in New York City. Nevertheless, Edwin Forrest still dominated the American stage, and another six years would pass before Edwin Booth would be duly recognized as a contender for the position held by Forrest in the American theater.

Booth was approaching the zenith of his career in 1865 when his hopes and dreams were shattered by the assassination of President Lincoln. In deep remorse for his brother's deed and in abject shame for the blight cast upon his profession, Booth went into voluntary retirement. However, on January 3, 1866, he resumed his career before a New York audience that accorded him a standing ovation. In 1869, Booth opened the sumptuous Booth Theater in New York. In reconstructing the opening night, Eleanor Ruggles writes:

> The auditorium was as big as a meadow and shaped like a horseshoe. From the ceiling a monster gasolier hung, its jets lighted by electric sparks. A fan worked by steam pressure agitated the atmosphere in a stately way. There were seats for almost two thousand people, most of whom couldn't as yet be induced to sit down, they were so busy admiring the painted Apollo, god of poetry and music, on the vaulted ceiling; the freshly gilded cupids and initial B in gold over the doors of the boxes; the busts of Garrick, Talma, Kean, Cooke, and Betterton along the walls and the noble statue of Shakespeare enshrined over the proscenium arch. . . . The orchestra began to play soft strains; the fringed curtain stole upward and arranged itself artfully in a series of festoons framing the stage, and the audience sank back into its plush chairs to wait for its money's worth.
>
> It got what it came for. With a loud alarm and clanging of bells a full hundred young men of the rival houses of Montague and

Capulet shot out from the wings and up and down the unusually wide and deep apron, their steel blades weaving and chattering—a professional maître des armes had been rehearsing them for weeks in the gymnasium upstairs. In the masque at the Capulets, which was gorgeously staged, a corps of trained dancers performed. The balcony scene had two balconies. Romeo bounded over the garden wall wearing a yellow satin tunic, a rolling collar of green silk, flowing sleeves, and a pointed hat of silk and solferino velvet with a plume of cock's feathers. When he took his hat off, his blond hair gleamed in the stage moonlight, which also shone on Juliet's form in white satin, leaning on the rail of the lower balcony, her skirt looped with pearls. More pearls were twined around her neck and a tiara of diamonds rested on her streaming, waist-long black hair.*

Romeo and Juliet set the standard for productions to come: *Hamlet, Richelieu, The Winter's Tale,* and *Julius Caesar.* Unfortunately, production costs and building debts were not offset by box-office receipts. Nor did his presentation of other stars, Charlotte Cushman, Joseph Jefferson, and Lotta Crabtree, provide Booth with the money he needed to meet operating costs. Sorely pressed for funds at a time when the nation was gripped by a financial panic, Booth filed for bankruptcy on January 26, 1874. Shortly thereafter, he resumed his career as an actor under the sponsorship of more astute theater managers.

d. Henry Irving

In England, meanwhile, Henry Irving was on the brink of theatrical fame and fortune. Unlike Edwin Booth, Henry Irving's parents were simple country folk who disapproved of the theater because of their religious training. To gratify his mother's wishes that he enter a respectable profession and to supplement the family income, he took a position as a law clerk. At the conclusion of each working day, however, he attended the City Elocution Class in an attempt

---

* Reprinted from *Prince of Players, Edwin Booth* by Eleanor Ruggles. By permission of W. W. Norton & Company, Inc. Copyright 1953 by W. W. Norton & Company, Inc.

to overcome a speech defect, stammering, and to learn acting techniques. When an inheritance gave him the needed financial security to embark upon a theatrical career, Irving terminated his employment with the law firm. Part of his inheritance was invested in a wardrobe, which he deemed important to his career. An additional three guineas was spent in purchasing the role of Romeo in a local production so that he could prove his ability to sustain a long emotional role. It was at this point, too, that Henry Irving acquired his professional name—he had been christened John Henry Brodribb at birth. From 1856, when he joined his first professional acting company, until 1866, when he became an established London actor, Henry Irving played over 600 roles in provincial stock companies based in Edinburgh, Birmingham, Liverpool, Glasgow, Manchester, and Dublin. The parts ranged from Scruncher (the Wolf) in *Little Bo-Peep* (a pantomime) to the title role in *Hamlet;* from a cook in *The Enchanted Lake* (an extravaganza) to the title role in *David Copperfield;* from Fernando and Villabella in *The Maid and the Magpie* (a burlesque) to George Barnwell in *The London Merchant.* To Henry Irving, each part, large or small, whether in comedy, farce, melodrama, or tragedy, was an exercise in learning his art. Like Edwin Booth, Irving forged his craft in the crucible of the rigorous training demanded by the theater.

In 1871, Edwin Booth rejected an opportunity to lease the Lyceum theater in England. At the time, Booth was too beset with the problem of operating his New York theater to undertake a season of plays abroad. Moreover, the Lyceum theater had acquired a reputation of being a house of failures as a result of the long string of theatrical disasters that opened and closed the house regularly. Superstitious theater producers refused to believe that any undertaking at the Lyceum could end successfully. Fortunately for Henry Irving, Hezekiah Linthicum Bateman, an expatriate American who had left the United States because of his sympathy with the Southern cause, was not of this mind. In need of a theater in which to launch the career of his third daughter, Isabella, Bateman leased the Lyceum for the 1871–1872 season.

Bateman hired Henry Irving to play the leading male roles in the plays featuring Bateman's daughter. When the initial offering,

Fanchette, proved of little box-office value, and when the next production, *Pickwick,* drew little attention, Bateman was at a loss as to how to keep his theater open. At this point, Irving reminded Bateman of his promise to mount a production of *The Bells* with Irving in the lead role. Reluctantly, the theater manager agreed to put the play into rehearsal under Irving's direction. His hesitancy was based on his limited knowledge of Irving's talent and his feeling that a talented comedian could not portray the guilt-ridden Mathias. The play opened on November 25, 1871, to resounding acclaim from the press and the public. Like so many great actors before him, Henry Irving became a star overnight.

In 1881, ten years after that eventful evening and during which time Irving became the actor–manager of the Lyceum theater, the career of Edwin Booth merged with that of Irving to provide the theater with one of its most brilliant productions, *Othello,* with each actor alternating in the roles of the Moor and his nemesis, Iago. The suggestion for the production came from Henry Irving when Edwin Booth, having completed an unsuccessful season of plays at the Princess theater, proposed a series of matinees at the Lyceum. In all probability Irving desired the production because he realized he would never again have an opportunity to play either role opposite an actor of Booth's stature. Additionally, Henry Irving had once supported the actor when he made his first tour of England, and he had a tremendous admiration for Booth professionally. The first performance occurred on May 2, 1881, at which time Booth played Othello, Irving, Iago, and Ellen Terry, Desdemona. Booth played Iago to Irving's Othello when the second week of performance began. Neither actor produced an Othello that was satisfactory to the critics or the audience. Physically, Irving was too tall and Booth too short to suggest the Moor's massive physique. In addition, both stars lacked the inner turmoil and fire that motivated the compulsive behavior of the Moor. Iago, however, was another matter. Both actors overwhelmed the audience and the critics with their interpretation of the role. Booth presented a quiet, brooding Iago who assiduously exploited the weakness of Othello's character. In Booth's hands, Iago became an evil force that silently chipped away at its victim. In contrast, Irving presented an active, scheming Iago who studiously sought to penetrate and destroy Othello's armor. In Irving's hands, Iago became an evil force that openly worked at taunting and ruining its victim. Whereas Booth's Iago calculated the next move, Irving's Iago catapulted the next situation. When the engagement ended on June 17, Booth went to Germany where he captivated audiences with his performances as Hamlet and King Lear. Irving, putting aside forevermore the costumes he had worn as Othello and Iago, went on to score additional triumphs with his exquisite productions of other plays by Shakespeare.

Today, the comparative greatness of the two actors is only a matter of academic interest. It is very likely that each would be out of place on a twentieth-century stage. Their grand manner of acting would not be in keeping with a style of acting that approximates life as completely as does our acting today. What is of interest and significance is the contribution that each actor made to his art and to his profession.

At a time when an energetic but youthful American theater was just beginning to develop its own actors and playwrights, Edwin Booth brought to the American stage a manner of acting that was comparable to the great acting of the past. Working within the limitations of a traditional style that stressed heroic acting, Booth added a degree of naturalness that identified the character as a human being. Regardless of the number of times he had played a part, Booth diligently studied each role as if he were playing it for the first time. He was, for example, never completely satisfied with his impersonation of Shylock and he repeatedly reviewed his performance and searched the script for additional nuances and clues to Shylock's character. In contrast, Henry Irving discarded the traditional concept and substituted an approach that dramatized the inner emotions of the character through detailed business. Audiences sensed the fear that throbbed within Mathias as Irving, bent forward to buckle his shoe, slowly moved his hands the full length of his body when he imagined that he was hearing the sleigh bells which had long ago pronounced the doom of the man he had murdered. Audiences read Iago's mind as he ate grapes, spewed out the seeds, and picked his teeth with his dagger while he eavesdropped on the conversation between Cassio and Desdemona. Irving's psychological approach portended an acting style that related external behavior to inner feelings at a time when artificial acting dominated the English stage.

As producer-directors, each actor brought to the theater of their time an artistic integrity that elevated the standard of play production and performance. The Booth and Lyceum theaters were showplaces, appealing to the eye and conducive to enjoyable playgoing. Productions were lavishly staged and accurately costumed. Henry Irving surrounded himself with the most talented actors available and did not hesitate to drill them like soldiers, regardless of their years of experience and status in the profession. Booth, in contrast, imaginatively staged and mounted his productions, but did not always extend the same effort and concern to selecting his actors. Too often one reads the criticism that while his productions were lavish and creative in execution and design, the actors were frequently inferior to their star and their surroundings. Perhaps this failure can be attributed to Booth's early experience as an itinerant actor which required him to tolerate the inadequacies of a stock-company cast.

Finally, each actor advanced his profession in the eyes of the public. Despite the scandals and the misfortunes that haunted Booth during his entire life, the public could not help but admire his fortitude in the face of adversity. Nor could the public deny their pride in his conquest of the European theater. Booth earned his reputation as America's greatest actor. Similarly, Henry Irving had taken his place in the long line of great English actors that had begun with Richard Burbage. His confrontation with the Church paved the way for molding positive public response toward the profession. His contribution to his art and his profession was recognized in 1895 when he was knighted by Queen Victoria.

9. Constantin Stanislavski

A revolt against the existing practices in the commercial theater occurred in the last quarter of the nineteenth century. Underlying the revolt was an objection to the established playwright who presented an artificial view of life and to the lack of a forum for the new playwright who responded to the impact of Charles Darwin's *The Origin of the Species.* The imagination of the playwright was stimulated by the idea that man was an appropriate subject for scientific investigation and observation. Consequently, the playwright envisioned the theater as a kind of laboratory for studying man in his habitat. In Norway, the revolt gained impetus from the plays written by Henrik Ibsen, who, in theatrically sound and well-constructed plays, depicted common man in the moments of personal crises that stemmed from his environment, heredity, and the social mores of the community. In France, the revolt was pressed by Émile Zola, who proclaimed in the preface to the play version of his novel, *Thérèse Raquin:*

> . . . It is by no means my intention to make my play a rallying standard. It has striking shortcomings, toward which no one is more severe than myself; if I were to criticize it, there would be only one thing I should not attack: the author's very obvious desire to bring the theater into closer relation with the great movement toward truth and experimental science which has since the last century been on the increase in every manifestation of the human intellect. The movement was started by the new methods of science; thence, Naturalism revolutionized criticism and history, in submitting man and his works to a system of precise analysis, taking into account all circumstances, environment, and "organic cases." Then, in turn, art and letters were carried along with the current: painting became realistic—our landscape school killed the historical school—; the novel, that social and individual study with its extremely loose framework, after growing and growing, took up all the activities of man, absorbing little by little the various classifications made in the rhetorics of the past. These are all undeniable facts. We have now come to the birth of the true, that is the great, the only force of the century. Everything advances in a literary epoch. Whoever wishes to retreat or turn to one side, will be lost in the general dust. This is why I am absolutely convinced that in the near future, the Naturalist movement will take its place in the realm of the drama, and bring with it the power of reality, the new life of modern art.
>
> In the theater, every innovation is a delicate matter. Literary revolutions are slow in making themselves felt. And it is only logical

that this should be the last citadel of falsehood: where the true belongs. The public as a whole resents having its habits changed, and the judgments which it passes have all the brutality of a death-sentence. But there comes a time when the public itself becomes an accomplice of the innovators; this is when, imbued with the new spirit, weary of the same stories repeated to it countless times, it feels an imperious desire for youth and originality.

I may be mistaken, but I believe that this is the situation of our public to-day. The historical drama is in its death-throes, unless something new comes to its assistance: that corpse needs new blood. It is said that the operetta and the dramatic fantasy have killed the historical drama. This is not so: the historical drama is dying a natural death, of its own extravagances, lies, and platitudes. If comedy still maintains its place amid the general disintegration of the stage, it is because comedy clings closer to actual life, and is often true. I defy the last of the Romanticists to put upon the stage a heroic drama; at the sight of all the paraphernalia of armor, secret doors, poisoned wines and the rest, the audience would only shrug its shoulders. And melodrama, that bourgeois offspring of the romantic drama, is in the hearts of the people more dead than its predecessor; its false sentiment, its complications of stolen children and discovered documents, its impudent gasconnades, have finally rendered it despicable, so that any attempt to revive it proves abortive. The great works of 1830 will always remain advance-guard works, landmarks in a literary epoch, superb efforts which laid low the scaffoldings of the classics. But, now that everything is torn down, and swords and capes rendered useless, it is time to base our works on truth. To substitute the Romantic for the Classic tradition would be a refusal to take advantage of the liberty acquired by our forbears. There should no longer be any school, no more formulas, no standards of any sort; there is only life itself, an immense field where each may study and create as he likes . . .*

Émile Zola's pleas for reform had little or no effect upon the commercial theater of the time and were not answered until André Antoine opened the Théâtre Libre in Paris in 1887. An impover-

---

* From *European Theories of the Drama* by Barrett H. Clark.

ished actor who eked out a livelihood as an employee of the Paris Gas Company, Antoine's original intent was personally motivated. He longed for a career in the theater. To his surprise, he found himself an overnight success and an innovator with his naturalistic mounting of *Jacques Damour,* an adaptation of a story written by Émile Zola. In subsequent mountings of plays by Ibsen, Strindberg, Hauptmann, Becque, and others, Antoine established the principles we associate with naturalism: plays that were loosely constructed, dialogue that reflected the speech of the common man, characters that were drawn from everyday life, acting that required the actors to live the characters, and stage settings that were replicas of the locale. Frequently, the playwright resorted to sordid situations in order to present a clinical study of life. The result was a "slice of life" on stage.

Encouraged by Antoine's success, other free theaters developed in Berlin, London, and Moscow. In 1889, for example, Otto Brahm opened the Freie Bühne with a production of *Ghosts* by Henrik Ibsen. Although the theater closed after two years, it did introduce an important new playwright, Gerhart Hauptmann. In 1891, J. T. Grein opened the Independent Theater in London. The prize playwright of the theater was George Bernard Shaw. In 1897, Vladimir Ivanovich Nemirovich-Danchenko and Constantin Stanislavski organized the Moscow Art Theater after an eighteen-hour conference in a coffee-house.

One of the lasting effects of Naturalism is the system of acting devised by Constantin Stanislavski. The "System" is based on Stanislavski's experience as an actor, his experience as a director and teacher of actors, and his observation of the great actors of the time, particularly Tommaso Salvini. The "System" offers the actor a valid approach to preparing a role in *any play.* It advocates a detailed analysis of the script and the character. The actor is urged to study the overall structure of the play and to understand how each scene contributes to the structure. The actor must research the historical background of the play and relate his findings to the role. In analyzing the role, the actor is cautioned not to accept the surface traits of the role as outlined by the playwright. Instead, the actor is exhorted to look within the character to discover the inner motivations that provoke the actions and behavior of the character in the play. The actor is stimulated to discover the "spine" of the role, that is, the basic desire, the motivation, the emotion, the objective, the goal that prods the character throughout the course of the play. The actor is then expected to relate this "spine" to individual scenes and the play as a whole. The actor is encouraged to imagine what he would do *if* he were placed in the same situation as the character he is representing. Exercises that develop the imaginative *if* provide the actor with an "emotional memory" he can recall while playing the role. Similarly, the actor's sense of observation is sharpened by exercises based on personal experiences and life-studies. The actor is urged to concentrate on each scene as it unfolds, responding to it as though it were a first experience. The actor does not "live the role" in actual performance as much as he imagines himself behaving and reacting as the character would in the situation. Training in basic stage techniques aids the actor in projecting his role.

Stanislavski recorded his ideas in *My Life in Art* (1924), *An Actor Prepares* (1926), *Building a Character* (published 1950), and *Creating a Role* (published 1961). Although the writings of great actors reveal an approach similar to that of the "System," Stanislavski's contribution to the understanding of acting theory is unique in that it represents a written, systematic approach to acting that can be practiced by any actor in preparing a role for any play. The "System," however, will not produce an actor, if the basic ingredient, talent, is lacking. On the other hand, the "System" will enhance the talent of a gifted actor.

B. CUES FOR THEATERGOERS

1. Evaluating the Performance

With self-identification, the theatergoer views the actor as lean, tall, thin, short, wide, fat, muscular, flabby, paunchy, masculine, virile, feminine, lovely, handsome, stately, ugly, dignified, beautiful, cute. With self-identification, the theatergoer studies the actor curiously, joyfully, amusingly, suspiciously, irritatedly. With self-identification, the theatergoer reacts with laughs, stomps, catcalls, whistles, screams, cheers, coughs, boos, yawns, sighs, applause. With self-identification, the theatergoer judges the actor brilliant, inadequate, fair, obscene, dull, amateurish, boring, witty, sobering, impossible, wonderful, magnetic, spellbinding. The presence and response of the theatergoer nurtures and unleashes the creative effort of the actor.

Acting is an ephemeral art. Unlike the creative effort of the composer, the painter, and the sculptor, whose talents are expressed and remembered through a tangible legacy, the creative effort of the actor is momentary and fleeting. It is ever-changing. Its duration in time is a scant two hours or less. Its total effect is cumulative because of its transient nature. It exists only in the presence of an audience, and it must be recreated for each new audience. It demands a critical skill on the part of the theatergoer if the creative effort is to remain a lasting memory. In viewing a performance, the theatergoer should consider:

a. Did the casting of the actors meet the performance needs of the play?

All plays have specific performance needs that must be solved by casting the right actor in the role. For example, *Death of a Salesman* needs an actor who has the gift of gab of a salesman, and one who behaves like a braggart. *A Streetcar Named Desire* needs an actress whose physical stature belies her fragile spirit. *Othello* needs an actor who can project brute strength and a passionate soul, and another actor who can project pure villainy. *Born Yesterday* needs an actress who can play a dumb chorus girl intelligently. *You Can't Take it with You* needs a cast of actors who can project the image of a family whose eccentricities and philosophy of life nearly ruin the romance of one of its members. Consequently, a theatergoer, after seeing a play, would do well to begin his appraisal of the performance by first considering whether the actors were properly cast. If all the actors have met the vocal, physical, emotional, intellectual, and spiritual needs of the roles written by the playwright, then the theatergoer can begin his criticism of the performance with the statement, "The play was well cast. The performance needs of the play were met."

b. Did the company achieve an ensemble effect in its performance?

After determining whether each role was properly cast, the theatergoer should consider whether the actors functioned as a team in performing the play. Did each actor perform his role in concert with the other actors? Did each actor listen and react to what was being said, whether or not he was being addressed? Did each actor become part of the scene, either as a participant directly involved in the action, or as bystander observing the action? Did each actor interpret his role in consonance with the overall concept of the play? Did the acting communicate totality in performance by the company, or individuality in performance by the actor? If the talents of the company were directed toward emphasizing the essence of the play, then it may be said that the company gave a demonstration of ensemble acting.

Ensemble acting in the theater today is the result of the influence wielded by George II, Duke of Saxe-Meningen, upon other theater reformers at the end of the nineteenth century. The Duke initiated ensemble acting when he began to direct his troupe of unknown German actors. A talented scene designer, the "theater Duke" took upon himself the responsibility of overseeing all phases of interpretation, performance, and production. Indeed, the play became paramount as the Duke bent all efforts and talents toward realizing the essence of the play. The status or talents of the actors were subordinated to the needs of the play. For example, an extremely versatile actor often found himself performing a small but key role rather than a lead part. In addition, the Duke subjected his actors to lengthy rehearsal periods and dictated the interpretation of the role. The movements of the actor were planned in detail by the Duke. Each actor was expected to dovetail his characterization with that of his fellow actor. In a day and age when the star dominated the performance and interpretation of the play, European audiences were stimulated and intrigued with the group performance of the Meningen players. Henry Irving and Constantin Stanislavski were moved to emulate the Duke's approach to play interpretation and production. The modern-day director was born as a consequence.

All productions strive to achieve a totality in performance, but ensemble acting is generally realized when a company of actors work together over a period of time to attain an acting style that serves the needs of the play. The recent offering of *Love for Love* by William Congreve is an example of the epitome of ensemble acting as offered by the National Theater of Great Britain. Sir Laurence Olivier, one of the great actors of our times, was cast in a minor role. In spite of Olivier's professional reputation, his performance was blended into the performance of the entire company in realizing the quintessence of Congreve's play. In his review of the performance, Dan Sullivan, drama critic for *The New York Times,* remarked that "to name the outstanding players would be to name the entire cast." Mr. Sullivan's comment might well be remembered by the theatergoer in judging the performance of a company of actors.

c. *Did the actor reveal the inner character of the role he played?*

If the playwright has written a fully developed character, the actor has many opportunities to reveal the inner character of the role he is playing. A play consists of many units and each unit generally affords the actor an opportunity to reveal another facet of the character. At the onset, the actor usually establishes the outer character of the role so that the audience can identify with the part. Then, as scene after scene is unfolded, and the plot develops, the actor exposes the inner character. His versatility can be judged by his ability to lay bare the character.

The part of Amanda in *The Glass Menagerie* by Tennessee Williams is an example of a role whose complex nature provides an actress with an opportunity to reveal the inner character. It is a difficult but challenging role for an actress to portray, because the performer must probe within Amanda to evoke understanding and empathy from the audience for her behavior. Amanda's outer character belies her many faceted inner character as the play moves to its climax. The actress must surmount the problem of playing scenes that present Amanda in an unsympathetic light. Outwardly, the actress has virtually no difficulty in establishing Amanda as a mother, a widow, a hostess, a faded beauty, and a saleslady. Inwardly, however, the actress must sense that Amanda is lonely, apprehensive, insecure, and defeated. In contrast to the demands of the inner character, the scenes in which Amanda appears overtly suggest that she is spiteful, foolish, vain, impulsive, selfish, cruel, and possessive. Unless the actress can successfully communicate the inner Amanda through the demeanor and deportment of the outer Amanda as a mother, widow, hostess, faded beauty, and saleslady, Amanda emerges as an unsympathetic character—domineering, demanding, and complaining—who has earned rejection and desertion by her family. It is a taxing but rewarding role that enables a gifted actress to demonstrate her skills in baring human nature before an audience.

It is important, therefore, that the theatergoer, in judging and appraising a performance by an actor, learns to criticize the performance on the basis of the actor's grasp of the role in relation to the entire play, in relation to the other roles of the play, in relation to the time of the play, and in relation to human behavior. Moreover, the theatergoer should learn to discern whether the actor has grasped and utilized the emotional needs, mental responses, and physical appearance of the character. Finally, the theatergoer should develop his skill in judging whether the actor's characterization of the part is merely superficial and external, or one that penetrates the veneer of a recognizable type and probes in depth to discover and bring forth a human being.

d. Did the actor effectively use his voice, body, and intellect in creating the role?

In creating a role, the actor draws upon such natural attributes as his voice, body, and intellect. Through his voice, the actor speaks the dialogue written by the playwright, expresses the emotions of the character, and reveals the inner responses of the role he is performing. The actor's diction should be free of defects because each sound must be well articulated, each word properly pronounced, each utterance clearly enunciated. The actor's delivery should indicate his knowledge and mastery of the oral techniques that aid in the projection of meaning: emphasis, rate, pause, phrasing, timing, and inflection. The actor's voice should be equal to the vocal demands of the dialogue: he should be able to speak the poetry of Shakespeare, the prose of Shaw, and the everyday speech of the modern playwrights. Last, but not least, the actor must be audible to all theatergoers, not only to those sitting in the first ten rows. Through his body, the actor presents a visual picture of the character, reacts to emotional stimuli, and suggests the mental state of the role he is portraying. The posture and stance of the actor should be suitable to the character. The physical movements of the actor should be graceful, coordinated, and under control. The gestures of the actor should be meaningful, natural, and appropriate to the time in which the play is set. The facial expressions of the actor should mirror the thoughts and emotions of the character. The actor should use his physical attributes to convey the outward response to what is happening within the character.

Through his intellect, the actor deliberates and interprets his role. The actor analyzes the play for its meaning, views his role objectively in relation to the meaning, and determines the forces and situations that motivate the character throughout the play. The actor conjures a mental image of the physical presence of the character, his dress, his reponses to given situations, and his social alliances. The actor searches the script for clues to the inner life of the role—analyzing his behavior in various scenes and noting the responses of other characters to the role he is enacting. The actor draws upon his own attributes and experiences to serve the demands of the role. Finally, the actor weaves all the elements together and, through his voice, body, and intellect, breathes life and vitality into the playwright's printed words.

In appraising the effective use of voice, body, and intellect, the theatergoer should consider the truth of the characterization. Did the voice of the actor seem appropriate to the age, social position, and circumstance of the character? Did the actor make effective use of his voice to project emotional responses and nuances of meaning? Did the body of the actor become the body of the character, and convincingly establish a physical silhouette in consonance with the circumstance, age, and occupation of the character? Did the gestures of the actor emanate from within, flowing out of a response to the situation, or did the gestures of the actor appear contrived, artificial, and superfluous? Did the actor's face reveal the proper reaction to the situation? Did the actor penetrate the surface of the role he performed? Finally, did the actor through his intellect and his creative imagination mold a character whose actions carried the consistency of truth throughout the entire play?

e. Did the creative effort of the actor touch the heart and conscience of the theatergoer?

In *Rosencrantz and Guildenstern Are Dead* by Tom Stoppard, the Player King upbraids Hamlet's two friends for walking out during a performance by the players. The Player King lectures them on the senselessness and futility of an actor performing without an audience, and the necessity for the actor to feel the presence of an audience. The actor must be assured that someone is watching, someone is listening, someone is responding, someone is evaluating his creative endeavors. The actor must sense a rapport with his audience while he is exhibiting his talents. The actor's intuitive awareness of the presence and approval of the theatergoer motivates his performance. The player experiences a personal sense of pride and achievement when he literally has the theatergoer in the "palm of his hand"—when he experiences that inner security of knowing that he has drawn the theatergoer into the performance, that the theatergoer has reacted to the character interpreted by the player, that the theatergoer has had an emotional response to his creative talents.

The theatergoing experience is rewarding only if the theatergoer leaves the theater with an emotional response to what he has seen on stage. He must be fascinated yet repelled by the evil and depravity of the Master of Ceremonies in *Cabaret;* amused by the folly of Monsieur Jourdain in *Le Bourgeois Gentilhomme;* upset by the bickering and violence of George and Martha in *Who's Afraid of Virginia Woolf?;* disturbed by the hopelessness of the derelicts in *The Iceman Cometh;* bothered and embarrassed by the plight of the black family in *A Raisin in the Sun;* or delighted by the antics of Sakini in *Teahouse of the August Moon*. He cannot, however, be fascinated, amused, upset, disturbed, bothered, delighted, or embarrassed without the creative effort of the actor. The theatergoer may be moved by the theme of a play, but his sensibilities are touched and awakened by the player who is the catalyst that makes the theme of the playwright a reality.

2. The Actor Today

The actor today seeks training at a university or at a professional acting school because the provincial and traveling stock company, which once was the source of on-the-job-training, no longer exists. Consequently, the actor today, unlike his predecessor who frequently had little or no formal education, generally possesses a Bachelor or Master of Arts degree in Theater Arts. In the United States, he may have attended Yale University, the University of Miami, the University of Minnesota, the University of Denver, Stanford University, the University of Washington, the University of Hawaii, or any of the more than fifty colleges and universities offering theater arts training. The actor today may also possess a certificate of completion of a program of study from any of several professional acting schools such as the Neighborhood Playhouse, the American Academy of Dramatic Arts, the Pasadena Playhouse, and the Goodman Memorial Theater and School of the Drama. It is probable, too, that the actor's training includes summer stock and community theater experience, and it is quite likely that the actor was introduced to the theater through secondary-school dramatic activities.

In preparation and performance, the actor works at achieving a truthful and natural portrayal of the role he is playing. It does not matter whether his approach is presentational, that is, characterization based on skillful reproduction of actions, manners, behavior, and emotions, or representational, that is, characterization based on self-identification with psychological and emotional motivation, as long as the end result is a truthful realization of the character, in accordance with the script, and emotionally moving to the spectator. Nor is the actor today satisfied to rest on his laurels and coast on his talent. Rather, the actor, whether employed or otherwise, constantly works at improving his skills and extending his range by studying with professional coaches who specialize in voice, body, and acting techniques. These professionals broaden the actor's knowledge of his art through exercises, drills, discussions, and observations that stretch his imagination and prepare him for a truthful approach to characterization on stage.

The man who chooses acting as a profession soon learns that the theater is a "fabulous invalid" whose health does not materially improve from one season to another. He soon realizes that he cannot eat the memory of applause and that he must seek other means of employment to sustain himself and his family while he is "at liberty." The theater season in New York City, the center of theater activity in the United States, lasts from September through May. Regardless of the number of new productions and the number of holdovers from the previous season, a large percentage of actors remain unemployed. Approximately 15,000 actors throughout the United States and Canada belong to Actors Equity. At the peak of a season, approximately one-third of the membership is engaged in theater activity. Although repertory companies in major cities outside of New York have relieved the necessity of seeking employment in the overcrowded New York City market, the supply of actors is still in excess of the demand. In their book, *Performing Arts: The Economic Dilemma,* William J. Baumol and William G. Bowen offer the statistics to be found in the table on page 123 on the income of performers during 1964.*

Occasionally, the actor finds himself in a long-run play such as *Abie's Irish Rose, Tobacco Road, Born Yesterday,* or a long-run musical hit such as *Oklahoma, My Fair Lady,* and *Fiddler on the Roof.* When this rarity occurs, the actor is generally reluctant to relinquish his windfall because the security of steady employment makes him feel, as one actor stated, like "other people." It is then

* From William J. Baumol and William G. Bowen, *Performing Arts: The Economic Dilemma,* Twentieth Century Fund, New York (1966); p. 133.

		For Performers Having Any	
Source of Income	*Percent Having Any*	*Median*	*Interquartile Range (Range of Middle 50%)*
Professional Sources:			
Live Performances	99	$4,877	$3,100–$7,586
Television and Related Sources	49	250	150– 1,000
Teaching and Coaching	34	1,000	300– 2,000
Total from Professional Sources	100	5,771	3,395– 8,700
Unrelated Sources	20	813	327– 1,476
Spouse	22	4.300	2,000– 8,900
Other Income	40	450	300– 1,000
Total Income	100	7,275	4,128–10,500

that the actor can realize the full benefits of his Equity contract: a one-week paid vacation after one year with a given production and additional vacation time in proportion to the additional time he remains with the production; pension and welfare coverage paid by the employer; insurance coverage for the loss of personal property; and one day per month sick leave. On the debit side, however, the actor runs the risk of impeding his artistic growth and acquiring a reputation of being a "one-role" performer. James O'Neill, father of Eugene O'Neill, is a classic example of the actor whose artistic growth was stunted by success in a single role. For almost twenty years, O'Neill toured the United States playing the lead role in *The Count of Monte Cristo*. Although the financial returns made it possible for him to support an ailing wife and two growing sons, O'Neill was unable to surmount the professional injury he sustained from his identification with the part. Too late in his career, O'Neill realized that he had been trapped professionally by a money-maker. The actor today tries to avoid this pitfall by signing a contract for a limited run with the option of renewing the contract if he feels that his development as an actor will not be jeopardized by continuing with the production.

The actor today is a respected member of his community and a participant in its activities. His children attend the local school and are usually admired because of their father's profession. Like most parents, the actor zealously safeguards his spare time so that he can spend it with his family. The respectability that the actor enjoys today, however, is not a recent phenomenon, but one that stems from the patterns of conduct displayed by members of the profession toward the end of the nineteenth century. For example, when it became obvious that the Edwin Forrest Home for Actors could not adequately care for members in distress, Edwin Booth, Joseph Jefferson, Lawrence Barrett, and other leading members of the profession established The Actors Fund of America in 1882 to give aid to ailing and indigent actors. In 1888, Edwin Booth established The Players, a club whose avowed purpose was "to represent all that is best in the dramatic profession, to foster the dramatic art, and to exalt the standard of personal worth among the actors of America." During the 1890s, Maude Adams, Julia Marlowe, and Viola Allen impressed Americans with their virtuous off-stage lives. Miss Allen in particular commanded the respect of the public because she taught Sunday School. The prestige of the actor was further enhanced in 1915 when Charlotte Cushman was elected to the Hall of Fame. Ten years later, Edwin Booth was accorded the same honor.

Actors have continued to follow the pattern of civic responsibility set by their predecessors. For example, Helen Menken has been actively involved with the work of The Institute for the Crippled and Disabled and The Institute for the Facially Disfigured. Katharine Cornell is chairman of the National Committee of the American Foundation for Overseas Blind, which is affiliated with the Helen Keller World Crusade for the Blind. Fredric March, Florence Eldridge, June Havoc, and Helen Hayes have been cultural emissaries to Europe, the Near East, and South America on behalf of the U.S. State Department. For his "courage and leadership toward integration in the performing arts," Frederick D. O'Neal was the recipient of the Canada Lee Foundation Achievement Award. Helen Hayes has served as a member of the Board of the Girl Scouts of America and as National Chairman of the Women's Division of the March of Dimes Campaign. Nanette Fabray received the Eleanor Roosevelt Humanitarian Award.

In recognition of their contribution to the art of the theater, Lynn Fontanne, Alfred Lunt, Katharine Cornell, and Eva Le Galliene have been awarded honorary degrees by universities. For the same reason, Tyrone Guthrie, Michael Redgrave, Alec Guinness, John Gielgud, and Laurence Olivier have been knighted and the honor of Dame Commander of the British Empire has been conferred upon Judith Anderson and Edith Evans by the Queen of England.

The actor today has come a long way since he was proclaimed to be a rogue and a vagabond!

C. THEATER SPOTLIGHTS

I. *Theater Terminology:* Define the following:

improvisation	impersonation	sense memory
justification	caricature	spine
motivation	concentration	circle

II. *Theater Who's Who:* Identify the following:

Lewis Hallam and Company	Joseph Jefferson
Ira Aldridge	Minnie Maddern Fiske
Friedrich Schröder	Eleonora Duse
François Delsarte	Sarah Bernhardt

III. *Theater Investigation:* Discuss the following:

1. "Yet acting is the most exact and exacting of arts. In it nothing can ever be left to chance—to an inspiration of the moment—after the performance has begun." . . . David Belasco

2. "A carefully trained voice, able to follow all the 'windings of all the lengthened *oh*,' is, of course, of great importance to the

actress, yet it would seem to me, from observing great players, that they achieve their most impressive results through depicting in the countenance 'the events of the soul.' " . . . Julia Marlowe

3. "A man isn't an actor until he commands a technique which enables him to get an impression across into the hearts of an audience without reference or relation to his own individuality." . . . John Barrymore
4. "We create in the imagination the character we wish to express. If it is real and vital to us in imagination, we will be able to express it with freedom and surety. But we must conceive it as a whole before we begin to express it." . . . Laurette Taylor

IV. ***Theater Projects:*** Prepare the following:

1. Read *Acting: The First Six Lessons* by Richard Boleslavsky. With a classmate, present one of the lessons to the class. In your presentation, act the concept Mr. Boleslavsky teaches.
2. Prepare a short paper in which you compare the acting and costuming of the Greek actor with that of the Kabuki actor.
3. Select a scene with five or more characters from a contemporary play, and:
   a. Perform the scene for a contemporary audience.
   b. Perform the scene for a Victorian audience using Delsarte's system of acting.
   c. Perform the scene for a Greek theater audience.
   d. Perform the scene as a pantomime.

V. ***Theater Bibliography:*** Read the following:

Allen, John. *Great Moments in the Theater.* New York: Roy Publishers, 1958.

Boleslavsky, Richard. *Acting: The First Six Lessons.* New York: Theater Arts Books, 1949.

Cole, Toby. *Acting: A Handbook of the Stanislavski Method.* New York: Lear Publishers, Inc., 1947.

Duerr, Edwin. *The Length and Depth of Acting.* New York: Holt, Rinehart and Winston, 1962.

Lelyveld, Toby. *Shylock on the Stage.* Cleveland, Ohio: Western Reserve University, 1960.

Lewes, George Henry. *On Actors and the Art of Acting.* New York: Grove Press, 1957.

Matthews, Brander. *Papers on Acting.* New York: Hill and Wang, 1958.

IV

Theater on Stage: The Playwright

This writing of plays is a great matter, forming as it does the minds and affections of men in such sort that whatsoever they see done in show on the stage, they will presently be doing in earnest in the world, which is but a larger stage.

GEORGE BERNARD SHAW, *The Dark Lady of the Sonnets*

A. SETTING THE SCENE: THE PLAYWRIGHT YESTERDAY

The playwright in the theater is a commentator whose themes are drawn from personal experiences, past and present events, the manners and morals of society, the nature of human beings, and our basic need for entertainment. The playwright's examination of personal experiences might yield such plays as *A Long Day's Journey into Night, The Glass Menagerie,* or *Years Ago*. The playwright's study of current events in which he sees a parallel in history might result in such plays as *The Trojan Women, The Crucible,* or *Indians*. The playwright's observation of the manners and morals of society might produce such plays as *Le Bourgeois Gentilhomme, The School for Scandal,* or *How to Succeed in Business Without Really Trying*. The playwright's investigation of the nature of human beings might beget such plays as *Oedipus Rex,*

Hedda Gabler, or *Who's Afraid of Virginia Woolf?* The playwright's recognition of our basic need for entertainment might spawn such plays as *Charley's Aunt, Three Men on a Horse,* or *Ladies' Night in a Turkish Bath.* Throughout the ages, the playwright has been an observer of the contemporary scene, a spokesman for his generation, and a recorder of the times in which he lived.

1. The Mighty Greeks

a. Aeschylus

At the time that Pisistratus invited Thespis to perform at the Great Dionysia Festival, Athens was a city-state on the brink of developing a democratic form of government. Although a tyrant ruled the land and dictated the needs of the populace, an elected Senate, Council, Assembly, and Court legislated and administered the laws under which the people lived. The transition from a monarchy to a benevolent despotism that contained elements of democracy was the result of reforms introduced by Draco and Solon. Draco provided Athens with its first written codified laws at a time when harsh laws and severe penalties were needed to bring order to a chaotic society bent on self-destruction. Solon revised Draco's laws and instituted other reforms that conferred equality upon all free men, and the right of participation in government to the lower classes. Slavery as punishment for debt was abolished, and those so enslaved were freed. All free men were subject to the same restrictions and penalties, regardless of their financial status. To balance the power held by the wealthy upper classes whose members comprised the Senate and the Council of Four Hundred, Solon revived the Assembly. Pisistratus wisely retained the governmental framework established by Solon, and he became involved with the work of the Senate and the Council only when he wished to promote his own program. His sons, Hippias and Hipparchus, were not as astute when they came into power upon the death of their father in 527 B.C. Hippias ruled harshly because of his brother's murder at the hands of assassins. His tyranny provoked turmoil within the city-state. In 508 B.C., two years after Hippias was driven into exile, Cleisthenes was proclaimed leader of the Athenians when he successfully defeated an attack by Sparta. The reforms undertaken by Cleisthenes set Athens on the road to developing a democratic society which would flourish and attain its zenith during the Age of Pericles.

Against this atmosphere of Athenian society emerging from the rule by one to the rule by many, Aeschylus wrote approximately ninety plays, seven of which are extant: *The Suppliant Women, The Persians, Seven Against Thebes, Prometheus Bound,* and the *Oresteia* (*Agamemnon, Choephoroi, Eumenides.*) An aristocrat who sensed a decline of the power enjoyed by the aristocracy and an increase in the power of the middle and lower classes, Aeschylus was a conservative who constantly examined and appraised Athenian man in relation to his religion, his society, and his government. Each play is more than a dramatized legend; rather, it is a search for the meaning of the legend in order to comprehend the significance of the society in which Aeschylus lived. Viewed against the background of the time in which they were written, the plays by Aeschylus disclose much pertinent information about Greek civilization during the fifth century B.C.

The son of a prominent member of the aristocracy, Aeschylus was twenty-six years old when he entered the Great Dionysia play competition; he was forty-one when he won his first prize in 484 B.C. In the interim, he and his brothers had become national heroes because of their bravery during the Battle of Marathon. Athenians acknowledged their glorious deeds with a commemorative painting. Four years after he won his first playwriting award, Aeschylus participated in the defense of Salamis, helping Athenians to defeat the Persians. In 472, at a time when Athens was exercising its control of the first Delian League, Aeschylus wrote *The Persians,* a play that demonstrates how the mighty fall from power when an excess of pride (*hubris*) blinds the Persians to a moral course of action. A single unit rather than a trilogy, *The Persians* was a patriotic glorification of Athens written when the city-state was a rising empire engaged in extending her colonies throughout the Mediterranean and competing with Sparta for leadership of the lesser city-states.

In 467 B.C., Aeschylus won the award with a trilogy that included two lost plays, *Laius* and *Oedipus,* and one extant play *Seven Against Thebes.* In this retelling of the legendary curse that haunted Laius and his progeny, Aeschylus examined the tragic effect upon society of political ambition whetted by personal hate as exemplified by the conflict between Eteocles and Polynices. The play was produced at a time when Athens was in the throes of political upheaval. From 480 to 462 B.C., three ambitious men vied for control of political power in Athens. Aristides, one of the ten generals who successfully fought in the Battle of Marathon, became chief archon of Athens in 489 B.C. Six years later, he was exiled because he opposed another popular general, Themistocles, who was then declared chief archon. However, Aristides gave his support to Athens during the defense of Salamis, and he helped Cimon form and organize the Delian League in 478. Themistocles ruled Athens until 471 when he was deposed by Cimon who became the leader of Athenian aristocracy. The ascendancy of Pericles brought about the decline of power held by Cimon. The quest for power by these three leading Athenian generals during Aeschylus' lifetime was in many ways similar to the quest for power by Eteocles and Polynices in *Seven Aganst Thebes.* It is probable that Aeschylus saw the parallel and sought to comment upon its effect on a society that was in the process of achieving a high degree of civilization.

In 460, Athenians saw *Prometheus Bound,* one part of the trilogy that included two lost plays, *Prometheus Unbound* and *Prometheus, the Fire-Bringer.* Written two years after the death of Ephialtes who had curbed the powers of the Areopagus senate, Aeschylus, through the retelling of the legend of Prometheus and Zeus, examined the heights to which Athenian man had risen, the god-like image he held of himself, and his need to reconcile himself with the existence of a higher power. It is conceivable that Aeschylus was attempting to evaluate Athenian society in terms of its achievements and in terms of the danger of losing those achievements as it marched forward with little regard to the pain and turmoil of the past. Two years later, Aeschylus took his final and thirteenth award with the *Oresteia,* a trilogy consisting of *Aga-*

memnon, Choephoroi, and *Eumenides.* Written at a time when Pericles was on the threshold of leading Athens toward its Golden Age, the *Oresteia* leads man to realize that in a civilized society he cannot be the dispenser of justice but, rather, that man must submit himself and his deeds to a higher order of judgment. In this tragic legend of the House of Atreus, Aeschylus makes a strong plea for the need to recognize the importance of the Areopagus senate in Athenian society: in the *Eumenides,* the protagonist, Orestes, is tried before a jury of twelve Athenian citizens whose deep sense of justice assures Orestes that he will be accorded an unbiased trial.

b. Sophocles

From 462 to 429 B.C., Athenian life was dominated by Pericles, an almost perfect man. Pericles caught the attention of the populace in 462 when he joined those democratic leaders who sought to free the city-state from the control of the powerful and conservative Areopagus senate. A year later, Pericles assumed leadership of the people when Ephialtes, who had purged the senate, was assassinated. Thereafter, for nearly thirty years, Pericles was elected and reelected one of the ten *strategoi,* or commanders, who governed Athens. During his long stay in power, Pericles initiated a plan for the beautification of Athens, innovated an economic program for the unemployed, extended payment for services to include jurists and the military, and raised the cultural sights of the multitude by providing each citizen with the price of admission to the play festivals. His illustrious career came to a disastrous end in 432, when members of the Athenian Empire rebelled against Athenian control of their economic life. In support of the rebellion, Sparta demanded that Athens relinquish her empire and free the city-states under her control. When Athens refused, war was declared. Primarily a sea power, Athens counted on a naval victory to defeat Sparta. The overcrowded city soon found itself infected by a plague that raged for three years. A fearful citizenry turned on Pericles, charging him with the misappropriation of funds and the responsibility for the predicament that had befallen them. Pericles was deposed. His fall from grace was accompanied by charges of impiety leveled against his mistress, Aspasia, and he was forced to bare his private life before the public in her defense. In 429 B.C., the people recalled Pericles, but it was too late for him to offer the needed leadership. The plague claimed him, and he died a few months after returning to office. Coincidentally, Sophocles' *Oedipus Rex,* a play about an almost perfect man, was premiered that same year.

Sophocles was one of the many talented men whose creative genius had helped make Athens the envy of the other city-states. A skilled athlete, a graceful dancer, and an able performer, Sophocles, at the age of sixteen, was chosen to lead Athenian youth in celebrating the victory over the Persians at Salamis. Twelve years later, Sophocles won his first play award. His chief opponent was Aeschylus. An established member of Athenian political and social life, Sophocles served Athens as its Imperial *strategoi.* In his long span of years, he enjoyed the acquaintance of the mighty Greeks who dominated and influenced Athenian life and thought. His contemporaries included the playwrights Aeschylus, Euripides, and Aristophanes; the historians Herodotus and Thucydides; the philosopher Socrates; the sculptor Phidias; the architects Ictinus and Callicrates; the statesman and general Alcibiades; and the physician Hippocrates. Living at a time when Athenian life hinged upon the character and the deeds of her leaders, Sophocles wrote plays that reveal a keen perception of human nature and character. *Ajax* is the study of a nobleman who must die as he lived, nobly. *The Trachinian Women* details the tragic effect of jealousy. *Electra* looks with psychological understanding at mother-hatred. *Philoctetes* examines deception and patriotism. *Antigone* explores arrogance and self-righteousness. *Oedipus at Colonus* reconciles the dignity of man with the harsh and realistic world in which he lives and dies. Like Pericles, each protagonist is an almost perfect man whose magnificent rise and tragic fall arouses pity and fear in the spectator.

Sophoclean tragedy is close-knit in its structure, simple in its development of plot, character and theme, and relentless as it builds toward a stunning conclusion. Excessive pride (*hubris*) causes the protagonist to make a decision that generally proves to be an error in judgment (*hamartia*). The decision propels the action of the play forward. A moment of recognition (*anagnorisis*), or a sudden reversal of fortune (*peripetia*), leads to punishment or retribution (*nemesis*). Pity and fear arouse the theatergoer who experiences a purging of emotions (*catharsis*) at the outcome. For example, excessive pride in his accomplishments causes the heroic Oedipus to ferret out the murderer of Laius to appease the gods and to rid Thebes of the plague that is destroying it. Oedipus's search leads him to realize that he is the culprit who has brought shame and pestilence to Thebes. No longer an honored king, Oedipus inflicts self-punishment by gouging his eyes. He seeks retribution through self-banishment. Sparse in detail, crisp in dialogue, ironic in circumstance and utterance, Sophoclean tragedy is self-contained, compact, and complete in its delineation of character and event. Unlike Aeschylean tragedy, Sophoclean tragedy employs the single play form rather than the trilogy or tetralogy to trace the rise and fall of the protagonist. Still, *Oedipus Rex, Oedipus at Colonus,* and *Antigone,* each written at a different period in the life of the playwright, may be considered a trilogy because collectively they relate the story of the house of Oedipus. Each, however, is a complete unit that may be performed independently of the others.

The most popular playwright of his day, Sophocles won twenty play awards and never placed less than second in the play contests. He wrote approximately 113 plays, seven of which have withstood time and are part of our universal drama heritage. His contributions to the development of the Greek theater were many. He increased the number of actors to three, and he increased the size of the chorus to fifteen without adding to its function or its prominence in the play. He rejected the trilogy and tetralogy as playwriting forms, popularizing instead the single play unit. Sophocles is said to have introduced painted scenery. He died at the age of ninety, shortly after the demise of Euripides.

c. *Aristophanes*

After the death of Pericles in 429 B.C., the foreign policy of Athens was determined by Cleon, a dealer in raw hides and leathers;

Nicias, a wealthy and pious aristocrat; and Alcibiades, the mercurial, opportunistic statesman-general. Each attempted to revitalize a demoralized Athens; but instead, each contributed to the defeat and eventual demise of the great city-state.

Cleon, characterized as a vulgar demagogue by both Aristophanes and Thucydides, was the acknowledged (although not the most revered) leader of a group of rising businessmen who called for a short and decisive war against Sparta in order to guarantee their commercial interests abroad. Initially successful in his prosecution of the war against Sparta, Cleon was mortally wounded at Amphipolis in 422 B.C. Leadership passed to Nicias, a cautious and superstitious man who had opposed Cleon. In 421, Athens and Sparta signed the Peace of Nicias, each city-state agreeing to respect the territorial integrity of the other for the next fifty years. The terms of the treaty, however, were soon forgotten when Alcibiades, a ward of Pericles, evinced an active interest in Athenian political life. A brilliant statesman whose magnetic personality charmed his admirers, Alcibiades had little difficulty instigating a sub-rosa revolt against Sparta, justifying the sacking of Melos, and persuading Athens to undertake the conquest of Syracuse. However, his immoral behavior and his hold upon the populace infuriated his enemies, and, in time, he became the victim of a political situation that he had created. An opportunist who saw in Athenian imperialism the gratification of personal whims and ambitions, Alcibiades died at the hands of an assassin in 404 B.C. Sparta then ruled Athens.

On stage, Athenians saw their political leaders caricatured, the war policy ridiculed, the new morality questioned, and human gullibility exposed in the plays written by Aristophanes. He was born in 446 B.C., at the time when Pericles was molding a democratic Athens and when the writers of comedy were applauded for using the theater as a podium for criticizing the current events of the day. A conservative who was dismayed by what he considered to be deteriorating influences upon Athenian political and social life, Aristophanes was a brilliant theater cartoonist who used bold comic strokes to comment upon the political, social, and moral issues affecting the Athenian populace. His plays fall into two categories: satirical political plays and satirical philosophical plays. The political satires are represented by *The Acharnians* (425), *The Knights* (424), *The Wasps* (422), *The Peace* (421), *Lysistrata* (411), and *The Ecclesiazusae* (392). With the exception of the latter, each play is a devastating criticism of the Peloponnesian War, an outrageous lampooning of public officials, a caustic exposé of governmental agencies. In *The Acharnians,* Dicaeopolis, a simple farmer, makes a separate peace treaty with the enemy because he finds the war personally inconvenient and unrewarding, and because the Assembly has failed to meet his needs in representing him. In *The Knights,* one of the lead characters, "The Tanner," so closely resembled Cleon that Aristophanes played the role himself because other actors were afraid to run the risk of political retaliation. In *Lysistrata* and *The Ecclesiazusae,* women prove superior to men in solving political and social problems. The philosophical satires are represented by *The Clouds* (423), *The Birds* (414), *The Thesmophoriazusae* (411), *The Frogs* (405), and *Plutus* (388). In *The Clouds, The Thesmophoriazusae,* and *The Frogs,* Aristophanes assaults the character of those whom he believes are responsible for undermining Athenian morality. Socrates is the target in *The Clouds;* Euripides is the victim in *The Thesmophoriazusae* and *The Frogs.* In *The Birds* and *Plutus,* Aristophanes comments upon democracy as an ideal form of government.

Aristophanic comedy, or Old Comedy, is logical in its structure although loosely connected in plot development. The structure resembles that of the problem-solution speech, thus giving credibility to an incredible solution. The play generally begins with a prologue in which the problem is defined and a happy solution is conceived by the leading character. The solution is then debated and worked out in the episodes that follow. Intermingled with the episodes and the debates are songs and dances by the chorus. Extravaganza, obscene and witty dialogue, and slapstick situations provoke laughter and provide entertainment for an audience that is forced to think about the folly of a prevailing situation.

Lysistrata, Aristophanes' attempt to make Athenians see the senselessness of the Peloponnesian War, provides an illustration of the structure of Old Comedy:

STRUCTURE	PURPOSE	LYSISTRATA
Prologue	Define problem, determine solution	Problem: stop the war Solution: no sexual relations
Parados	Entrance of Chorus	The male members of the chorus beseige the female members of the chorus . . . and lose in a spectacular battle between the sexes
Agon	A debate of the solution	Lysistrata and the Commissioner debate woman's place in the home, on the battlefield, in public life, etc.
Parabasis	The Chorus airs the views of the playwright	The battle of the sexes continues
Episodes	Application of solution	A number of episodes demonstrate how war interferes with the love-life of the sexes
Exodos	Resolution of the problem; a bringing together of opposing parties; exit of the Chorus	Peace is declared. Man and woman are reconciled. Life goes on

Aristophanic comedy is usually salacious in making the point. For example, consider the following oath administered by Lysistrata to the women of Athens, which is later upheld by Myrrhine in a scene with her husband when he comes a-wooing.

LYSISTRATA:

Lampito: all of you women: come, touch the bowl, and repeat after me—remember, this is an oath—: I WILL HAVE NOTHING TO DO WITH MY HUSBAND OR LOVER

KALONIKE:

I will have nothing to do with my husband or lover

LYSISTRATA:
THOUGH HE COME TO ME IN PITIABLE CONDITION

KALONIKE:
Though he come to me in pitiable condition
(Oh Lysistrata! This is killing me!)

LYSISTRATA:
IN MY HOUSE I WILL BE UNTOUCHABLE

KALONIKE:
In my house I will be untouchable

LYSISTRATA:
IN MY THINNEST SAFFRON SILK

KALONIKE:
In my thinnest saffron silk

LYSISTRATA:
AND MAKE HIM LONG FOR ME.

KALONIKE:
And make him long for me.

LYSISTRATA:
I WILL NOT GIVE MYSELF

KALONIKE:
I will not give myself

LYSISTRATA:
AND IF HE CONSTRAINS ME

KALONIKE:
And if he constrains me

LYSISTRATA:
I WILL BE COLD AS ICE AND NEVER MOVE

KALONIKE:
I will be cold as ice and never move

LYSISTRATA:
I WILL NOT LIFT MY SLIPPERS TOWARD THE CEILING

KALONIKE:
I will not lift my slippers toward the ceiling

LYSISTRATA:
OR CROUCH ON ALL FOURS LIKE THE LIONESS IN THE CARVING

KALONIKE:
Or crouch on all fours like the lioness in the carving

LYSISTRATA:
AND IF I KEEP THIS OATH LET ME DRINK FROM THIS BOWL

KALONIKE:
And if I keep this oath let me drink from this bowl

LYSISTRATA:
IF NOT, LET MY OWN BOWL BE FILLED WITH WATER.

KALONIKE:
If not, let my own bowl be filled with water.

LYSISTRATA:
You have all sworn?

MYRRHINE:
We have.*

Although the plays of Aristophanes may abound in obscenity and vulgarity, the viewpoint is always stated with wit and perception, the language and imagery are frequently lyrical, and the intent is always commendable. If Aristophanes prods our insides and touches our lust, he also stimulates our intellect and appeals to our intelligence in making us aware of the folly of our ways.

d. Euripides

Externally, the Peloponnesian War threatened the very existence of Athens. Internally, the city-state was challenged by the growing

* From Aristophanes' *Lysistrata,* translated by Dudley Fitts, copyright, 1954, by Harcourt, Brace & World, Inc., and reprinted with their permission.

number of enlightened thinkers who questioned the traditional beliefs in ethics, religion, and politics. Ironically, these enlightened men had once been welcomed by wealthy Athenians who had sought the best in education for their young sons. Shortly after the Persian Wars, these scholarly men began to make their way into the life of the community. Admired for their knowledge and their skill in imparting their learning, these "teachers of wisdom"—collectively known as Sophists—became the mentors of young Athenians. In time, they acquired a following and rose to prominence because of their beliefs. When their pupils began to follow their teachings and questioned the traditional order of things, older Athenians became alarmed and fearful of this manifestation of their influence upon the younger generation. Steps were taken to rid the community of some of these "teachers of wisdom." In 429 B.C., Cleon brought charges of impiety against Anaxagoras, who had dared to take issue with the accepted explanation of the origin of the universe. The famed philosopher was banished from the city-state. In 411 B.C., the Athenian Assembly brought charges against Protagoras because he had dared to question the existence and the justice of the gods. The sixty-nine-year-old philosopher fled the city and was drowned while enroute to Sicily. Only Socrates remained to question, challenge, and enlighten Athenians in their homes, in the street, and in the marketplace. In time, he, too, would face charges before the Athenian Assembly. As if there were no escape from the spirit of free inquiry that permeated Athenian thought and discussion, the theater, too, became a forum for challenging the established concepts of ethics, religion, and politics. The apostle of wisdom who dramatized his philosophy was the playwright Euripides.

Alcestis, Medea, Hippolytus, Andromache, and *Electra* provide examples of the philosopher–playwright's interest in the status of woman in a male-dominated society. In *Alcestis,* a husband, Admetus, accepts the willingness of his wife, Alcestis, to sacrifice herself to the gods so that Admetus may live. In *Medea,* an ambitious man, Jason, casts aside the mother of his children to achieve his goals. In *Hippolytus,* the natural passions of a woman, Phaedra, are forced to conform to the standards of a male society. In *An-*

dromache, a woman of royal background is reduced to slave status when she becomes a booty of war. In *Electra,* a girl of noble birth is forced into a marriage beneath her station in life. Each play also represents an attempt to penetrate the feminine mystique. *Alcestis* examines the nobility of womanhood. *Medea* reveals the fury of a female scorned by the male. *Hippolytus* analyzes female passions and desires. *Andromache* studies female jealousy, and *Electra* investigates the female psychological motives that lead to revenge and murder. The penetration is deep and the findings are not always flattering. Consequently, in a society that considered the female to be an incubator for the male seed, it is not surprising to discover that Athenians were shocked by a viewpoint that proclaimed the nature of woman to be the same as that of man, the rights of woman to be the same as those of man, and the needs of woman to be the same as those of man. Tradition-bound Athenians rejected the views of the playwright and branded Euripides a misogynist because he revealed woman as she is, not as Athenians thought she should be.

The folly of war, the horror of war, and the hypocrisy of war are exposed by Euripides in *The Children of Heracles, Hecuba, The Suppliants, The Trojan Women,* and *Iphigenia in Aulis.* The first three plays were written during the early part of the Peloponnesian conflict, when Cleon sought a decisive military victory over Sparta and when Nicias sought a peaceful termination of the war between the city-states. These early war plays are a blend of patriotism that glorified Athens as a haven for the oppressed, and pacifism borne out of a realization of the human misery caused by war. A stronger indictment of war occurs in *The Trojan Women* and *Iphigenia in Aulis.* In 416, the Athenian fleet besieged the island of Melos in order to force the inhabitants to become members of the Athenian Empire. At first, the Melians resisted, but when reinforcements from Athens arrived upon the scene, the Melians surrendered and placed themselves at the mercy of the Athenians. The invaders decimated the male population and sold the women and children into slavery. Alcibiades defended the action of the invaders and Athenians rejoiced in the "victory." Euripides, incensed by the wholesale slaughter of the male population, and moved by the plight of women and children in captivity, wrote *The Trojan Women,* an account of the sacking of Troy. Produced in 415 B.C. on the eve of the sailing of the Athenian fleet to Sicily, the play incensed the populace, and they were firmly convinced that Euripides should be banished. In 405 B.C., Euripides wrote *Iphigenia in Aulis,* a moving anti-war play that questions the price of patriotism exacted from people. The play was written while the poet was in exile and it was produced posthumously by the playwright's son.

In addition to espousing a recognition of the role of women in Athenian society and pricking the conscience of Athenian warmongers, Euripides debunked the greatness of the legendary hero as well as the power and justice of the mythological god. The result was an increased awareness of human behavior and a criticism of religion. The plot of each play is derived from a legend; the dramatis personae are the characters in the legend—but with a difference that permitted theatergoers to identify with the plight of the protagonist. For example, Agamemnon in *Iphigenia in Aulis* is not simply the great Athenian warrior as he appears in the legend and history, but a very human being trapped in a situation that tests Agamemnon as a man, a husband, a brother, a father, and as a military leader. He must make a decision that affects his child, his wife, his country. He must appease the Goddess Artemis, by sacrificing his daughter Iphigenia, or else the winds will not blow and the Athenian fleet cannot set sail for Troy. Wretched and bitter, he cries out:

> Woe, woe is me, unhappy, caught by fate,
> Outwitted by the cunning of the gods!
> O that I were base-born! Then I could weep.
> What can I do, a King? Our dignity
> Still rules our lives, and still we serve the mob.
> I shame to weep, and yet I shame to weep not,
> In this sore strait. What shall I tell my wife?
> How can I greet her, look her in the face?
> She has undone me, coming now, uncalled,
> Coming to wed her daughter, full of love,
> To find me thus, a murderer. And she,

Poor hapless maiden, now the bride of Death!
The Pity of it! I hear her call to me,
"Father, O father, would you slay your child?
A bitter bridal have you made for me:
I would you had the like!" and he, the boy,
Little Orestes, he will cry with her,
Knowing and knowing not. Accursed Paris,
Thy rape of Helen hath destroyed me! *

For the moment, the theatergoer sees Agamemnon without his military armor and without his royal garb. The theatergoer identifies him as a parent and empathizes with him in that relationship. The cause of Agamemnon's predicament emphasizes the negative role that the gods frequently play in the lives of men. It is difficult for the spectator not to conclude that the ways of the gods are not always just. Subtly, Euripides has made his point—the legendary hero is not a superhuman being, but rather a man like all men; human feelings characterize and motivate all men, regardless of their station in society; the gods cannot be trusted to understand the nature of man and, therefore, cannot be expected to always do that which is in the best interest of man. Such innovative thinking, however, had to be approached cautiously, lest the playwright arouse the hostility of the theatergoer and incur the wrath of the Athenian Assembly. Thus, many plays by Euripides seem to have two endings, one which logically concludes the action of the hero, and another which employs the *deus ex machina* to bring a god on stage as a just arbiter in the affairs of the protagonist.

Euripides was born on the island of Salamis, supposedly on the day that Athens defeated Persia. His parents were respected and prominent members of the community, although Aristophanes would have us believe otherwise. A lonely and melancholy man, Euripides voiced the sentiments of that segment of Athenian society which sought truth and understanding of man and the world in which he lived. Euripides wrote approximately ninety-two plays or twenty-three tetralogies. Only five of his plays won first awards.

---

* From *Iphigenia in Aulis,* translated by F. M. Stawell. Copyright © G. Bell & Sons, Ltd., London. Reprinted by permission of the publisher.

Usually, he placed second or third when his plays were chosen for production. His extant plays include:

Alcestis (438 B.C.)
Medea (431 B.C.)
Hippolytus (428 B.C.)
Children of Heracles (427 B.C.)
Andromache (ca. 426 B.C.)
Hecuba (ca. 425 B.C.)
Cyclops (ca. 423 B.C.)
Heracles (ca. 422 B.C.)
The Suppliants (421 B.C.)
Ion (ca. 417 B.C.)
The Trojan Women (415 B.C.)
Iphigenia in Tauris (414 B.C.)
Electra (413 B.C.)
Helen (412 B.C.)
The Phoenician Women (ca. 410 B.C.)
Orestes (408 B.C.)
Iphigenia in Aulis (?405 B.C.)
The Bacchae (?405 B.C.)

In 408 B.C., two years after he was acquitted by the Athenian assembly of charges of perjury and impiety, the playwright voluntarily sought asylum in Macedonia. There he wrote *Iphigenia in Aulis* and *The Bacchae,* a play that attempts to reconcile man and his religious beliefs. Death came to the playwright in 406 B.C. at a time when Athens was on the brink of defeat at the hands of Sparta. Honor and reverence came to him when the people began to realize that he had not only spoken for his times, but for all men in all times.

2. The Lusty Romans

Roman comedy and Roman tragedy began in 240 B.C. when a Greek tragedy and a Greek comedy were presented at the *Ludi Romani* to commemorate the First Punic War. The plays were translated into Latin by Livius Andronicus, an actor and manumitted slave from Tarentum, a city in Roman-conquered Magna Graecia. Entertainment-hungry Romans eagerly accepted the new genre as a welcome relief from the usual program of dances and recitations. Other playwrights and poets, namely Gnaeus Naevius, Quintus Ennius, Marcus Pacuvius, and Lucius Accius followed Livius Andronicus in developing a body of dramatic literature that served the needs of professional actors and the literary needs of a growing populace. In the course of time, Romans came to identify a tragedy based on Greek themes as *fabula crepidata;* a comedy in Greek dress as *fabula palliata;* a play in Roman dress as *fabula togata;* and a historical play as *fabula praetexta.* Unfortunately, only fragments of these plays written by these early playwrights and poets remain. To understand the characteristics of Roman comedy and the audience for which it was written, we must examine the plays of Titus Maccius Plautus (whose name may be freely translated as "flatfoot") and those written by Publius Terentius Afer. Similarly, we must examine the *fabula crepidata* written by Lucius Annaeus Seneca for an appreciation of Roman tragedy.

a. Plautus

Plautus was born ten years after the onset of the First Punic War in 264 B.C. He was fifty-four years old when he began his career as a professional playwright. Earlier, he had failed as a businessman and had worked as a millhand. In his relatively short career as a playwright, he wrote more than a hundred plays, twenty of which are extant: *Amphitryon, The Comedy of Asses, The Pot of Gold, The Two Bacchides, The Captives, Casina, The Casket, Curculio, Epidicus, The Twin Menaechmi, The Merchant, The Braggart Soldier, The Haunted House, The Girl from Persia, The Carthaginian, Pseudolus, The Rope, Stichus, The Three Penny Day,* and *Truculentus.* The plays are adaptations of Greek comedies written by Demophilus, Diphilus, Menander, Philemon, and other writers of Greek New Comedy. Each play is fashoned to suit the intelligence of the Roman theatergoer and to satisfy his search for lively entertainment.

Despite the fact that he was not an educated man and frequently did not comprehend the refinements of Latin, the Roman theatergoer attended a performance of a play by Plautus confident that he would have little or no difficulty understanding the play. As a matter of fact, he might even learn to think and express himself better as a result of the playgoing experience. The theatergoer knew from having seen other plays by Plautus that he could expect a simple plot and that the playwright would clearly explain any complications that might arise during the course of the play. The Roman theatergoer expected that the play would begin with a prologue that outlined the plot and identified the main characters. He recalled that as the play progressed, new characters would introduce themselves when they came on stage, or would be introduced by others. He likewise expected that the playwright would tell him how to behave during the performance. Also, that he would probably be instructed to applaud the actors when the play ended. For example, the Prologue to *The Captives* identifies the scene, outlines the plot, introduces the two main characters, and lectures an audience member:

PROLOGUE

(*Philocrates and Tyndarus are chained in front of the house of Hegio*)

This pair of captives you see standing here,
They do not sit, because they have to stand;
I think you all are witness of that.
Hegio, the old man dwelling in this house,
Is father of the one (*pointing to Tyndarus*); but how it is
He is his slave, that's what I'll tell to you.
He had two sons; and one of them was stolen
By a slave, when four year old, who flying hence
Sold him, in Elis, to the father of
This man (*pointing to Philocrates*) that one you see here;
I think you take me;
'Tis good! But there's a man in the back seats
Who says he does not; please, sir, come this way.
If there's no seat, you're free to walk about,
Since thus you force an actor to strain his voice
As if he were a beggar asking alms.
But I'll not break my voice to pleasure you.
To you who can afford to pay your rates
And taxes, and take seats, I'll pay my debts;
I hate to owe to any one at all.
This slave then, as you know already, fled
And sold the young boy he had stolen to
The father of this man (*indicating Philocrates*); who when he'd bought him
Gave him to this his son, to be his playmate,
Because their ages were the same. He thus

Becomes the slave of his own father, though
He knows it not. For often thus the gods
Make shuttlecocks of men. And now you know
How he lost one of those his sons that were.
But later, when there was a war between
The Aetolians and the Eleans, as oft happens,
The other son was taken prisoner.
Menarchus, a physician, bought him there.
Then Hegio began to buy up captives,
To see if he could find one to exchange
For his lost son; he knows not even now
He has one safe at home. When yesterday
He heard that there was an Elean knight
Of highest place and family, he spared
No money, if so be that he might win
His son, and bring him back again to home.
Accordingly, he bought these prisoners here
At the quaestor's sale. But they between themselves
Arranged a plot, by which the master (*indicating Philocrates*) might
Return to his home, the slave alone remain
They then proceed to change their dress and name.
He's called Philocrates (*indicating Tyndarus*), he Tyndarus (*indicating Philocrates*);
Today each passes for the other man.
The slave today will carry out this plot,
Will set his master free, and by the same means
Will serve his brother, and return him too
To his own country, to his father's house,
Not knowing what he does, for oftentimes
One does more good by chance than by design.
So by their own wit and unknowingly
They've so arranged and prepar'd their plot
That this man should remain his father's slave;
Although, as I have said, he is his son;
And so, in ignorance of the fact, he is.
Ah, when one thinks, what paltry things we are!
This is the subject of the present play
We are about to represent to you,
For you a story only. There's one point
On which I wish to warn you. 'Twill be well

To give your close attention to the play.
It is not in the hackneyed style, like others.
There are no filthy verses that one can't
Repeat; no perjured pimp appears today,
No infamous abandoned courtesan,
No braggart soldier. Don't alarm yourselves,
Because I said there was a war at hand.
The battles will be all fought off the stage;
'Twould be unfair for a comic company
Of a sudden to attempt a tragedy.
Therefore, if any one has set his heart
Upon a battle, he must go to law;
And if he get one stronger than himself
To fight, I promise him a battle he
Won't like, and will not want to see again.
And so good-bye, kind critics, here at home,
Good Fighters all if the day of battle come.

(*The Prologus and the Captives depart.*) *

Generally, however, Plautus did provide the Roman theatergoer with an earthy witticism that he could repeat as his own, or a moment of low burlesque that he could relate to his friends. For example, Roman theatergoers never wearied of seeing performances of *Casina* because of that moment in the play when Olympio, a slave, and Lysidamus, his master, attempt to bed Chalinus, a slave disguised as the bride, Casina.

Roman audiences applauded the adaptations by Plautus because the playwright provided the theatergoer with the robust, earthy, holiday entertainment. Jokes, jests, puns, name-calling, and comic insults pepper the humorous dialogue written by Plautus and provoke gales of laughter from an audience. Mistaken identity (*Amphitryon* and *The Twin Menaechmi*) and good intentions gone awry (*Epidicus*) produce farcical situations that delight and amuse the spectator. Identifiable and stereotyped characters (Euclio in *The Pot*

---

* From *The Captives,* trans. by Sir Robert Allison, in George E. Duckworth. *The Complete Roman Drama,* vol. I (New York: Random House, 1942), pp. 227–229. Copyright © 1942 by Random House, Inc. Reprinted by permission of the publisher.

of Gold and Pyrgopolynices in *The Braggart Soldier*) engender comic anticipation of plot and character development. Song and dance (*The Rope*) enliven the merriment of a fast-paced show. Asides, monologues, and soliloquies involve the audience in the development of the plot. Best of all, fertility, a component of comedy and the nature of man, underscores plot and theme. Invariably, the hero in Plautine comedy wants to either wed the heroine (*Casina*) or acquire a mistress (*Truculentus*). His attempt to wed (*Curculio*) or bed (*The Two Bacchides*) is complicated by others who either remove, or add, obstacles to satisfying his sexual yearnings. A righteous parent withholds his approval (*The Casket*). A slave-servant conspires to aid his master and a knavish pimp makes unreasonable demands (*Pseudolus*). A philandering father competes with his son (*The Merchant*). The vain soldier makes a claim (*The Carthaginian*). Of course, love, sex, and romance triumph in Plautine comedy: the hero and his bride or mistress are happily united as the play ends. A prolific people conscious of family ties and responsibilities, Romans acclaimed Plautus because the playwright presented life in an entertaining manner.

Plautus is an example of the playwright who applies his talents to writing plays designed to amuse rather than to enlighten an audience. His subject matter is life itself—coarse and vulgar, reproductive and procreative—a continuation of the species. His characters are stereotypes initially introduced by the writers of Greek New Comedy and recognized by the audience as prototypes of everyday society (although to Roman audiences, they seemed removed because the actors were garbed in Greek dress). His aim is convulsive laughter at possible, but highly improbable, situations. His techniques are a bag of dramaturgical tricks guaranteed to cause his audience to exit laughing. He is concerned neither with the current political or social events affecting the life of the theatergoer, nor with penetrating and analyzing the nature of man so that the viewer can better understand himself. Rather, he is concerned with man's desire to laugh his troubles away, to escape momentarily into a topsy-turvy world where a happy solution is the inevitable answer to all problems. And why not? Man needs laughter as well as enlightenment to cope with the problems that beset him.

b. Terence

Publius Terentius Afer, generally known as Terence, was born in Carthage, ca. 195 B.C. He was a young boy when he was brought as a slave to Rome by Publius Terentius Lucanus, a Roman senator. The boy's intelligence and talents were such that his master was moved to provide him with an education and to grant him manumission. In gratitude, the young Carthaginian took the name of his benefactor. A chance acquaintance with Caecilius Statius, the playwright, led to the granting of patronage by the Scipionic circle, a group of aristocratic Romans headed by Publius Cornelius Scipio, a Roman general and patron of the arts, and his close friend, Caius Laelius. In his brief playwriting career, from 166 B.C. to 160 B.C., Terence wrote six plays, all extant: *The Woman of Andros, The Mother-in-Law, The Self-Tormentor, The Eunuch, Phormio,* and *The Brothers.* Although each play is an adaptation of a Greek original, each bears the trademarks associated with Terentian comedy:

1. A prologue that defends the playwright against charges of plagiarism rather than a prologue that summarizes the plot, identifies the dramatis personae, and lectures the audience on its behavior. A typical example is the prologue that opens *The Eunuch:*

PROLOGUE

> Our poet wishes his name to be enrolled among those writers who make it their object to please as many good people and hurt the feelings of as few as possible. If any writer thinks that he has been harshly spoken of by our poet, he ought to consider that the words were an answer to him, not an attack upon him, because he began the strife. It is he who by translating well but writing badly has made feeble Latin plays out of good Greek ones. Of late he has put upon the stage Menander's *The Phantom,* and in *The Treasure* makes the defendant who has got the money show cause why it should be his own, before the claimant has set forth why it belongs to him, and how it found its way into his father's tomb. Now, for the future, that he may not deceive himself, or think "I have got rid of him, there is

nothing that he can say to me," I warn him to behave himself and plague me no more. I have many more things to tell about him, which I will spare him now, but which shall be brought out hereafter if he goes on attacking me as he has begun to do.

As for the play which we are now about to act, Menander's *The Eunuch,* after the aediles had bought it, he got permission to read it. When it was being rehearsed in the presence of the magistrates, he cried out, "It is a thief, not a poet, that has written this play, but he has not deceived me for all that." He said that there was an old play, *The Flatterer,* by Naevius and Plautus, and that the characters of the parasite and the soldier were borrowed from it. If this is a crime, it was committed by the poet unwittingly, not because he intended to plagiarise. You may prove the truth of this for yourselves. *The Flatterer* is a play of Menander's; in it there is a flattering parasite and a swaggering soldier; he does not deny that he transferred these characters into his *The Eunuch* from the Greek play; but he utterly denies that to his knowledge, they ever appeared before this day in Latin plays. If he may not use these characters, why should he be any more allowed to describe a slave running, or to put on the stage virtuous matrons, vicious courtesans, hungry parasites, swaggering soldiers, babies substituted, old gentlemen tricked by their slaves, love, hatred, or suspicion? In short, nothing is said now that has not been said before; you ought to reflect upon this, and pardon us new writers if we practice the same tricks as the old ones. Now pray make up your minds to listen in silence, that you may learn the meaning of *The Eunuch.**

2. A dual plot that complicates the action as the result of combining two plays rather than a single plot which becomes complicated as a result of incidents conceived or contrived by the playwright. For example, *The Woman of Andros* combines two plays by Menander: *The Lady of Andros* and *The Lady of Perin-*

---

* From *The Eunuch,* in George E. Duckworth, *The Complete Roman Drama,* vol. II (New York: Random House, 1942).

thos. The heads of two households, Simo and Chremes, agree to cement their lifelong friendship by arranging a marriage between Simo's son, Pamphilus, and Chremes' daughter, Philumena. Pamphilus, however, has committed himself to Glycerium, and Philumena is in love with Charinus, a close friend of Pamphilus. A pivotal character, Davus, a slave of Simo, complicates the situation further when he attempts to bring the lovers together. Crito, a neutral bystander, provides the solution when it is learned that Glycerium, the woman from Andros, is the long-lost daughter of Chremes. *Contaminatio,* the device of combining the plot of one play with the plot of another, is employed by Terence in all his plays. Always *A* wants *B, B* wants *D*, and the efforts of *E* and *F* make it possible. A diagram, such as the one that follows, can help the reader understand the dual plots which are characteristic of Terentian comedy:

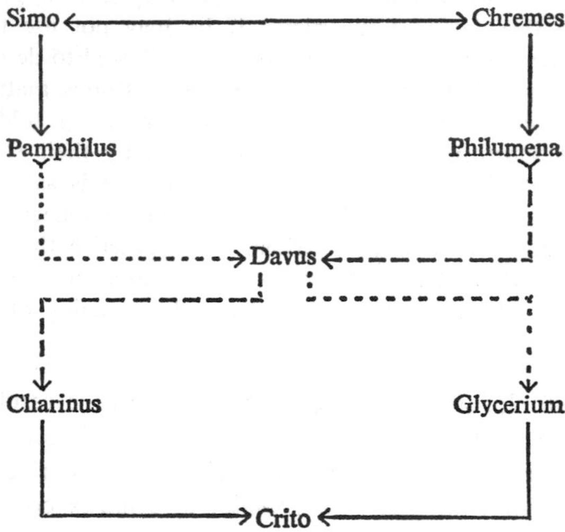

3. Dialogue that is notable for its continuity of thought, its polished sentences and paragraphs, its frequent epigrammatic sayings:

It is a plan fit for lunatics rather than for lovers.

The Woman of Andros, Act I, Scene 3

Well, it is a great proof of the mistress's innocence when those who run her errands are so ill-cared for; for it is the regular practice of those who laying siege to the mistress begin by bribing the maids.

The Self-Tormentor, Act II, Scene 3

I am a human being; I am interested in everything human.

The Self-Tormentor, Act I, Scene 1

Do you go hunting for game, when you're a hare yourself?

The Eunuch, Act III, Scene 1

I know the ways of women; they won't when you want them, when you don't want they're eager for it.

The Eunuch, Act IV, Scene 7

Who ever saw anyone taken for adultery in a brothel?

The Eunuch, Act V, Scene 4

Frequently it is not the greatest injuries that cause the greatest quarrels; something which would not ruffle another man's temper will often make a hasty man your bitterest foe.

The Mother-in-Law, Act III, Scene 1

All mothers-in-law are of one mind in hating their daughters-in-law.

The Mother-in-Law, Act II, Scene 1

A courtesan is an enemy to a married woman who is separated from her husband.

The Mother-in-Law, Act V, Scene 2

It is, indeed, a true saying: if you are absent anywhere, or chance to stay longer than ordinary, better those things happen to you, which your wife says, or fancies in her resentment, than what indulgent parents are apt to suspect.

The Brothers, Act I, Scene 1

I bid him look into all men's lives as into a mirror, and make others serve as examples of himself.

The Brothers, Act III, Scene 3

Somehow all those who are unsuccessful in life are prone to suspicion; they take everything as an insult, and believe that they are being slighted because they are helpless; so you are more likely to win their pardon if you defend yourself in person before them.

The Brothers, Act IV, Scene 3

The life of man is like playing with dice: if you don't throw exactly what you want, you must use your wits to make shift with what you have thrown.

The Brothers, Act IV, Scene 7

There are many signs in people's characters whereby you may easily guess, when two of them are doing the same thing, how it will affect them so that you can often say: "It will do this one no harm, it will do that one harm"; not because the thing that they are doing is different, but because their characters are different.

The Brothers, Act V, Scene 3 *

In addition to enjoying the polished prose and the subtle humor, Roman aristocrats probably enjoyed the plays of Terence because they could identify with the characters in the plays. What Roman father was not concerned about the education of his son? What Roman father did not desire to appear indulgent, understanding, and forgiving of his son's peccadillos? What Roman father did not

---

* From *The Plays of Terence,* in George E. Duckworth, *The Complete Roman Drama,* vols. I and II (New York: Random House, 1942). Copyright © 1942 by Random House, Inc. Reprinted by permission of the publisher.

wish to create his son in his own image? What Roman matron did not wish the best for her son, did not want him to make a good marriage? What Roman young man did not wish to sow his wild oats without hurting himself or his parents? What Roman son really understood his parents or, for that matter, what Roman parents really understood their progeny? Roman aristocrats probably enjoyed the plays written by Terence because, in recognizing the characters, they recognized a serious theme beneath the surface of an otherwise farcical comedy. For the same reason, Roman plebeians rejected Terence's plays as too subtle, too thought-provoking, too removed from a world they were not likely to enter.

c. Seneca

Lucius Annaeus Seneca was born into a family of prominent Romans who resided in Cordoba, Spain. Annaeus Seneca, his father, was a reputable orator, rhetorician, and author of two major writings on rhetoric: *The Controversia* and *The Suasoriae.* Gallio Seneca, his brother, was the Roman prefect before whom Paul the Apostle was interrogated. Seneca was a young man when he came to Rome to study law. He remained in Rome to become a leading Roman senator, famed for his eloquence in speech-making. His oratorical skill so perturbed the vicious Caligula that the Emperor plotted to have him murdered. He refrained from carrying out his plans, however, when others convinced the Emperor that Seneca's poor health portended a short life. The Emperor Claudius, however, was not concerned with Seneca's longevity on this earth. When he was "advised" that the popular senator was having an affair with the Emperor's sister, Julia, the brilliant orator was banished from Rome in A.D. 41. Eight years later, Seneca was recalled at the behest of Agrippina, Claudius's niece and fifth wife, to tutor her son, Nero, for whom she had ambitious plans—Emperor of Rome. In A.D. 54, Claudius died from eating poisoned mushrooms prepared by Agrippina. Nero succeeded to the throne and Seneca became his chief adviser. The two men severed relationships in A.D. 62, three years after Nero had his mother murdered so that he alone might rule the Roman Empire. In A.D. 65, the Emperor successfully brought charges of conspiracy against the man who had once tutored him as a child and had advised him as a man.

Stoically, Seneca complied with the command of his Emperor to commit suicide: he slit his veins. In a world gone mad with licentious living, moral decadence, and political corruption, Seneca was an enigma. In private life, he was a proponent of Stoicism, capable of brilliantly arguing the virtues of the good life. In public life, he was a government official who composed a merciless satire on Claudius, as well as Nero's letter to the Roman Senate defending the murder of Agrippina. Seneca would have made an ideal protagonist in a tragic drama—a man neither all good, nor all bad, but a little of both to gain our sympathy and understanding.

Seneca's nine tragedies, all of which are extant, are adaptations of originals written by Greek playwrights. One, *Agamemnon,* is a restatement of the tragedy written by Aeschylus. Two plays, *Oedipus* and *Hercules on Oeta,* are based on tragedies written by Sophocles. Five plays, *Medea, Phaedra, The Phoenician Women, The Trojan Women,* and *Mad Hercules,* are adaptations of plays written by Euripides. *Thyestes* is from an unknown source.

Seneca's tragedies were not produced within his time, although the Emperor was enamored of the theater and fancied himself a skilled and brilliant actor. The supposition is that the plays were written while Seneca was in exile during the reign of Claudius and were intended for reading, not for performance. It is likely, however, that Romans would have applauded the plays because Seneca's treatment of the subject matter was appropriate for the times—bloody, sensational, horrendous, and melodramatic. Thrill-seeking Romans probably would have enjoyed the blood-curdling scenes depicted in view of the audience: Phaedra pouring out her sorrow to the mangled corpse of Hippolytus; Hercules stunned by the sight of the wife and children he had murdered in a moment of madness; Thyestes vomiting over the chopped and roasted bodies of his sons! Occult-minded Romans would have been enveloped in the incantations chanted by Manto and Tiresias in *Oedipus.* Too, speech-conscious Romans probably would have listened intently to the bombastic debates that passed for dialogue in all the plays. Undoubtedly, a woe-begone ghost would have held a Roman spectator enthralled with its frightening forecast of doom. Likewise, superhuman heroes and heroines who faced death with courage probably would have won the admiration of Roman spectators.

The Roman playwrights are not considered great because their plays do not have range or scope; their works are without original creativity; their plays are adaptations, not originals. The Roman playwright, however, is assured an important niche in the history of the theater because he is a link with the playwrights of antiquity. He is the source and inspiration of subsequent playwrights, and his plays are representative of the theater of his time. For example, Plautus is the source for *A Funny Thing Happened on the Way to the Forum* by the twentieth-century playwright Burt Shevlove. *The Twin Menaechmi* by Plautus is the inspiration for Shakespeare's *The Comedy of Errors.* In turn, Richard Rodgers, Lorenz Hart, and George Abbott based *The Boys from Syracuse* on Shakespeare's play. In short, a Greek New Comedy became Plautus' Roman Comedy, became Shakespeare's Elizabethan farce, became American musical comedy! Similarly, *The Woman of Andros* by Terence is the inspiration for Thorton Wilder's novel, *The Woman from Andros,* written in the 1930s; *Phormio* is the source for Molière's *Les Fourberies de Scapin;* the plot of William Wycherley's *The Country Wife* contains elements of *The Eunuch* by Terence. The Elizabethan playwrights turned to Seneca for inspiration. Thomas Kyd, Christopher Marlowe, William Shakespeare, and John Webster were quick to imitate his themes of love, hate, and revenge; his stoical heroes and heroines who had a will of their own and who faced death courageously; his use of the ghost as a portending figure of doom; his stichomythic dialogue with its brilliant shower of epigrams and proverbs. Although the Roman playwrights do not compare favorably with either the great Greek playwrights who preceded them, or with the great playwrights who followed, the Roman playwrights did provide subsequent writers with a blueprint for continuing the development of comedy and tragedy, and they did advance the separation of the theater from its religious ritualistic origins by concentrating on the needs of the audience for entertainment rather than on a need for spiritual guidance.

3. The Propagandist Medieval Playwright

The Greek theater was born out of the cult worship of the god of wine and fertility, Dionysus. It came into being when Pisistratus realized that the popular worship of Dionysus could be used to unify Athenian political life. It materialized when Pisistratus organized the City Dionysia Festival in 534 B.C. Its playwrights refined the religious ritualistic presentations into an art form that had ethical intent. It lost some of its religious aura when man's interest in his gods and his relationship to them shifted to interest in himself and to discovering solutions to the realities of everyday living. In contrast, the Roman theater had no religious roots. It sprang from the rustic plays and games of a people and from novelty, or from the search for entertainment to celebrate a holiday. Its plays were adaptations of plays written by the Greek dramatists. Its architecture imitated Greek theater architecture. The Roman theater mirrored the rise and fall of Roman civilization. Its popularity paralleled the growth of the Roman empire, and it fell into disrepute when it became the plaything of Emperors and when public behavior began to ape the immorality of its leaders. The medieval theater was born because of a felt need on the part of the Church to propagate the doctrines of Christianity and to educate an illiterate congregation in the tenets and rituals of the Church. It came into being when the Church employed dramatization to vitalize the religious services celebrating the birth and the resurrection of Christ. Its playwrights were lay people, priests, monks, and nuns. Its physical environment was, at first, the aisles and altar of the Church itself and, later, the marketplaces and streets of the city. It was separated from the Church when clerical intent was engulfed by theatrical production and secular influence. It became commercial theater when the Crown banned the performance of religious drama in order to establish its authority with the populace. It became professional theater when the professional actor returned to perform plays written by professional playwrights for a secular audience. The medieval theater marks the beginning of our theater today.

Little is known about the identity of the medieval playwright. It is generally assumed that a member of the clergy was responsible for the first dramatizations of religious rituals and Biblical incidents, and that a member of the congregation was later responsible for the humanization of Biblical characters, the introduction of facets of everyday life, and the elaboration of production effects. It is likely that the secular playwright assumed full responsibility for preparing the scripts in 1264 when the guilds in England, the religious societies in France, and the city corporations in Germany and Switzerland took over the production and presentation of religious dramas in celebration of a new religious holiday, Corpus Christi Day, proclaimed by Pope Urban IV. The religious dramas written by the anonymous medieval playwright may be classified as Mystery, Passion, Miracle, and Morality plays.

A Mystery play is based on a Biblical incident from either the Old or the New Testament. As dramatized by the medieval playwright, the Mystery play frequently seems like an everyday occurrence because the Biblical characters speak and behave like people in medieval society. For example, in the dramatization of the Biblical story *Noah and the Ark,* Noah and his family are portrayed as a medieval family unit involved in a domestic crisis because Noah's wife refuses to board the ark. She refuses to believe that the ark has been built at God's bidding, and she is piqued that Noah has left her sitting alone each night:

NOYE:
Dame, forty days are nearhand past
And gone since it began to rain;
Alive shall no man longer last
But we alone; that is full plain.

WIFE:
Now, Noye, 'faith, thou grows fond too fast.
I ask no more, nor will remain.
Thou are night mad. I am aghast.
Farewell! I will go home again.

NOYE:
O woman, art thou mad?
Of my works knowest thou nought.
All that has bone or blood
Shall be overflowed with the flood.

WIFE:
In faith, ye were as good

As let me go my gate.
Oh! Out! Haro!

NOYE:
What now? What cheer?

WIFE:
I will no nearer for no kin's need.

NOYE:
Help me, my sons, to hold her here,
For to her harms she takes no heed.

SECOND SON:
Be Merry, mother, and mend your cheer.
This world will all be drowned indeed.

WIFE:
Alas! That I this lore should hear.

NOYE:
Thou spoils us all—ill might thou speed!

THIRD SON:
Dear mother, wend with us;
There shall nothing you grieve.

WIFE:
Nay, nay; needs home I must
For I have tools to truss.

NOYE:
Woman, why dost thou thus,
To make us more mischief?

WIFE:
Noye, thou might have let me wit,
Early and late when you went out,
And aye at home you let me sit,
To look not what you were about.

NOYE:
Dame, hold thou me excused of it;
It was God's will, without a doubt.

WIFE:
What? Thinkest thou so for to go quit?
Nay, by my troth, thou gettest a clout.*

The humanization of Biblical characters and stories is characteristic of medieval playwriting and of a purpose. It not only brought the Biblical characters and stories alive for an audience that could not read, but it taught the religious concepts by permitting the audience to identify with the characters and the situation. Although it is not likely that the clergy took exception to the broad humorous treatment of Noah and his family, it is quite possible that they did take exception to the domestic bliss that permeates the scene between Joseph and Mary in the playlet based upon the purification of Mary after the birth of Christ. Except for the fact that the characters are identified by name as members of the Holy family, Joseph and Mary seem like any married couple discussing the fulfillment of religious obligations after the birth of a child. However, the simple poetic language, the naiveté of Joseph's reasoning, and the quiet love that passes between Joseph and Mary give the scene a simple religious dignity appropriate to the subject matter and appropriate for an audience that required oversimplification and personal identification in order to grasp the meaning:

MARY:
Joseph, my husband and compeer,
Take to me now ready intent.
I will show you in this manner
What I will do; thus have I meant.
Full forty days are come and went
Since that my babe Jesus was born;
Therefore, I would he were present
As Moyses' law tells us before,
Here in this Temple before God's sight,

* From *The Fisshers and the Marynars,* in J. S. Purvis, *The York Cycle of Mystery Plays* (London: The Society for Promoting Christian Knowledge), pp. 51–52. Copyright by The Society for Promoting Christian Knowledge, Holy Trinity Church, London, England. Reprinted by permission of the publisher.

As other women do appear,
So methinks is good skill and right
The same to do now with good cheer,
After God's law.

JOSEPH:

Mary, my spouse and maiden clean
This matter that thou moves to me
Is for all these women, I mean,
That have conceived with sin fleshly
To bear a child.
The law is hedged for them right plain;
They must be purified again,
For in man's pleasures for certain
They were defiled.
But, Mary bride, thou needst no so
For this cause to be purified, lo,
In God's Temple.
For sure thou art a clean virgin
For any thought thy heart within,
Nor never wrought no fleshly sin,
Nor never ill.

MARY:

That I my maidenhood have kept still
Is only through great God's own will;
That be ye bold.
Yet to fulfil the law, I wis,
That God almighty would express,
And for example of meekness,
Offer I would.

JOSEPH:

Ah, Mary! Blessed be thou aye;
Thou thinkest to do after God's will.
As though has said, Mary, I say;
I heartily consent theretill,
Without a doubt.
Therefore now dress we forth our way,
And offering make to God this day,
Even likewise as thyself did say,
With hearts devout.

MARY:
Thereto am I full ready dight;
But one thing, Joseph, I would move.

JOSEPH:
Mary, my spouse and maiden bright,
Tell on heartily, what grieves my love?

MARY:
Both beast and fowl must we needs have,
A lamb and two dove birds also.
Lamb have we none, nor none can crave.
Therefore, Joseph, what shall we do?
What is your rede?
If we do not as custom is
We are worthy to be blamed, I wis;
I would we did nothing amiss,
As God me speed.

JOSEPH:
Ah, good Mary, the law is this—
The rich to offer both lamb and bird;
And the two turtles, as I wis,
Or two dove birds shall with good word
Our offering be.
And Mary, we have done birds two,
As falls for us there where we go;
They are herein a pannier, lo,
Ready to see.
And if we have not both to bear,
The lamb, the birds, as rich men have,
Think then that we must present here
Our babe Jesus as we vouchsafe
Before God's sight.
He is our lamb, Mary; fear not;
For rich and poor none better sought;
Full well thou hast him hither brought,
This our offering dight.
He is the lamb of God, I say,
That all our sins shall take away
Of this world here.
He is the lamb of God very
That must defend from all affray,

Born of thy womb, our joy today
And all our cheer.*

Usually, a number of Biblical incidents were strung together to form a cycle of playlets. For example, the York Cycle consists of forty-eight Biblical playlets, ranging from *The Creation of the Heavenly Beings* to *The Last Judgment.* Each playlet was performed by a different guild and mounted on a pageant wagon that was drawn to a specific station where the playlet was performed for the audience. When the performance was completed, the pageant wagon moved on to the next station where the performance was repeated. At a given moment, ten to twelve playlets were performed simultaneously. The York Cycle was revived in 1957 with great success.

The Passion play is related to the Mystery play in that its subject matter is based upon a Biblical incident. However, the Passion play is concerned only with those incidents that surround the death and resurrection of Christ, rather than with a series of Biblical stories. Today, the Passion play is performed at such places as Oberammergau, Germany, and at Lake Wales, Florida. The Miracle play is based upon the suffering or the martyrdom of a saint. It is not concerned with Biblical incident or Biblical characters. T. S. Eliot's *Murder in the Cathedral,* the retelling of the martyrdom of Thomas à Becket, is an example of the Miracle play written in the twentieth century. The Morality play is not concerned with either Biblical incident or sainthood. Rather, it is concerned with man living the good life now in order to prepare for the good life in the hereafter. The characters in the Morality play are usually personifications of abstractions such as good and evil, vice and virtue, ignorance and knowledge, avarice and generosity, love and hate, and so on. Invariably, the protagonist is summoned to meet his Maker and is asked to account for his deeds on earth. *Everyman*

---

* From *The Hatmakers, Masons and Laborers,* in J. S. Purvis, *The York Cycle of Mystery Plays* (London: The Society for Promoting Christian Knowledge), pp. 125–126. Copyright by The Society for Promoting Christian Knowledge, Holy Trinity Church, London, England. Reprinted by permission of the publisher.

is the classic example of the Morality play. It relates the summoning of Everyman to his death. As Everyman moves toward his inevitable fate, he discovers that his boon companions on earth, Fellowship, Beauty, Discretion, Strength, and Material Wealth, for example, will not accompany him on his journey. Only Knowledge accompanies him to the end, and only Good Deeds pass into death with him. The play concludes with the following note of impending doom for those who do not lead the good moral life:

> This moral men may have in mind.
> Ye hearers, take it of worth, old and young,
> And forsake pride, for he deceiveth you in the end;
> And remember *Beauty, Five Wits, Strength,* and *Discretion,*
> They all at last do *Everyman* forsake,
> Save his *Good Deeds* there doth he take.
> But beware and they be small,
> Before God he hath no help at all.
> None excuse may there be for *Everyman.*
> Alas, how shall he do then?
> For after death amends may no man make,
> For then mercy and pity doth him forsake.
> If his reckoning be not clear when he doth come,
> God will say, *Ite maledicti in ignem aeternum!*
> And he that hath his account whole and sound,
> High in Heaven he shall be crowned.
> Unto which place God bring us all thither
> That we may live body and soul together.
> Thereto help, the Trinity!
> Amen say ye, for Saint Charity.*

Today, *Everyman,* or *Jedermann,* is performed annually at the Salzburg Festival in Austria. *J.B.,* by Archibald MacLeish, is an example of the twentieth-century Morality play.

Theater was reborn when the Church employed theater techniques to revitalize religious ritual for the edification of the congregation. The result was the reappearance of the playwright, the

---

* From *Everyman,* in John Allen, ed., *Three Medieval Plays* (London: Heinemann Educational Books Ltd.). Reprinted by permission of the publisher.

play actor, the play producer, and the play presentation. The playwright was reborn to meet the need for script preparation and dramatization. Like the playwrights who had preceded him, he chose his material from a source close to the audience, in this case, the Old and New Testaments. The playwright placed everyday speech in the mouths of the Biblical characters and embellished the Biblical incidents with everyday situations, thereby making the scriptures more significant and realistic for the congregation. His treatment of his subject matter resulted in a dramatic literature that includes the Mystery, Miracle, Passion, and Morality plays, and each gives evidence of the interest that dominated the life of the congregation, namely, religion. The play actor was reborn in the person of the amateur player, a guild member or citizen, whose enthusiastic participation in the plays stemmed from the instinct of man to act. The play producer reappeared when the Church first sponsored the presentation of religious drama and when the guilds and city corporations assumed the responsibility for the presentations as a community service. All the elements of theater reappeared in the cause of propagating the faith and saving men's souls: production of a written script that was performed by living actors before a live audience. Unwittingly, the Church, in serving its own cause, had served the cause of an art form that it had condemned and damned to perdition.

4. The Vigorous Elizabethans

The Wars of the Roses were terminated with the death of Richard III in 1485. Henry VII, the first of the mighty Tudor monarchs, faced the arduous task of making England into a first-rate power. During his twenty-four-year reign, Henry VII suppressed recalcitrant nobles by making effective use of the Star Chamber as a means of dispensing justice; encouraged trade and commerce by arranging a commercial treaty with Holland; developed a navy to protect England against invasion; and allied England with Scotland and Spain by arranging marriages between his progeny and the heirs to the Scottish and Spanish thrones. When Henry VII died at the age of fifty-two, he bequeathed to his heir, Henry VIII, a full exchequer and a tradition of autocratic rule.

Henry VIII was eighteen years old when he ascended the throne. He ruled England in traditional Tudor fashion: his word became law enacted by Parliament. Upon his death in 1547, Henry VIII bequeathed to his heirs Edward VI, his son by Jane Seymour; Mary I, his daughter by Katherine of Aragon; and Elizabeth I, his daughter by Anne Boleyn, a nation confused and divided because of the religious break with Rome, and a depleted exchequer because of the religious war against France and Scotland.

Elizabeth I was twenty-five years of age when she came to the throne of England in 1558. From her half-brother Edward VI (1547–1553) and her half-sister Mary I (1553–1558) she inherited a kingdom that was torn by religious strife, troubled by widespread idleness and unemployment, and threatened by foreign adversaries. From her grandfather, Henry VII, and from her father, Henry VIII, she inherited the political acumen needed to solve her nation's problems and to deal wisely with her rivals. Personable but vain, magnanimous but unforgiving, strong-willed but yielding, regal but human, Elizabeth I personified the spirit of the Renaissance. She was an avid reader, a linguist, and a patron of the arts who surrounded herself with men of intellect and genius. She was *the* monarch of her time, and she is generally considered to be the greatest of all English monarchs.

Elizabeth I resolved the religious question by proclaiming the Church of England and Protestantism to be the church and the religion of the land. Through royal decrees and legislation that made her seem unaware of and indifferent to human life and the freedom of worship, she gradually converted Catholic England to a Protestant nation. By 1590, all churches were conducting Protestant services. Elizabeth managed to keep England at peace with her adversaries for nearly thirty years. Exercising her diplomatic skill, she retained Spain and France as allies by flirting with the heads of state of both countries, alternately offering her hand in marriage to Francis, Duke of Alençon, and to Phillip II of Spain. She disavowed any support of Sir Francis Drake's piracy of Spanish ships on the high seas while she secretly encouraged his harassment and his sacking of Spanish ports. In 1588, however, when she was confronted with no alternative but war, Elizabeth permitted Drake to undertake the defeat of the Spanish Armada which theoretically should have been able to invade England with little effort. Drake's victory over the Spanish fleet seriously damaged the prestige of Spain in the eyes of her rivals and caused England to emerge as a power to be reckoned with. After a century of political turmoil and religious strife, life in Elizabethan England bristled with excitement and anticipation born of the prospect of a young nation successfully meeting the challenge of her more powerful rivals, Holland, France, and Spain.

The Elizabethan playgoer was stimulated by the personalities and the current happenings of the day. He admired Queen Elizabeth because the gossip surrounding her romances aroused romantic feelings in his heart and because her feminine ways proved an effective weapon for operating in what was essentially a man's world. Seemingly, both the Queen and her subject lived by their passions and their wits. He worshipped Sir Francis Drake because of his daring deeds and because the Admiral had achieved in fact what the playgoer dreamed in fancy: he had sailed around the world and had played havoc with the Spaniards while en route. He respected, perhaps even envied, Sir Walter Raleigh's business acumen and his ability to acquire lands and amass wealth while serving the Queen. He identified with the high-spirited and virile Earl of Essex. He took pride in the defeat of the Spanish Armada and he enthusiastically supported the war against Spain. He sensed an impending empire, consequent national wealth, and the prospect of individual prosperity in the eventual defeat of Spain. Books and pamphlets whetted his curiosity about himself and the world in which he lived. He attended the theater expecting that the excitement and adventure which characterized the times would be incorporated into the play.

The Elizabethan playwright, influenced by the Renaissance and stimulated by the world around him, did not disappoint the playgoer. He devised plots that were complicated by subplots, replete with sudden twists and turns and unexpected and surprising reversals that enabled the playgoer to examine the theme and to analyze the characters in depth. He selected strong themes and powerful emotions to demonstrate the meaning of life and to reveal the nature and character of man. He created characters that bore magnetic and magnificent personalities, comparable to those of national leaders and heroes. He endowed his characters with human instincts and human passions with which the playgoer could identify and relate. He devised a drama that reiterated and reaffirmed the Renaissance viewpoint that man was free to determine his fate, that life was to be enjoyed here and now, and that man succeeded or failed according to his strength or weakness of character. The playwright wrote poetic dialogue that aroused emotions and elevated the theme. He sacrificed the unities of time, place, and action so that his play might develop without restriction. He studied the architecture of his theater and used it wisely in placing and alternating the locale of his scenes. He mingled comedy with tragedy, tragedy with comedy, farce with melodrama, melodrama with fantasy, to create a play that was as varied as life itself. He gave the audience what it wanted: ghosts, supernatural beings, music, dance, sword-play, spectacle, blood-curdling crimes, and lusty humor. The Elizabethan playgoers rewarded the playwright with attendance and applause when he gave them pleasure; catcalls, boos, and apple cores when he did not meet their needs or anticipations.

The flowering of the playwright during the reign of Elizabeth I represented the final shift from religious to secular drama. Although religious drama continued to be performed during the sixteenth century, secular drama was in the ascendency as a result of a revival of interest in the play form. For example, John Rastell produced and wrote a number of plays in the early part of the century that reflected the influence of the humanist movement. In 1534, John Heywood wrote a number of interludes that were designed to entertain an audience rather than to edify it. Universities and schools began to produce and perform the plays of Plautus and Terence rather than use the texts merely for the teaching of Latin. In or about 1540, Nicholas Udall wrote and produced *Ralph Roister Doister,* the first English play to imitate the structure and the character of a Roman play. The play is an adaptation of Plautus' *The Braggart Soldier* to a local scene. Soon after Elizabeth acceded to the throne, *Gammer Gerton's Needle* (playwright anonymous), another farce that imitated Roman comedy, was produced at Cambridge. In 1562, *Gorboduc,* the first English tragedy, was written by Thomas Sackville and Thomas Norton. It was produced at the Inns of Court, the residences and training centers for lawyers.

It is the first English play to be written in blank verse, and marks the beginnning of the influence of Seneca upon the writing of popular Elizabethan drama. John Lyly, a graduate of Oxford, contributed to the evolution of Elizabethan drama by creating a style of prose, euphuism, that appealed to the listener because of the beauty and ring of the language. His first play, *Alexander and Campaspe,* was produced in 1584. Lyly's plays reflected the wit, grace, and the elegance of the royal court, and were primarily written to please and gain favor with the Queen. Despite his popularity with the public and the court, Lyly failed to win the post of Master of Revels. Between 1586 and 1588, three plays, *The Spanish Tragedy* by Thomas Kyd, *Tamburlaine the Great* by Christopher Marlowe, and *Arden of Feversham,* frequently attributed to Thomas Kyd, excited and thrilled Elizabethan audiences. These three plays set the style and tone of Elizabethan drama that flourished until the death of the Queen in 1603.

During his brief but brilliant career as a playwright, Christopher Marlowe wrote four outstanding tragedies: *Tamburlaine the Great* (ca. 1587), *The Tragical History of Dr. Faustus* (ca. 1588), *The Jew of Malta* (ca. 1589), and *Edward II* (ca. 1592). Each play contributed to the development and acceptance of blank verse as the vehicle for dramatic dialogue, and each play established the nature and character of the protagonist as the motivating forces for plot and action. A graduate of Cambridge, where he supplemented his livelihood by spying for the Queen, Christopher Marlowe was a personal friend of Thomas Kyd whose play, *The Spanish Tragedy,* set the pattern for Elizabethan play structure. The two playwrights were roommates and members of a group who allegedly held atheistic beliefs. In 1593, Thomas Kyd was brought up on charges of heresy. Under torture, he implicated Marlowe. However, before Marlowe could defend himself against the charge, he was stabbed during a brawl in a pub and died. Thomas Kyd died the following year, 1594, in poverty and disgrace as a result of implicating Marlowe. In their brief playwriting careers, both Kyd and Marlowe made major contributions to the development of Elizabethan drama.

At best, the facts concerning the life of William Shakespeare and his career in the Elizabethan theater are a sketchy outline of a man who attained success as a playwright. Born in Stratford-on-Avon in 1564, Shakespeare was the third child of a respectable merchant who was actively engaged in community affairs. When the playwright was eighteen years old, he married Anne Hathaway who was eight years his senior. It is believed that the young husband and father left his wife and family in 1585 to journey to London where it is thought he eked out a living as a poet, an actor, and a play doctor before becoming a successful playwright. The records indicate that in 1592, Philip Henslowe paid him for writing *Harry the Sixth* for Edward Alleyn. The play is assumed to be Shakespeare's *Henry VI, Part 1.* Two poems, *Venus and Adonis* (1593) and *The Rape of Lucrece* (1594), established Shakespeare's reputation as a poet. By 1594, he was a paid member of the Lord Chamberlain's Players who were managed by the Burbage family. By 1599, he was declared a partner in the operation of The Globe theater and had written nearly a dozen plays as well as appearing as an actor in Ben Jonson's *Every Man in His Humour.* Shakespeare retired from the theater in 1613, two years after completing his last comedy, *The Tempest.* He died three years later at the age of fifty-two.

The plays of Shakespeare may be broadly categorized as chronicle plays, tragedies, and comedies. The chronicle plays include *King John, Richard II, Richard III, Henry IV, Parts 1 and 2, Henry V, Henry VI, Parts 1, 2, and 3,* and *Henry VIII.* The tragedies include *Romeo and Juliet, Julius Caesar, Hamlet, Troilus and Cressida, Othello, King Lear, Macbeth, Antony and Cleopatra, Coriolanus, Titus Andronicus,* and *Pericles.* The comedies, which range from farce to fantasy, from romantic to tragic comedy, include *Love's Labor's Lost, A Midsummer Night's Dream, The Merchant of Venice, Much Ado About Nothing, As You Like It, Twelfth Night, Measure for Measure, The Winter's Tale, The Tempest, The Merry Wives of Windsor, The Taming of the Shrew, The Comedy of Errors,* and *Two Gentlemen of Verona.*

Shakespeare relied upon Raphael Holinshed's *Chronicles of England, Scotland,* and *Ireland* (1577) for factual information in writing the chronicle plays. Similarly, the playwright borrowed from Sir Thomas North's translation of *Plutarch's Lives* in writing the Roman tragedies. The other tragedies and many of the comedies were derived from poems, folk tales, mythology, novels, and other plays. Some seem to have been inspired by a contemporary personality or situation. For example, *A Midsummer Night's Dream* was reportedly written in honor of a royal marriage, and *The Merry Wives of Windsor* was written at the request of Queen Elizabeth who had expressed a desire to see Falstaff, the character initially introduced in *Henry IV, Parts 1 and 2,* but eliminated from the action in *Henry V,* revived on the stage. Puritanism undoubtedly inspired the creation of Malvolio in *Twelfth Night.* It is sometimes thought that the wave of anti-Semitism that permeated London as a result of the charge leveled against Rodrigo Lopez, a Jew, and personal physician to the Queen, that he had accepted a bribe to poison the Queen, inspired Shakespeare to write *The Merchant of Venice.* It seems likely, too, that the chronicle plays were written to arouse a feeling of patriotism at a time when England was engaged in a major conflict with Spain. One of the chronicle plays, *Richard II,* gained political significance when a special performance was given at the request of the Earl of Essex on the eve of his projected plan to lead a group of subjects against the Queen. Many of the plays contain topical allusions that were meaningful to an Elizabethan audience, but that have virtually no meaning for today's audience. For the most part, Shakespeare's plays are plays of character rather than plays of social significance.

Shakespeare is considered by some to be the greatest of all playwrights. Others, however, believe that he shares such accolades with Aeschylus, Sophocles, Euripides, and Molière. Shakespeare's reputation in the theater rests upon his use of the English language, his poetic imagery, his range of subject matter, his blend of comedy and tragedy, his tapestry of characters, his insight into human behavior, and his compassionate understanding of mankind.

Ben Jonson is an example of the playwright who is perturbed by the behavior of the society in which he lives and who seeks to expose the foibles and the follies of mankind through his plays. Jonson was a graduate of the Westminister School where, under the influence of William Camden, he became acquainted with the works of the classicists. Upon graduation, however, it was necessary for him to follow the vocation of his stepfather, that of a bricklayer, to supplement the family income. This he did for a period of seven years. He was happy to answer the call to arms in the war against Spain because he considered military service preferable to bricklaying. He began his theatrical career as an actor in 1597 but soon found himself in trouble with the law when, as a collaborating playwright with Thomas Nash, he wrote a play called *The Isle of Dogs*. The Privy Council deemed the play seditious and slanderous and ordered Ben Jonson jailed. In 1598, Jonson wrote his first successful comedy, *Every Man in His Humour,* which was produced at The Globe with Shakespeare appearing as one of the actors. The play initiated a style of comedy based on the ancient medical theory that the physiology of man consisted of four body fluids, namely, blood, phlegm, black bile, and yellow bile. The theory was first enunciated by Hippocrates, who believed that an imbalance of the fluids resulted in pain and disease. Later, Galen advanced the theory that the four body fluids were indicative of four basic temperaments, namely, buoyant (blood), sluggish (phlegm), dejected (black bile), and quick-tempered (yellow bile). Robert Burton revived the theory in his publication *The Anatomy of Melancholy*. Elizabethans referred to the fluids as "humors." Jonson utilized this theory to endow his characters with a spccific humor representative of one of the body fluids. The result were characters who were eccentrics, ideal for exposing vice, but hardly human, because they represented only one aspect of human nature. Success as a playwright did not prevent Jonson from becoming entangled with the law for a second time. Shortly after the opening of the play, he quarreled with another actor and killed him in a duel. He was imprisoned, and branded on his thumb as an indication that he was a second offender. His property was confiscated.

After his release from prison in 1599, London audiences saw a second "humor" play, *Every Man Out of His Humour*. The year 1605 was another year of success and adversity. *Volpone, or The Fox* established Jonson as the leading satirist of his day. A second play, *Eastward Ho!,* written in collaboration with John Marsten and George Chapman, two playwrights with whom he had carried on a literary duel, and which was produced the same year as *Volpone,* resulted in the arrest of the playwrights on the ground that the subject matter of the play insulted James I. The playwrights were imprisoned with the threat that their noses and ears would be severed from the rest of their persons. Jonson continued to expose the follies and foibles of Jacobean society in *Epicene, or The Silent Woman,* a play about a hypochondriac who marries a "dumb" wife because the hypochondria manifests itself in an inability to cope with noise; *The Alchemist,* a play that satirizes gullibility and greed; and *Bartholomew Fair,* a play that caricatures the Puritans because of their attack upon his plays. Although Jonson, whose measure of conceit is indicated by the fact that he dropped the letter "h" from the spelling of his name to make it distinctive, wrote several tragedies and masques, his forte was satirical comedy. Despite the fact that his characters are stereotypes, albeit brilliant ones, collectively they represent the spectrum of human behavior. An adherent of the principles of classical playwriting, Jonson frequently criticized his contemporaries, especially Shakespeare, for ignoring the criteria for classical playwriting. After the death of Shakespeare, Jonson became the literary lion of England and its unofficial poet laureate. He was pensioned by the government despite his altercations with the law in his early years. He died in poverty in 1629 and was honored in death by burial in Westminster Abbey.

In addition to enjoying the plays written by Christopher Marlowe, William Shakespeare, and Ben Jonson, Elizabethans applauded the plays written by Thomas Dekker, Thomas Heywood, Francis Beaumont and John Fletcher, and John Webster. Elizabethans in 1600 were delighted with Dekker's *The Shoemaker's Holiday,* a domestic comedy with music that celebrated the antics of Simon Eyrie, the master shoemaker who became the Lord Mayor of London. In 1603, a domestic tragedy, *A Woman Killed with Kindness,* by Thomas Heywood, held the attention of London theatergoers. Francis Beaumont and John Fletcher won favor with their romantic tragicomedies. John Webster startled, stunned, and shocked audiences with two sensational revenge plays entitled *The White Devil* and *The Duchess of Malfi.*

Despite the fact that his play drew at the box office, the status of the Elizabethan playwright was no better than that of the actor. Although he might be a university graduate and an intimate of royalty, he, too, was considered a rogue and a vagabond because of his association with the theater. Unless he was a member of the company, he netted little profit from his creativity. Generally, his play was purchased by the company and became its property. Frequently, his authorship was omitted when the play was published and usually publication of the play was prevented by the company lest the work be pirated by a rival. If he was a member of the company, he did have an opportunity to share in the box-office receipts as a result of the success of his play. The Elizabethan playwright was subjected to a degree of censorship through the requirement that his play be registered with the office of Master of Revels who ruled upon the propriety of the subject matter. Consequently, most Elizabethan plays do not reflect the events of the time. When they did, the allusions were shrouded. If, in performance, they became obvious, the play was closed by the Privy Council and the playwright was punished. In his day, the Elizabethan playwright was second to the importance of the actor.

5. Two Neoclassicists and a Rebel

During the greater part of the sixteenth century, France was wracked by civil and religious strife: noble fought noble for power; Catholicism fought Protestantism for recognition as the official state religion. It was not until 1598, when the Edict of Nantes, granting religious rights to the Huguenots, was signed by Henry IV, the first of the Bourbon kings, that the future of France was assured a measure of tranquility. The economic and political conditions of the country were not conducive to the establishment of a professional theater. Additionally, the *Confrèrie de la Passion* held a monopoly on theater production in Paris, thus preventing actors from developing a permanent French theater in the capital. Moreover, French theatergoers preferred the entertainment offered by the Italian *commedia dell'arte* players to the works of such playwrights as Alexandre Hardy. Although his plays were specifically written to cater to the entertainment needs of the French theatergoer, Hardy's plays were of too little literary consequence and too insufficient in character delineation to warrant enthusiasm for a national and professional theater. As a result, the theater in France during the early part of the seventeenth century was not as professionally advanced as the theater in England or Spain. It was not until the reign of Louis XIII that the professional theater, through the offices of Cardinal Richelieu, received encouragement from the Crown. It came about because of the Cardinal's desire and plan to promote and enrich French culture.

Cardinal Richelieu became chief minister of France in 1624. The Cardinal assumed full control of the government in 1630 when Louis XIII exiled Marie de Medici because he was weary of his mother's political intrigues and her ambition to rule France through his office. In addition to providing France with a foreign policy that extended the prestige and power of France abroad, and in addition to strengthening the royal power by crushing rebellious nobles at home, Cardinal Richelieu established the French Academy to raise the standards of French culture. The idea was not entirely a new one, but a revival of classicism in France. As early as 1553, a group of French poets had organized themselves into a group called The Pléiade. The purpose of these early neoclassicists was to establish French, rather than Latin, as the language of national literature, and to establish a national literature that was comparable to the literature of other countries. Étienne Jodelle, a playwright who wrote the first modern French tragedy, *Cléopatre Captive,* was one of its members. In 1635, the French Academy received its royal patent, and it was formally registered in 1637 by Parlement. The purpose of the seventeenth-century neoclassicists was to set the criteria for French literature, grammar, and rhetoric. Its criteria for dramatic criticism were based upon Greek and Roman criticism, principally that of Aristotle and Horace. *Le Cid* by Pierre Corneille offered the Academy its first opportunity to apply its criteria for judging the literary merits of a play.

Pierre Corneille was practising law in 1629 when he entrusted the production of his first play, *Mélite,* a comedy, to Montdory, the leading French tragedian of the day. The play was initially produced in Rouen, the birthplace of Corneille. A performance of the play was repeated in Paris the following year, and proved to be more than just a hometown success. Nevertheless, although Parisian theatergoers enjoyed the play, French poets criticized *Mélite* because the playwright had ignored the playwriting principles adhered to by the Italian playwrights whom the French poets admired.

A second play, *Clitandre,* was written to please the critics, but failed to please the audience. During the next seven years, Corneille alternated between playwriting in Paris and practising law in Rouen. At the end of the 1636–1637 season, the Hôtel de Bourgogne produced Corneille's *Le Cid.* The play was an instantaneous success and gave rise to the French proverb "Beautiful as le Cid." The play, an adaptation of *Las Mocedades del Cid* by Guillen de Castro, told the story of Rodrique and Chimène, whose love for each other almost comes to a tragic end when Rodrique slays Don Gomez, Chimène's father, to avenge the honor of his own father. Parisians applauded the deeds of the noble hero who put honor before love, and they responded to the emotional dialogue written in Alexandrine verse. However, despite the positive audience reaction to the play, the French Academy, while admitting that the play had popular appeal, criticized the work on the grounds that it did not adhere to the principles of good playwriting. In a "position paper" prepared by Jean Chapelain, considered to be the greatest French poet of his day, the French Academy stated its opinion. It allowed that Corneille had observed the classic unities, which require that the action occur in one place, that it be completed within a twenty-four-hour period, and that it not be complicated by a second plot. It allowed that the protagonist was of noble character and intent. It allowed, too, that the characters behaved according to their station in life. However, the Academy objected to the fact that Corneille had written a tragic comedy and not a pure tragedy. In the end, the lovers are reconciled, despite the fact that the hero has killed the heroine's father. The French Academy held the viewpoint that one could write either a tragedy or a comedy, but that one could not write a play that combined the elements of tragedy and comedy if one were to successfully imitate the classics of Greece and Rome. Moreover, the Academy ruled that Chimène's decision to marry Rodrique violated the principles of verisimilitude and decorum. It was incredible and not within character that the heroine could fall in, out, and in love again in so short a time and in view of the circumstances. Additionally, although *Le Cid* does not contain any strong secondary plots, the number of events that occur within the twenty-four hours violated the principle of verisimilitude. In short, Corneille had written a popular box-office success, but one that did not meet the criteria for playwriting set by the French Academy. In subsequent plays such as *Horace, Cinna,* and *Polyeucte,* Corneille succeeded in meeting the prescribed criteria. In 1647, he was elected to the French Academy. Corneille's reputation as a playwright waned with the passing years, and he grew increasingly embittered as Jean Racine surpassed him both in public acclaim and in recognition by the Academy.

Jean Racine was twenty-five years old when his second play, *Thébaïde,* was produced by Molière in 1664. The established playwright sought to befriend Racine who had come to Paris after deciding upon a career in the theater rather than one in the Church. A first play, *Amasie,* had been purchased by the players at the Hôtel de Bourgogne, but had remained unproduced. A third play, *Alexandre,* was first produced by Molière at the court of Louis XIV. Although the presentation was successful, Racine was dissatisfied with the quality of the acting and he offered the play to the Bourgogne company for public presentation. Molière was offended by this slight and never spoke to the playwright again. Two years later, in 1667, the Bourgogne players presented *Andromaque.* Its success established Racine as the leading writer of French tragedy and as the rival of Corneille. Thereafter, in rapid succession, Parisians saw *Les Plaideurs* (1668), a satire on the French legal system; *Britannicus* (1669), *Bérénice* (1670), *Bajazet* (1672), *Mithridate* (1673), *Iphigénie* (1674), and *Phèdre* (1677). Each tragedy conformed to the criteria established by the French Academy. Racine's tragic heroes and heroines differ from Corneille's in that Racine is usually concerned with man's passions, whereas Corneille is usually concerned with man's ideals. Too, the protagonist in Racine's tragedies are more human. Each is prevented from doing what is morally correct because of a conflict with an inner instinct. The heart rules the mind in Racine's dramas. In contrast, the protagonist in Corneille's tragedies seemingly has no inner conflict, but is always at work to achieve the ideal. The nobility of man motivates the behavior of the protagonist in Corneille's tragedies.

In 1677, at the height of his career, and after he had been elected to the Academy in preference to Molière, Racine withdrew from the theater because he could not accept any censure or criticism, however slight, from either his colleagues or admirers. He retired to write a history of Port-Royal and to fulfill his duties as historian to King Louis XIV. In 1689, Racine emerged from retirement at the request of Mme. de Maintenon, the morganatic wife of King Louis, to write *Esther. Athalie,* a second religious drama, was written in 1691 to honor another request by Mme. de Maintenon. There are many who believe that his last play, *Athalie,* is his masterpiece. Others believe that *Britannicus* or *Andromaque* deserve this honor. His most popular play, if not his masterpiece, is *Phèdre,* a play that is to an actress what *Hamlet* is to an actor.

While Corneille and Racine sought to win the favor of the French Academy by writing plays that adhered to the Academy's interpretation, and sometimes misinterpretation, of the playwriting criticisms written by Aristotle and Horace, Molière ignored the French Academy and wrote his plays from first-hand knowledge of the theater. While Corneille and Racine reached into the past for source material, Molière looked at his French society and drew his material from the contemporary scene. While Corneille and Racine created characters who were too noble or too passionate, Molière created characters who were too foolish for their own good.

Molière was christened Jean Baptiste Poquelin on January 15, 1622, a date frequently given as his birthday. His father was an upholsterer who nine years later became *valet tapissier* to Louis XIII with the assurance that the assignment would revert to his son when the father retired. Until such time when the young Poquelin would assume the position of bedmaker to the King, Molière was educated at the Collège de Clermont, a Jesuit institution. In 1643, despite his education, which is thought to have included training for the bar, Molière joined the Béjart family to organize the L'Illustre Théâtre. The lack of the company's success in Paris led to traveling the provinces from 1648 to 1658. In that year, Molière persuaded Philippe, the brother of Louis XIV, to become the patron of the L'Illustre Théâtre. Philippe's patronage led to a performance before Louis XIV on October 24, 1658. For the occasion, Molière chose Corneille's *Nicomède* and an afterpiece that he had written, *Le Docteur Amoureux.* Fortunately, the brilliant success of the afterpiece counterbalanced the dismal failure of the performance of *Nicomède*. L'Illustre Théâtre was assigned a hall in the Petit-Bourbon to alternate with a group of Italian players.

Molière's plays reveal a society that sought to emulate the manners and morals of King Louis XIV, who had declared "I am the State." It was a society of rising nouveau riche whose members flaunted their wealth to achieve status. It was a society that was obsessed with fashion, manners, and money. *The Precious Young Women* (1659) and *The Scholarly Ladies* (1671) ridicules the affected manners and ostensible erudition of young women. *The School for Husbands* (1661), *The School for Wives* (1662), and *George Dandin* (1668) are concerned with love and marriage. The first raises the question of how to train a young woman to be a good wife; the second questions the wisdom of forcing a young woman to marry her guardian; and the third ponders the effect of jealousy upon a marital relationship. *Tartuffe* (1664) exposes the hypocrite; *Dom Juan* (1665) analyzes the cynic; and *Le Misanthrope* (1666) portrays the idealist. *The Miser* (1668) unmasks the hoarder; and *Le Bourgeois Gentilhomme* (1670) satirizes the manners and morals of the nouveau riche. *The Flying Doctor* (1648?), *Love, the Doctor* (1665), *The Doctor in Spite of Himself* (1666), *Monsieur de Pourceaugnac* (1669), and *The Imaginary Invalid* (1673) are concerned with doctors and their patients. Each of the plays takes to task the false values, the vain obsessions, and the foolish quests of the society in which Molière lived—and, indeed, our own as well.

The comedy of Molière is the comedy of detached laughter. The playwright dangles his hero before our eyes so that we may see his foibles exposed at a distance. We laugh at what we see because we believe the foibles are his exclusively, and not ours. But the more we look, the more we realize that his foibles bear a marked resemblance to our own. For example, Alceste in *Le Misanthrope* is disillusioned by the society in which he lives when the heroine, Célimène, cannot bring herself to put aside the joys of her world to marry Alceste. The hero responds by withdrawing from society. We are amused by the inability of Alceste to compromise with life. And yet, how many times do we say to ourselves, "I wish I were on an island," or "I'd like to get away from it all," or some such similar comment. Consider the "plight" of Argan in *The Imaginary Invalid.* His life is one enema after another. His preoccupation with health leads him from one doctor to another and the scheme that "I would like to have a doctor as my son-in-law so that I can have all the treatment and prescription and free consultations I need without going outside the family." He denies that he is healthy, that his body is in extremely good condition, and that it is a small miracle that he hasn't died as a result of all the medication he has already consumed. Question: How far removed is the hypochondriac of the seventeenth century from that of the twentieth century? When we wish to be sick, do we not play the game of hunting for doctors who will agree with us? It has been said that comedy is serious business because it is concerned with the business of living. When our obsessions and our fears and our follies and our foibles get in the way of the realities of living, then it is the serious business of comedy to laugh us back into the real world. Underlying the comic twists and turns, the slapstick action, the humorous dialogue, the *commedia dell'arte* characters, the songs and dances, and the satirical wit is the serious business of Molière's comedy: life and common sense.

Molière's last play, *The Imaginary Invalid,* provided him with his final role as an actor. It was during the fourth presentation of the play on February 17, 1673, that Molière was taken with a coughing seizure that he managed to overcome so that he could finish his performance as Argan. Immediately after the play ended, he was taken home by his wife. He died suddenly after the onset of another coughing spell. Funeral arrangements were delayed while his wife sought an audience with King Louis XIV because the Church would not grant permission for him to be buried in consecrated ground. The decision by the Church recalled "L'Affaire Tartuffe." Shortly after King Louis had appointed Molière to be the organizer of the entertainment at Versailles in 1664, Molière presented *Tartuffe* for the King's pleasure. Although the liberal-minded monarch enjoyed the play, he withheld permission for its public presentation because it had anti-religious overtones. When it seemed that the King was about to change his mind a month later, a Church official denounced Molière as a libertine and praised the King for prohibiting a public presentation of the play. Three years later, the King gave his approval before going off to fight in Flanders. The show opened on August 5, 1667, at the Palais Royal. The next morning, the theater was closed by the President of the Parlement, and a week later the Archbishop of Paris forbade the reading, the hearing, or performance of the play, either in public or in private. Two years later, on February 5, 1669, the play was presented to the public with the consent of the King. This was the basis for the strained relationship that existed between Molière and the Church at the time of his death. Only the intervention of King Louis XIV made it possible for a compromise to be reached: Molière was buried without religious rites, at dusk, in the cemetery of Saint Joseph in the Rue Montmartre.

In addition to providing examples of the playwright who writes to entertain and enlighten his audience and who writes to comment upon the age in which he lives, Corneille, Racine, Molière, and their contemporaries are examples of playwrights whose works are encouraged by the government for a specific national purpose. The plan to raise the standard of the French language and literature through the creative effort of the playwright was introduced by Cardinal Richelieu, nurtured by Cardinal Mazarin, and brought to fruition by Jean Baptiste Colbert, chief adviser to Louis XIV from 1661 to 1683. The government's use of the theater through its playwrights was similar to that of the development of the Greek theater by Pisistratus and Pericles with Aeschylus, Sophocles, Euripides, and Aristophanes as chief playwrights. The growth and development of the French Academy and the response of the playwright, particularly Corneille and Racine, to the revival of classicism were basic factors in the establishment of Paris as the cultural capital of Europe. In effect, Paris became a second Athens —a city to be emulated and reproduced by lesser monarchs in other countries. The role of the government in the development of the French professional theater and the French playwright was the reverse of the role played by the English government in the development of the English theater. In France, a national theater emerged at the end of the seventeenth century. In England, a commercial theater continued to grow and develop with the government serving only as patron and protector. The French government honored Corneille, Racine, and Molière with pensions. It also gave financial assistance to acting companies. The French Academy honored Corneille and Racine with membership, but denied Molière a similar honor because his plays did not conform to their criteria for playwriting. On the other hand, King Louis XIV was a great admirer of the comic playwright and frequently defended him in his skirmishes with critics and clergy. In the last analysis, Molière emerged triumphant. Seven years after his death, King Louis XIV united the players of the Hôtel de Bourgogne with those of Molière's company to form the Comédie-Française which, even today, is often referred to as La Maison de Molière.

6. The Restoration Wits

After the death of Shakespeare in 1616, and after the comic genius of Jonson had spent itself, London theatergoers, now consisting of a prosperous middle class, were dependent upon the works of lesser playwrights for entertainment. Sensational and romantic tragedy replaced exalted tragedy as written by Shakespeare. Pert and saucy comedy superseded the pungent comedy of humors written by Jonson. Nevertheless, theatergoers were moved by *The Changling* by Thomas Middleton and William Rowley. Its story of intrigue and murder was based upon a story taken from *God's Revenge Against Murder,* an anthology of murder cases compiled by John Reynolds in 1621. Audiences were similarly touched by the plays of John Ford, whose treatment represented a psychological interpretation of Robert Burton's *The Anatomy of Melancholy. The Broken Heart* and *'Tis Pity She's a Whore* are concerned with the tragedy that results from a consuming obsession with sex and love. There are many who believe that Ford's plays mark the beginning of modern psychological drama. For example, many of the plays of Tennessee Williams are thought to have their psychological roots in the plays written by John Ford. Philip Massinger was another playwright whose comedies and tragedies entertained pre-Restoration audiences. Additionally, London theatergoers were delighted and amused by the comedies of John Fletcher and James Shirley. *The Wild Goose Chase,* a romantic comedy that Fletcher wrote for the court of King James I, was sufficiently sophisticated and immoral to hold the attention of a Restoration audience when it was revived.

Unfortunately, most of these plays, as well as many of the Elizabethan plays, held little or no interest for a Restoration audience because two generations of potential theatergoers had been lost as a result of the closing of the theaters in 1642. A new body of dramatic literature had to be created for the society of the time, a society whose instincts and desires had heretofore been repressed by the austere code of living dictated by the Puritans, and which now sought release through entertainment that glorified the joys of being alive. It was not time for tragedy, but, rather, it was a time for sparkling and artificial comedy that reflected the manners and morals of the Merrie Monarch of England, Charles II, whose amorous dalliances inspired the behavior of high society.

The Comical Revenge; or Love in a Tub, by Sir George Etherege, set the theme, the dramatis personae, the structure, the dialogue, and the moral tone for Restoration comedy. The theme is ageless: the war of the sexes. The dramatis personae, unlike those in Jonson's comedies, are not representative humors, but members of Restoration society. In creating the character of Sir Frederick Frolick, Etherege presented Restoration society with its first view of one of its own members, the gallant. The structure follows that of the comedy of intrigue, quite suitable for a society that was frequently caught napping in the wrong bed. The dialogue is a combination of prose and poetry and reflects the wit and sophistication of an immoral society. The moral tone suggests that life is a game to be played without restrictions or consequences. In 1668, Etherege offered a second play, *She Would If She Could. The Man of Mode; or, Sir Fopling Flutter* is generally thought to be the best of Etherege's plays. Through marriage, the playwright moved in high social circles. Through diplomatic service rendered for the King, he mingled with members of royalty. His plays echoed the sophistication of his private life.

Seven years after the premiere of *The Comical Revenge; or Love in a Tub,* William Wycherley added a stinging bite to the comedy of manners innovated by Sir George Etherege. Wycherley's plays are more satirical in purpose, more pornographic in language and situation, more brutal in the exposure of a fashionable society that cloaked its coarseness and vulgarity with good manners. *Love in the Wood; or St. James Park* is a satire on contemporary life in London in 1671. *The Gentleman Dancing Master* employs disguise as a means for the hero to court the heroine. *The Country Wife* (1672) permits one of its lead characters, Mr. Horner, to pretend that he is a eunuch so that he can stalk his prey without suspicion. In part, the plot is derived from *The Eunuch* by Terence. *The Plain Dealer* (1674) is a bitter denunciation of Restoration society and resembles *Le Misanthrope* by Molière.

The Restoration comedy of manners approached perfection with the plays of William Congreve. Congreve made his playwriting debut in 1693 with *The Old Bachelor.* It won public acclaim and led to a friendship with John Dryden who was then the acknowledged literary leader of England. *The Double-Dealer* followed a year later, but it did not achieve the acclaim that had been accorded Congreve's first play. In 1695, he scored another hit with *Love for Love,* a satire on the vices and follies of the times. The play was applauded for its wit, and critically praised because of the manner in which Congreve developed the plot and the characters. *The Way of the World,* Congreve's last play, was produced in 1700. It is Restoration comedy at its best. It combines the frivolity of Etherege with the sting of Wycherley. Its brilliant sparkling dialogue established Congreve as a master of the comedy of repartee. Although Congreve pictures a world seemingly without moral values, obsessed with fashion and manners, and bent upon social intrigue, his characters enlist our sympathy because they live in a tinsel world of nothingness. We are moved by the two lovers, Mirabell and Millamant, who realize that mutual love is not enough to assure a successful marriage, that the ways of their society may affect their remaining as husband and wife. In Act IV, Scene 1, Millimant states the conditions under which she will accept Mirabell's proposal. In part, she says:

MRS. M.:

> Ah! idle creature, get up when you will—and d'ye hear, I won't be called names after I'm married; positively I won't be called names.

MIRABELL:
Names!

MRS. M.:
Ay, as wife, spouse, my dear, joy, jewel, love, sweetheart, and the rest of that nauseous cant, in which men and their wives are so fulsomely familiar—I shall never bear that—good Mirabell, don't let us be familiar or fond, nor kiss before folks, like my Lady Fadler and Sir Francis: nor go to Hyde Park together the first Sunday in a new chariot, to provoke eyes and whispers, and then never to be seen there together again; as if we were proud of one another the first week, and ashamed of one another for ever after. Let us never visit together, nor go to a play together; but let us be very strange and well-bred: let us be as strange as if we had been married a great while; and as well-bred as if we were not married at all.

MIRABELL:
Have you any more conditions to offer? Hitherto your demands are pretty reasonable.

MRS. M.:
Trifles!—As liberty to pay and receive visits to and from whom I please; to write and receive letters, without interrogatories or wry faces on your part; to wear what I please; and choose conversation with regard only to my own taste; to have no obligation upon me to converse with wits that I don't like, because they are your acquaintance; or to be intimate with fools, because they may be your relations. Come to dinner when I please; dine in my dressing-room when I'm out of humor, without giving reason. To have my closet inviolate; to be sole empress of my tea-table, which you must never presume to approach without first asking leave. And lastly, whereever I am, you shall always knock at the door before you come in. These articles subscribed, if I continue to endure you a little longer, I may by degrees dwindle into a wife.

MIRABELL:
Your bill of fare is something advanced in this latter ac-

count.—Well, have I liberty to offer conditions—that when you are dwindled into a wife, I may not be beyond measure enlarged into a husband?

MRS. M.:
You have free leave; propose your utmost, speak and spare not.

The play, however, did not win the approval of the audience. Possibly, its portrait of Restoration society was too close for the comfort of many of its members. Its failure to please caused William Congreve to withdraw from the theater. He spent his remaining years working for the government. He died in 1728 and was buried in Westminster Abbey.

The heroic play augmented the presentation of brittle comedy during the Restoration period. Its chief proponent was John Dryden, who sought to emulate the plays written by Corneille and Racine. A heroic play may be described as one containing a stalwart hero or heroine who is motivated by love and honor in overcoming the many obstacles that stand in his path. Invariably, the subject matter is derived from a historical incident and the locale is a far-away land. The dialogue is written in rimed couplets and the plot is intricate with manifold subplots. The use of spectacle to allow for songs, dances, and scenic effects gives the heroic play the aura of opera. Typical examples are Dryden's *The Conquest of Grenada, Part I* (1670) and *Almanzor and Almahide, or The Conquest of Grenada, Part II* (1670), in which the protagonist duels, murders, dances, and sings his way through three love plots and ten acts before he wins the hand of the heroine. A happy ending always awaits the hero. Other heroic plays conceived by Dryden include *The Indian Emperour, or The Conquest of Mexico by the Spaniards; Tyrannick Love, or The Royal Martyr;* and *Aureng-Zebe*. After proclaiming the appropriateness of rimed verse in composing heroic drama, Dryden grew weary of "his Mistress, Rhyme" and he turned to blank verse for the writing of *All for Love: or, The World Well Lost* (1677). The play is an attempt by Dryden to apply the principles of classicism to the story of Antony and Cleopatra. The ten days that shook the world of the great lovers in Shakespeare's play were telescoped into one day by Dryden. It was a world well lost for the cause of love. Many critics believe that it is an effective play and shares honors with Dryden's *Don Sebastian, King of Portugal,* another of his tragic dramas. Dryden also wrote a number of licentious Restoration comedies, the best of which is *Marriage à la Mode*. Frequently accused of being an opportunist who changed his religion to accommodate himself to the political leadership of his day, John Dryden was appointed Poet Laureate in 1670. He, too, lies buried in Westminster Abbey.

The Restoration playwright catered, and perhaps even pandered, to the entertainment needs of an elite and select society whose members sought to emulate the ways of a theatergoing and pleasure-loving king. The playwright did not write for a middle-class audience because its members absented themselves from the theater in the conviction that the theater spawned evil. And it did. It was the meeting place for the politically corrupt and the career opportunist, the socially ambitious and the philanderer, the courtier and the gallant, the mistress and the prostitute. It was the starting point for a night of carousing. Its audience came to see and to be seen. The playwright, a member of the society and learned in its ways, provided the audience with comic and romantic intrigue that paralleled the private lives of the viewers. The fact that actresses now played the female roles led to the development of romantic scenes that were frequently licentious and obscene. Too, the presence of women on stage whetted the amorous imagination of the male members of the audience. Despite the fact that only a thin line appeared to separate the fantasy on stage from reality, Restoration theatergoers never seemed to tire of seeing and hearing themselves through the words of the playwright. Restoration comedy began to wane at the end of the century as a more mature society evolved from the old one. Although the comedy of manners and intrigue continued to influence some writers of comedy early in the eighteenth century, its importance diminished with the development of sentimental comedy during the reign of Queen Anne. Today, Restoration comedy is a reminder of a tinseled past, a way of the world of another era.

7. The Sentimentalists

a. England

The political, economic, and social developments in England at the conclusion of the seventeenth century and during the eighteenth century set the pattern for similar developments in other European countries. For example, the Glorious Revolution in 1688 established the democratic principles that fostered the American and French Revolutions. Parliament, disturbed and angered by the autocratic behavior of King James II, offered the crown to William and Mary of Orange to assure that a Catholic would not succeed to the throne and to end, once and for all, the absolutism of kings of England. The decision by Parliament was justified by John Locke in his *Treatise on Civil Government.* In this treatise, Locke asserted that the people possessed natural rights to life, liberty, and property, that it is the people who create governments and grant authority for the purpose of protecting these rights, and that when governments fail in this purpose, the people may seek to institute change, by revolution if necessary. Locke's political theories had widespread influence. In America, Thomas Jefferson incorporated Locke's ideas into the Declaration of Independence. In France, Jean Jacques Rousseau was similarly influenced in writing *The Social Contract,* a book that contributed to the French Declaration of the Rights of Man. In Prussia, Austria, and Russia, monarchs were inclined to justify their absolutism by claiming to govern in the interests of the people. As a result, Joseph II of Austria, Frederick the Great of Prussia, and Catherine the Great of Russia were frequently referred to as "enlightened or benevolent despots."

In addition to the political revolution that was fomented in England, the Industrial Revolution also originated in that country and soon spread to other European nations. It was during the eighteenth century that the domestic system gave way to the factory system. The demand for goods from both domestic and foreign markets necessitated increased production. As a consequence, new inventions such as the flying shuttle, the spinning jenny, the water frame, the spinning mule, the power loom, and the cotton gin were created to meet the demands for manufactured goods. In turn, the steam engine was constructed to create a source of energy for the operation of machinery. Market demands and new inventions obviously required a labor force and capital for investment. Peasants, forced to relinquish their lands by the Enclosure Acts, flocked to the cities for employment in the factories. Wealthy aristocrats and successful merchants provided the capital for industrial expansion. As a result, a wealthy middle class emerged and influenced governmental policies. This pattern repeated itself as the Industrial Revolution spread to the Continent. In recognition of an audience that was now primarily composed of members of the new society, the eighteenth-century playwright fashioned plays to meet the emotional and entertainment needs of the eighteenth-century theatergoer.

Restoration comedy began to decline in popularity toward the end of the seventeenth century. With the ascension of William and Mary to the throne, and later Queen Anne, the theater became less of a toy for royalty and more of an entertainment outlet for the rising middle class. A new generation of theatergoers questioned the morality of the Restoration comedy, finding that they had little in common with the behavior of the characters depicted on stage. In 1698, the death knell was sounded when the Reverend Jeremy Collier ferociously attacked the theater in his essay, *A Short View of the Immorality and Profaneness of the English Stage.* A year later, William Congreve's *The Way of the World* failed to please the audience. The last proponent of Restoration comedy was George Farquhar, whose plays provided a transition from the brittle comedy of manners to the humorous but sentimental comedies written by later playwrights.

Sentimental comedy—comedy that extolled virtue with a smile and a tear—made its first appearance in 1696 with *Love's Last Shift; or, The Fool in Fashion* by Colley Cibber, the actor–manager whose career in the theater spanned more than half a century. The story of an errant husband who mends his ways at the conclusion of the play, *Love's Last Shift* was greatly admired by an audience that now consisted of tired businessmen, merchants, and their families. Sir John Vanbrugh, statesman, architect, and dramatist, found the play completely unrealistic and not in keeping with the nature of man. In reply, he wrote *The Relapse,* which revealed an errant husband returning to the pursuit of happiness. *The Relapse,* however, does contain a heroine who is the epitome of the virtuous wife who successfully manages to maintain her integrity and her morals in a world of licentiousness. Sentimental comedy gained popularity through the plays written by Sir Richard Steele of *The Tatler* and *The Spectator* fame. Deliberately written to purify the tone of the theater and to provide a play that extolled the virtues of the rising middle class, *The Funeral, or Grief a la Mode, The Lying Lover, or The Ladies' Friendship, The Tender Husband,* and *The Conscious Lovers* established the vogue for sentimental comedy on the English stage.

A brief respite from sentimental comedy occurred during the final quarter of the eighteenth century. In 1768, theatergoers accorded *The Good-Natured Man* by Oliver Goldsmith a mixed reception because the famed novelist, dramatist, poet, and essayist had attempted to write a comedy free of sentiment. Five years later, a warmer reception was accorded his new effort, *She Stoops to Conquer: or, The Mistakes of a Night.* A farce-comedy of incident, the play relates the humorous happenings that occur when the hero, a young man who is only successful in making love when the recipient of his affections is a servant-girl, mistakes the heroine for a barmaid. In the same year, 1773, Londoners also applauded Samuel Foote's *The Handsome Housemaid,* a burlesque of sentimental comedy. It remained, however, for the plays of Richard Brinsley Sheridan to restore the comedy of manners to the English stage. *The Duenna; St. Patrick's Day; or, The Scheming Lieutenant,* and *The Rivals* appeared in 1775 and established Sheridan as the leading playwright of the time. *The Rivals,* which introduced Mrs. Malaprop and the term "malapropism" into the English language, was followed by *The School for Scandal,* which is considered Sheridan's masterpiece. *A Trip to Scarborough,* a reworking of *The Relapse* by Sir John Vanbrugh, entertained theatergoers in 1777. *The Critic; or, A Tragedy Rehearsed,* Sheridan's last play, burlesqued and satirized contemporary sentimental drama. In 1780, Sheridan entered Parliament as a member of the Whig Party. He became one of the most brilliant orators of his time, and he was in the midst of an impassioned oration in 1809 when the Drury Lane theater, of which he was the owner and director, was destroyed by fire. In 1813, Sheridan was arrested for debts that he had incurred as a result of personal extravagances and financial reverses stemming from the loss of his theater. He died in 1816, materially and spiritually a bankrupt.

Despite the fact that the heroic tragedy continued to be written and produced during the eighteenth century, it was domestic tragedy that captured the interest of theatergoers. Although *Cato* by Joseph Addison, the essayist, playwright, poet, and statesman, aroused the patriotic emotions of both Whigs and Tories at a time when succession to the throne was in question, theatergoers generally found heroic tragedy difficult to accept because the leading characters were too far removed from their society. Moreover, heroic tragedy had been the target for satirists from the time of its introduction by John Dryden. In 1671, the Duke of Buckingham ridiculed Dryden's *Almazor and Almahide; or, The Conquest of Grenada* in a satire entitled *The Rehearsal.* In 1734, theatergoers guffawed at Henry Carey's *The Tragedy of Chrononhotonthologos: Being the Most Tragical Tragedy that ever was Tragediz'd by any Company of Tragedians.* Henry Fielding also lampooned heroic tragedy in his satirical play, *The Tragedy of Tragedies; or The Life and Death of Tom Thumb.* Parenthetically, it should be noted that Fielding's political satires, *Pasquin, A Dramatick Satire on the Times* (1736) and *Historical Register for the Year 1736* (1737) were responsible for the Licensing Act of 1737, which theoretically limited the legal number of theaters to three, but which assured play censorship at the source. In any event, eighteenth-century theatergoers clamored for heroes of the present rather than of the past. Such a hero appeared in 1731 when London audiences viewed a performance of *The London Merchant; or The History of George Barnwell* by George Lillo. With the exception of the prologue, the dialogue was written in prose rather than in verse. The plight of the apprentice who fell prey to the evils of city life moved and touched the emotions of the spectator. Lillo's moral was appropriate for the day: sin begets an ignominious end, virtue begets its own reward. The playwright's realistic portrayal of city life and his selection of a protagonist identifiable to the audience set the style for domestic tragedy. The play had widespread influence on playwrights abroad. Diderot and Lessing praised the virtues of this drama of the common man.

Unlike the Greek, Roman, Elizabethan, French, and Restoration playwrights, the eighteenth-century playwright was generally not a man of the theater per se. Rather, the eighteenth-century English playwright was a creative writer whose response to the literary movement of the times, neoclassicism, motivated him to experiment with the various forms of literary expression. For example, Joseph Addison and Sir Richard Steele are probably better known for their periodicals *The Tatler* and *The Spectator* than for their plays. Henry Fielding is more often remembered as a novelist than as a playwright. *The Vicar of Wakefield* by Oliver Goldsmith is as well known as *She Stoops to Conquer.* Too, the eighteenth-century playwright frequently led an active political life. For example, Addison, Steele, and Sheridan were at one time or another members of Parliament. Henry Fielding eventually became a Justice of the Peace and is said to have established the first detective force in England. Additionally, the eighteenth-century playwright, and this was particularly true of Addison and Steele, considered himself to be the guardian of public morals and the arbiter of that which was deemed English culture. With the exceptions of George Farquhar, Colley Cibber, and John Gay, who innovated the ballad opera, notably *The Beggar's Opera* and *Polly,* the eighteenth-century playwright was essentially a man of many literary talents. Perhaps this is why the eighteenth-century theatergoer enjoyed a potpourri of dramatic entertainments: heroic tragedies, sentimental comedies, domestic tragedies, dramatic satires, pantomimes, and ballad operas—and, for good measure, hacked-up versions of the plays of Shakespeare.

b. France

On January 21, 1793, Louis XVI, well intentioned but the least capable of the French Bourbon kings, was guillotined. Four years earlier, the Bastille had been destroyed by Paris mobs when rumors were circulated to the effect that the king had ordered soldiers to disperse the National Assembly. The members of the National Assembly had been drawn from the Estates-General, which had not met since 1614. Louis XVI had summoned the Estates-General to solve a national financial crisis that had arisen as a result of governmental policies during the reigns of Louis XIV and Louis XV, two monarchs who reigned from 1643 to 1774, a period of 131 years. When Louis XVI came to power, he continued the policies of his predecessors who had given financial support to the conduct of foreign wars, who had spent lavishly and excessively to maintain the court at Versailles, and who had steadfastly refused to tax the privileged classes. Unlike Louis XIV, whose forceful personality could quell all opposition by proclaiming *"L'état c'est moi,"* and unlike Louis XV who could shrug off all warnings of the need for reforms with the statement *"Après moi le déluge,"* Louis XVI was forced to face his predicament more realistically. Rule by divine right had reached its peak with Louis XIV and had rapidly declined after his death in 1715. One force that led to its demise and the circumstances in which Louis XVI found himself was the philosophy of the Enlightenment as expressed by Montesquieu, Rousseau, Voltaire, and Diderot. The dismissal of Turgot and Necker as Ministers of Finance did not help to strengthen the position of the King with his subjects. By 1788, France was in a state of bankruptcy. Louis XVI had no other choice but to call the Estates-General into session, thereby admitting the King alone could not solve the financial crisis confronting the country. The events which followed in rapid succession culminated in a series of interim governments that ended in 1799 with the establishment of a military dictatorship headed by Napoleon Bonaparte.

With the exceptions of *The Marriage of Figaro,* which was produced in 1784, and the highly inflammatory and emotionally charged plays written during the Revolution, the plays written during the eighteenth century conformed to the rules established by the French Academy and followed the development of sentimental comedy and domestic tragedy in England. Literary achievements, the development of play form, and the problems of the bourgeoise, not current events, motivated the playwrights to express themselves.

Heroic tragedy in the manner of Corneille and Racine continued to be written during the eighteenth century. Its chief proponent at the opening of the century was Prosper Jolyot de Crébillon whose bloody and tragic melodramas terrified the French theatergoer. Crébillon gained additional prominence when Mme. de Pompadour encouraged him to come out of retirement and compete with Voltaire. A social reformer who battled with the Church throughout his lifetime, Voltaire rewrote his first tragedy *Oedipe,* while imprisoned in the Bastille in 1717. Its successful presentation by the Comédie-Française won him fame, fortune, and the friendship of Mme. de Pompadour, who sponsored his election to the French Academy. Although Voltaire admired the works of Shakespeare, he criticized the playwright for not adhering to the rules established by the playwrights of antiquity. Denis Diderot also wrote for the theater. Deeply influenced by George Lillo's *The London Merchant; or, The History of George Barnwell,* Diderot introduced domestic tragedy, or *drame bourgeois,* in two plays, *Le Fils Naturel* and *Le Père de Famille.* Toward the end of the century, French theatergoers were introduced to the plays of Shakespeare. Unfortunately, the mangled translations and inept adaptations by Jean-François Ducis convinced French theatergoers that Voltaire was correct in referring to the great English playwright as a refined barbarian.

Although the plays of Molière continued to be revived, the writers of comedy employed their talents to develop *la comédie larmoyante et domestique* rather than the comedy of manners. The counterpart of sentimental comedy in England, *la comédie larmoyante* characterized the plays written by Pierre-Carlet de Chamberlain de Marivaux, Pierre Claude Nivelle de la Chaussée, and Philippe-Néricault Destouches. It remained for Pierre-Augustin Caron, or Beaumarchais, to recapture the comic spirit of Molière. A social reformer and a liberal who gave heavy financial support to the American Revolution, Beaumarchais wrote a number of plays, the most important of which are *The Barber of Seville,* and its sequel, *The Marriage of Figaro.* Both plays incurred the censorship of Louis XVI because Beaumarchais dared to criticize the nobility at a time when the populace was restless and discontent.

Although *The Marriage of Figaro* was accepted by the Comédie-Française for production in 1781, it was not until 1784 that Louis XVI permitted the company to mount a production. Its revolutionary sentiments made a deep impression on the public, and its bold satire of a decadent but powerful nobility resulted in public riots. In 1785, Marie Antoinette revived *The Barber of Seville* in the private theater she had persuaded Louis to build for her on the grounds of the Petit Trianon. The pretty Queen cast herself in the role of Rosine, the leading lady, and she invited Beaumarchais to the performance. Considering the reception that had been accorded *The Marriage of Figaro* only a few months earlier, and in view of the ill feeling that existed between the playwright and the King, it is not clear why the Queen invited the rebellious playwright to view her production of his play, or why she chose to produce the play at that particular time.

The professional French theater owed its existence and its popularity to the interest of a Court that extravagantly maintained its own theater. Culture-oriented ministers of state had rescued the French theater from obscurity and poverty early in the seventeenth century, and a king who was sympathetic to theater activity had protected the professional French theater from damnation by the Church. Louis XIV made the French theater a national institution when he organized the Comédie-Française after the death of Molière. The Court granted theater managers licenses and monopolies that limited the number of theaters to a favored few. Playwrights were rewarded with pensions, high government posts, and election to the French Academy. Actors were accorded honors by the government. Court subsidies helped theater companies through periods of financial crisis and made possible a living wage and a retirement plan for the actor. The public accepted the theater as an integral part of French society because the Court recognized and supported the professional French theater.

This paternalism extended by the Court naturally exacted "payment" from the professional. Theater managers thought not only in terms of the box office when new plays came up for consideration, but also in terms of the pleasure of the King, lest the play give offense and the monopoly be withdrawn. Actors were professionally frustrated by the bureaucracy that dictated their status in the company and that attended the assignment of roles. Actresses thought twice about their professional ambitions before refusing to grant their favors to members of the nobility. Nobles abused the privilege of purchasing tickets to sit on stage by interfering with the performance of the actor. Playwrights accepted the literary restrictions imposed by the French Academy and seldom questioned the censorship decreed by the King. Only Molière in the seventeenth century and Beaumarchais in the eighteenth dared to take issue with the censorship of the King; only Voltaire dared to remove the rude spectators from the stage. In the long run, however, the rewards probably balanced the limitations, because the eighteenth-century professional French theater flourished under, and in spite of, the control exercised by the Court.

In truth, the situation was not much different from the situation of the professional theater in England. There, the professional theater also looked to the Court for favors, protection, and patronage. Additionally, the French and the English playwrights responded similarly to the literary movement of the time: heroic tragedies that adhered to the principles of neoclassicism; sentimental comedies and domestic tragedies that catered to the entertainment needs and tastes of the rising middle class in both countries. However, unlike the fate that befell the professional English theater when the Puritans came to power in the middle of the seventeenth century, the eighteenth-century French theater survived the chaotic years of the French Revolution. Existing theaters remained open and many more appeared when the revolutionists removed the abuse of granting monopolies and privileges to a favored few. The actor became a compatriot of the revolutionist and was hailed as a hero if he gave a moving performance in a play that expressed the sentiments of the Revolution. Talma, the great French tragedian, gained early fame because of his exciting performance in *Charles IX,* a drama with revolutionary sentiments written by Marie Joseph de Chénier. Schooled in the works of Voltaire, Rousseau, and Montesquieu, caught up in the ideas and passions of the times, inspired by the success of the American Revolution, a new generation of French playwrights utilized their talents to serve the cause of the Revolution and, in so doing, turned propagandists. The French theater, once the toy and the joy of royalty, now became the forum for the voices that cried, "Liberty, Equality, Fraternity!"

c. Germany

In 1727, Carolina Neuber, actress and manager, and Johann Christoph Gottsched, professor and critic, formed an alliance to raise the standards of the professional theater in Germany and to improve the quality of German literature performed on the stage. At the age of fourteen, Carolina Neuber ran off with a childhood sweetheart. Apprehended by the police who returned her to her home, Carolina suffered another five years before she again sought to escape the harsh discipline of her tyrannical father. This time, she ran off with two young men, one of whom, Johann Neuber, she married. The trio found employment as actors with Johann Spiegelberg, an actor–manager of a touring company that could trace its beginnings to Johannes Velten, a seventeenth-century German actor. In 1727, Carolina and Johann Neuber assumed the management of the Karl Ludwig Hoffmann company of actors. The Neubers were given permission to call their company The Royal Polish and Electoral Saxon Court Comedians. Under her management, the actors were required to memorize their lines, adhere to carefully planned stage business, and to attend rehearsals. The Royal Polish and Electoral Saxon Court Comedians traveled the German countryside, attempting to improve public taste for dramatic fare by performing comedies and tragedies translated from the French by Johann Cristoph Gottsched and, when attendance was low, reviving the coarse and vulgar farces that featured Hans Wurst or Pickle-Herring, two stereotype comic figures that represented the German counterpart of the buffoon found in the *commeda dell'arte*. Gottsched, a University of Leipzig professor who attempted to mold German dramatic literature along the lines of French neoclassicism, broke with Carolina Neuber when he began to criticize his collaborator in favor of Johann Schoenemann, a former member of Carolina Neuber's company, who had now formed an acting company of his own. The actress and the professor carried on a vendetta that lasted throughout their lifetime. During this period, German theatergoers had come to enjoy the change in dramatic fare to which they were exposed and to appreciate the high quality of acting evidenced in the performances of Sophia Schröder, Konrad Ackermann, Friedrich Schröder, and Konrad Ekhof, "The Garrick of Germany."

On April 21, 1767, the Hamburg National Theater gave its initial performance. Organized by twelve businessmen at a time when Germany was not a unified country, the Hamburg National Theater was the new name for a company of actors headed by Konrad Ackermann. Its repertory consisted of plays by Molière, Voltaire, Marivaux, Destouches, Corneille, La Chaussée, and the German playwrights Lessing, Schlegel, and Weisse. Although the venture lasted only two years, it did bring into prominence the talent of Gotthold Ephraim Lessing. Lessing was educated for the ministry at the University of Leipzig. An interest in literary criticism, however, led him to a career in the theater. A production of a first play, *The Young Scholars* (1748), by Carolina Neuber, undoubtedly encouraged him to pursue his literary ambitions. It is also probable that his employment by Voltaire as a translator whetted his interest, although his association with the French philosopher ended in a quarrel and his dismissal. In 1755, Lessing wrote his first tragedy, *Miss Sara Sampson,* along the lines of George Lillo's *The London Merchant.* The success of *Miss Sara Sampson* influenced other German playwrights to abandon French neoclassicism in favor of plays that were more realistic and appealing to middle-class theatergoers. A third play, *Minna von Barnhelm,* a comedy played against the background of the Seven Years' War, appeared in 1767 and remains a classic standby in German repertory today. *Emilia Galotti* (1772) portrays the cruel and insolent practices of the German nobility, although the scene is set in Italy. *Nathan the Wise* (1779), Lessing's last play, is a plea for religious tolerance and brotherly love. When the Hamburg National Theater was in the process of being organized, Lessing was offered the post of stage poet, or playwright for the company. He refused because he did not believe that he could supply the company with the many plays it required to make up a season's program. However, he did accept the position of being its critic. The result was the *Hamburg Dramaturgy* (1767–69), a series of critical essays that, with *Letters Con-*

cerning the Newest Literature (1759–1765), have caused many to consider Lessing, as a critic, on a par with Aristotle. His belief that all art is but a reflection of nature and not the product of rules paved the way for the drama written by Schiller and Goethe.

"Sturm und Drang," the literary movement that received its title from a play by Friedrich Maximilian von Klinger, represents the revolt against the influence of French neoclassicism upon German literature. Influenced by the romanticism and emotionalism of Rousseau, German playwrights of the period sought to emphasize the freedom of the individual in political and social life. Generally, the protagonist is one who is in rebellion or trapped by the society in which he lives. For example, *The Tutor*, by Jacob Michael Reinhold Lenz, has as its protagonist an educated young man who rebels against the ill-treatment accorded him by the German nobility. The "Sturm und Drang" literary movement catapulted Goethe and Schiller upon the scene. Johann Wolfgang von Goethe made his playwriting debut in 1773 with the romantic tragedy entitled *Goetz von Berlichingen.* A good example of the "Sturm und Drang" play that dispensed with rules and that revealed the influence of Shakespearean structure, the play related the attempt of a German baron to remain free from the political and religious intrigue of his time. In its original version, the play contained fifty-four scenes with almost as many characters, not to mention the number of supernumeries who appeared on the stage in the crowd scenes. It was initially written in 1771 and revised for production in 1773, with great success. German theatergoers, moved by the temper of the times, cheered the hero's dying words: "Freedom, freedom!" Three other plays, *Egmont, Iphigenia in Tauris,* and *Torquato Tasso,* were premiered approximately fifteen years later. Each of the plays represents a refinement of the playwriting techniques Goethe employed in writing *Goetz von Berlichingen.* The play on which Goethe's reputation as one of the world's great playwrights rests is *Faust.* Goethe began writing the play in 1775. The first part was completed in 1808 and the second part was not released for publication until 1831, a year before his death. Although he was a director of the Court Theater in Weimar for twenty-six years, Goethe was not a man of the theater in the sense that Sophocles, Shakespeare, and Molière were. Too often, his plays are literature to be read rather than literature to be performed.

Johann Christoph Friedrich von Schiller was the third member of the trio of great German playwrights who contributed to the development of the German theater during the eighteenth century. The son of an army captain who agreed to the arbitrary decision of the Duke of Wurttemberg that young Schiller be given a military education, Schiller began his brief military career as an army surgeon when he was graduated from the Duke's academy, Karlsschule, in 1870. Two years earlier, the playwright had begun writing *The Robbers,* a typical "Sturm und Drang" play that focused attention upon a hero who joins a gang of robbers whose ethics are superior to those of the society in which he lives. The play was performed at the theater in Mannheim in 1782. Because of its anti-social viewpoint, the play created an uproar that caused Schiller to leave his military post in Stuttgart when the Duke ordered that he put an end to his playwriting. From 1783 to 1784, Schiller was resident playwright for the Mannheim Theater where he gained additional fame with two plays, *Fiesco* and *Intrigue and Love,* which continued to express his views of German military and social life. *Don Carlos, Prince of Spain,* the first of Schiller's five historical dramas, was written in 1787. The play is generally considered to be transitional in the career of the playwright, because Schiller takes a more mature and tolerant view of German society and the role of the individual within it. Although Schiller continued to romanticize and idealize his protagonists out of proportion to their actual character in real life, he began to endow his heroines and heroes in subsequent plays with a sense of moral obligation to adjust their personal needs to those of the society in which they lived and with a sense of moral responsibility for their deeds. Implied, of course, was the reciprocal need of the society to recognize and respect the rights of the individual. Toward the end of the eighties, Schiller accepted a professorship in history that had been obtained for him at the University of Jena by his friend, Goethe. In 1796, Schiller quit his post at the University to join Goethe at Weimar. In the interim, the playwright had completed two histories, *The Revolt of the Netherlands* and *The History of the Thirty Years' War.* Now aware that his severe tuberculosis threatened his life,

Schiller worked without rest to complete his projected works. It is often related that the playwright worked through the night, keeping himself awake by immersing his feet in a basin of cold water. In 1799, he completed *Wallenstein,* a trilogy based upon the career of the famous German general. In the ensuing five years, Schiller penned *Maria Stuart* (1800), *The Maid of Orleans* (1801), *The Bride of Messina* (1803), and *William Tell* (1804). He was in the midst of writing *Demetrius,* a play with a Russian historical background, when he died in May 1805.

A good example of Schiller's rearrangement of historical fact for dramatic effect occurs in *Maria Stuart,* Act III, when the Queen of Scotland pleads with Elizabeth to spare her life. History records no such meeting between the two Queens. Act III also contains a good example of the romantic spirit that permeates Schiller's plays. Mary's lyrical outburst in Scene 1 is typical of the romantic's view of nature and freedom:

Scene 1. (Mary, running, comes from behind a group of trees. Hannah follows her slowly.)

HANNAH:
You're running as if wings assisted you,
I cannot follow you so fast. Please wait.

MARY:
Let me delight in my precious new freedom,
Let me again be a child and rejoice
Testing the hurrying, light-footed step
On the green meadows' resilient carpet.
Have I escaped the gloom of my prison?
Am I released from my sorrowful tomb?
Let me then drink in long, thirsty draughts
Freedom's heady, heavenly air.

HANNAH:
Oh my dear Lady, your old prison
Has only been enlarged, its walls are still
Around us, even though the trees and shrubs
May for the moment shield them from our view.

MARY:

Oh, thank you, thank you, friendly trees,
Your kind green arms blot out my prison walls.
I want to dream that I am free and happy,
Why, Hannah, wake me from my sweet illusion?
I am surrounded by the vast, blue sky,
Free and unfettered my eye sweeps
Across the limitless expanse.
There where you see the clouds' grey mountains rise,
There is the boundary of my domain, my glance
Accompanies the clouds where southward lies
The goal they search beyond the ocean, France!
Hurrying clouds, ships of the sky!
That I could sail with you, that I could fly!
Take my love to the land of my youth.
I am a prisoner, I am in chains,
You be the messengers of my pains.
Freely you course in the infinite air,
No one your master, no queen your despair.

HANNAH:

Oh dearest Lady, you're beside yourself,
The air of freedom, missed so long, makes you extravagant.

MARY:

There is a fisherman tying his boat!
Frail as it is, it could be a tool,
To take me to lands under more friendly rule.
Scarce is the food that he catches afloat.
I would load up his boat with the richest of treasure,
Such fish he hauled never, try as he may,
In his nets he would find good luck without measure,
If his rescuing bark would take me away.

HANNAH:

A forlorn hope! Do you not see the spies
Who in the distance follow us?
A dismal cruel order chases
All sympathetic creatures from our path.

MARY:

No, Hannah. No, believe me, not in vain

Have they thrown open now my prison doors.
This little favor must announce
Still greater happiness. I can't be wrong
I see a loving hand at work,
The Earl of Leicester's mighty arm.
Yes, bit by bit they will expand the walls,
Preparing me with small for greater things
Until at last I stand before the man
Who will release me from my chains forever.

HANNAH:
I see no rhyme or reason in all this:
It was but yesterday that they announced
That you must die, and now, today, this privilege.
I've also heard it said that those
May benefit from slight concessions
Whom their eternal liberty awaits.

MARY:
Listen! The hunting horn! Did you hear
Its mighty call across meadow and forest?
Oh, how I wish I could mount my brave steed
To be part of the chase!
Again it sounds! How well I know its voice,
Full of memories, painful and sweet!
Often it filled my ear with delight
On the hilly heath of the highlands,
*When the boisterous hunters approached.**

Several factors contributed to the rapid development of the German professional theater during the eighteenth century. Except for the Seven Years' War (1756–1763), which erupted as the result of the seizure of Silesia from Austria by Frederick the Great, the political situation in Germany was relatively quiet and uneventful. For centuries, Germany had been the battleground for great religious wars that had left the country devastated. Now, however, while England sought to subdue the colonists in America, and while France was involved with internal problems, Frederick

* From *Maria Stuart* by Friedrich Schiller. *Classical German Drama,* translated by Theodore H. Lustig. Copyright © 1963 by Bantam Books, Inc.

the Great, who ruled for forty-six years, had an opportunity to organize and develop Germany as a nation. The moment was historically opportune for the development of a professional theater because the rise of the theater is generally a corollary of the rise and growth of a nation. In Germany, political stabilization was accompanied by the emergence and growth of large cities, many of which became cultural centers that supported professional theaters. Additionally, German nobility began to evince an interest in theatergoing. For example, the Elector Charles Theodore sponsored the theater in Mannheim and the Elector Charles Augustus not only supported the theater at Weimar, but developed that city as a center of German culture. Moreover, the rapid development of professional theater in Germany was the result of the simultaneous appearance of excellent actors and great playwrights whose combined talents vitalized the German drama of the time. The theatrical situtaion was similar to that which had made the Elizabethan theater and the seventeenth-century French theater exceptional in the annals of theatrical history. Despite the fact that the German professional theater did not begin until centuries after the professional theater had established itself in England, France, and Spain, the German theater was equal to, and perhaps in advance of, the professional theater in these countries at the conclusion of the eighteenth century.

8. The Revolutionaries

The nineteenth-century playwright in England, France, Norway, Germany, Russia, and the United States wrote against a background of wars, revolutions, political changes, social reforms, and developments in industry, science, and culture. In the early decades of the nineteenth century, a limited monarchy reigned and "ruled" through the Parliament in England; a republic in the United States sought to assert its freedom on the seas and its independence from foreign entanglements abroad; and a military dictatorship existed in France. The Age of Metternich, which followed the downfall of Napoleon, ended in the Revolution of 1848. At mid-century, the slavery issue in the United States portended civil strife as westward expansion brought new states into the

Union. The bombardment of Fort Sumter on April 11, 1861, signaled the beginning of the War Between the States; the four years of bloodshed culminated in the assassination of President Lincoln. Abroad, the unification of Italy proceeded under the leadership of Mazzini, Garibaldi, Cavour, and Victor Emanuel, who was crowned King of Italy in 1861. In Germany, Bismarck eliminated Austrian influence in 1866, and in 1867, he established the North German Confederation. In France, the Second French Empire began to crumble when Napoleon III, who had recently been defeated in his plans to control Mexico, attempted to oppose the unification of Germany. The Franco-Prussian War (1870–1871) led to the establishment of the Third French Republic with a president chosen by the legislature, and to the establishment of the German Empire, with William I as Emperor. Meanwhile, England, "the workshop of the world," had begun its acquisition of colonies around the world, and, in the Far East, Japan had begun to Westernize its government, its army, and its industry. As the century neared its close, the United States emerged as an imperialist power as a result of her victory in the Spanish-American War. In Russia, the rumblings of war and revolution could be heard. Many plays written during the century mirrored these ongoing world events.

Concurrently with the rise and development of great world powers, the second phase of the Industrial Revolution promoted changes that affected everyday living. The factory replaced the home as the center of production. Its location in populated areas contributed to the growth of the cities. The need for money to finance the costs of machinery, the importation of raw materials, the manufacture of goods, and the payment of wages led to the investment of private capital and the development of a capitalistic society. The periods of unemployment that were consequences of seasonal changes and unforeseen economic depressions and the abuses inherent in unfair hiring practices and miserable working conditions paved the way for the formation of labor unions and the enactment of legislation to protect the worker. In England, for example, the Factory Act of 1819 and the Factory Act of 1833 restricted the hiring age of children and the length of the working day of other minors. In 1824, Parliament permitted the formation of unions; and in 1867, city workers were granted the right to vote. Between 1883 and 1889, Germany enacted legislation dealing with social security, sickness, accident, and old-age insurance. During this period, Karl Marx and Friedrich Engels had written the *Communist Manifesto.* Later, Marx wrote *Das Kapital,* a critical study of the capitalist system and an enunciation of his socialist theories.

As markets increased and profits accumulated, there emerged an upper class that utilized its wealth to influence government legislation and seized upon every opportunity to solidify and increase its holdings. It was a materialistic society that created the illusion that anyone could succeed by dint of hard work. This upper strata enjoyed all the home conveniences and inventions of the time long before mass production made such appliances available to the public. This social class entertained lavishly, traveled luxuriously, dressed in high fashion, and hobnobbed with royalty. Their public image belied their private lives. Their peccadillos became sensational scandals when revealed in public. As working conditions improved and as wages increased, there also emerged a class-conscious society that sought to emulate the respectability and gentility of the leaders of upper-class society.

a. The Romantics

Generally, all segments of nineteenth-century society supported the theater because the playwrights offered heroes and heroines with whom, and themes with which, the audience could identify and empathize. In his treatment of theme, plot, setting, character, and speech, however, the nineteenth-century playwright was influenced by the literary trend of his day. During the early half of the nineteenth century, romanticism colored the works of poets, novelists, and playwrights. The antithesis of neoclassicism, romanticism permitted the playwright to express his disdain for literary rules, to reveal his opposition to authority, to reaffirm his belief in the individual, to sing the wonders of nature and beauty, to set the locale in far-away places and in another time, and, finally, to idealize and glorify the character of his hero or heroine. In England, the romantic poets, Samuel Taylor Coleridge, Lord Byron, Percy Bysshe Shelley, John Keats, and Sir Walter Scott, attempted to write romantic drama with little or no popular success, although a later dramatization of Sir Walter Scott's novel *Guy Mannering* did provide Charlotte Cushman, the great American actress, with one of her best roles. Perhaps the reason why romanticism failed to hold the attention and interest of the English theatergoer was that romanticism lacked novelty for the English audience. Despite their success in writing romantic poetry and romantic novels, the romantic poets could not surpass the romanticism of the Elizabethan playwright. Additionally, the political climate in England was sufficiently democratized to negate the connotation that romanticism had on the Continent.

In France, a Bourbon king ruled as a result of decisions reached at the Congress of Vienna. Although Louis XVIII had followed a middle-of-the-road policy, Charles X, his successor, attempted to restore the conditions that had existed under the old regime. Frenchmen did not enjoy the degree of democracy enjoyed by Englishmen. In February 1830, the Comédie-Française produced *Hérnani* by Victor Hugo. The premiere performance was a sensational success. There were riots in the audience and pitched battles in the streets. The play was sheer romanticism in every sense of the word. The playwright had completely broken with the rules and rigidity of neoclassicism and this shattered the sensitivity of the members of the French Academy. The public applauded wildly and considered Hugo a national hero. In July 1830, the middle class revolted and succeeded in overthrowing Charles X. The spirit of romanticism and the spirit of democracy seemed to be one and the same. Other important French romantic dramatists were Alexandre Dumas *père,* Alfred de Vigny, and Alfred de Musset.

b. The Realists

By mid-century, romantic drama had had its day of popularity at the box office. A new generation of theatergoers and a new generation of playwrights evinced little interest in supporting or retaining a genre that turned its back on the problems of the day: nationalism, social reform, industrialization, unions, mechanization, and public education. What had once been considered the virtues of romantic drama now became its vices. The glorified heroes in romantic drama seemed too far removed from the true nature of man. The idealized situations provided artificial solutions and bore no resemblance to the everyday problems that confronted man. The romantic dialogue did not speak the language of the people. What the theatergoers wanted was what theatergoers throughout the centuries have always wanted—heroes with whom they could identify, situations that they could recognize, and insights that provided them with an understanding of their problems. The playwrights, aware of the limitations of romantic drama, influenced by the new literary trend of the day, realism, and stimulated by *The Origin of the Species* by Charles Darwin, gave the audience what it longed for—plays that were a reasonable facsimile of life.

Although it is generally agreed that both Émile Augier and Alexandre Dumas *fils* pioneered the writing of realistic drama in France, the latter is credited with writing the first truly realistic play seen on the French stage, a dramatization of his popular novel, *La Dame aux Camélias.* The story of a noble and honorable "fille de joie," Marguerite Gautier, who sacrifices her life and her love to shield her lover's family from public scandal, *La Dame aux Camélias* shocked theatergoers because the playwright implied a criticism of French society: the courtesan-heroine was shown to have a greater sense of ethics than the society that had both fashioned and condemned her. A vehicle for a number of actresses and a popular attraction at the box office, the play seems overly sentimental today, although its operatic version, *La Traviata* by Giuseppe Verdi, is a popular draw at the opera, and its motion-picture version with Greta Garbo is considered a cinematic classic. In 1855, three years after *La Dame aux Camélias,* Dumas wrote *Le Demi-Monde,* a bitter and realistic account of the life led by those women who existed on the fringe and in the twilight of French high society. Three years later, theatergoers observed *Le Fils Naturel,* a play that dealt with the problem of illegitimacy. Dumas's didactic and moralistic demand for a change of attitude toward the illegitimate child established a new play genre, "pièce à thèse," or "thesis play," one that uses the theater as the forum for discussion of an idea through dramatization. Two other French playwrights of the period, Eugène Scribe and Victorien Sardou, contributed to the popularity of the realistic play by writing contemporary "well-made" plays. The close-knit play structure developed by Scribe enhanced the reality of what was happening on stage. In the hands of Sardou, the "well-made" play became such a pat formula that George Bernard Shaw was once moved to describe this kind of play as "Sardoodledum."

The success of realistic drama on the French stage influenced the creative efforts of playwrights in other countries. In the United States, Dion Boucicault, the Irish playwright whose career embraced both the English and the American theaters, combined realism and melodrama in writing plays about the American scene. In 1857, *The Streets of New York,* or, as it is sometimes called, *The Poor of New York,* established Boucicault as a popular playwright with American audiences. His ability to fashion a play from a current event that lent itself to sensational treatment satisfied the need of the audience for realism and thrills. For example, *The Streets of New York* utilized the Panic of 1857 as its dramatic framework for action and a tenement fire on stage for thrilling effect. *The Octoroon, or Life in Louisiana* aroused the nation to an even higher pitch at a time when slavery was an inflammatory subject. A realistic slave sale, a lynch trial, and a spectacular steamboat explosion punctured the romance between Zoe and George and excited the audience because of the realistic staging of each of the episodes. A touching scene that pertained to slavery occurs when George proposes to Zoe:

GEORGE:
Zoe, what have I said to wound you?

ZOE:
Nothing; but you must learn what I thought you already knew. George, you cannot marry me; the laws forbid it!

GEORGE:
Forbid it?

ZOE:
There is a gulf between us, as wide as your love, as deep as my despair; but, O, tell me, say you will pity me! that you will not throw me from you like a poisoned thing!

GEORGE:
Zoe, explain yourself—your language fills me with shapeless fears.

ZOE:
And what shall I say? I—my mother was—no, no—not her! Why should I refer the blame to her? George, do you see that hand you hold? Look at these fingers; do you see the nails are of a bluish tinge?

GEORGE:
Yes, near the quick there is a faint blue mark.

ZOE:
Look in my eyes; is not the same color in the white?

GEORGE:
It is their beauty.

ZOE:
Could you see the roots of my hair you would see the same dark, fatal mark. Do you know what that is?

GEORGE:
No.

ZOE:
That is the ineffaceable curse of Cain. Of the blood that feeds my heart, one drop in eight is black—bright red as the rest may be, that one drop poisons all the flood; those seven bright drops give me love like yours—life hung with passions like dew-drops on the morning flowers; but the one black drop gives me despair, for I'm an unclean thing—forbidden by the laws—I'm an Octoroon!

GEORGE:
Zoe, I love you none the less; this knowledge brings no revolt to my heart, and I can overcome the obstacle.

ZOE:
But I cannot.*

Northern audiences acclaimed the play as a great anti-slavery vehicle. Southern audiences accepted the play as a romantic study

---

* From Dion Boucicault, *The Octoroon* (New York: Appleton-Century-Crofts, 1953), p. 383. Copyright © 1953 by Appleton-Century-Crofts, Educational Division, Meredith Corporation. Reprinted by permission of the publisher.

of slavery in the south. Today, Dion Boucicault is recognized as a playwright whose contribution to the development of the American theater exceeded his stature and skill as a playwright. His use of a current event, realistic staging, and sensational incident influenced the growth of realism in the American theater. His plays paved the way for audience acceptance of the spectacle and realism of the motion picture. Several decades later, during the Golden Age of the American theater, Steele MacKaye, James A. Herne, Bronson Howard, William Gillette, Augustus Thomas, and David Belasco continued the development of realism.

In England, Thomas W. Robertson wrote several realistic comedies with laconic titles: *Society, Hours, Caste, Play, School,* and *M.P.* Each was a faithful representation of life, realistic in setting and performance. At the conclusion of the century, Sir Arthur Wing Pinero, influenced by the works of Henrik Ibsen, dominated the English stage with such plays as *The Second Mrs. Tanqueray, The Notorious Mrs. Ebbsmith, The Benefit of the Doubt,* and *The Profligate.* Each play realistically portrayed an aspect of English society and each play followed the play structure innovated by Scribe, perfected by Sardou, and refined by Ibsen. In a lighter vein, Oscar Wilde offered *The Importance of Being Earnest.* It remained, however, for George Bernard Shaw to literally shake the English theater free from its Victorian doldrums. In the interim, in Norway, Henrik Ibsen had set the standard for writing meaningful realistic dramas. In Sweden, Johan August Strindberg wrote a number of dramas that later had a direct influence upon many playwrights of the twentieth century. In Russia, Anton Pavlovitch Chekhov recorded the passing social and political scene. On the eve of the twentieth century, realism, and its close relative, naturalism, dominated the theater around the world.

c. The Naturalists

In contrast to the neoclassical playwright who attempted to write plays in the manner of the playwrights of antiquity and in keeping with the rigid rules of playwriting established by the French Academy, the romantic playwrights wrote plays that emphasized and idealized the human spirit and that were not constructed according to any rules. In contrast to the romantic playwrights, the realistic playwrights wrote plays that focused attention upon everyday people and everyday situations to show life as it is and, in some instances, to instigate the need for social change. For example, the double standard applied in judging the morality of women is the essence of the matter in such plays as *A Doll's House, Margaret Fleming, The Second Mrs. Tanqueray, Mrs. Warren's Profession,* and *Lady Windermere's Fan.* In contrast to the realistic playwrights, the naturalistic playwrights penetrated the surface realism dramatized by such playwrights as Alexandre Dumas *fils,* Dion Boucicault, Sir Arthur Wing Pinero, and Bronson Howard. Using their pens as scalpels, the writers of naturalistic plays revealed life in the raw. Rather than utilize the structure of the well-made play, the playwrights borrowed the procedure of the scientist: a recorded objective observation of man reacting to the stimuli about him. Events happened as a natural occurrence rather than as a prearranged course of action determined by the playwright. Consequently, a "slice of life" unfolded before the spectator as though some moment had been removed from life and placed on stage. No degree of sordidness or detail was omitted. Motivated by Darwin's *Origin of the Species,* and influenced by the realism of Ibsen, the naturalists created a drama that generally fascinated yet frequently depressed and repulsed the theatergoer because of the ugliness of the life depicted on stage.

In France, the naturalists were encouraged and inspired by Émile Zola, who believed that the continued existence of the theater depended upon an objective view of life. In 1887, André Antoine provided the writers of naturalism with a showcase when he opened the Théâtre Libre. The success of Antoine's venture spurred Otto Brahm to organize the Freie Bühne (free stage) in Germany. Gerhart Hauptmann, the outstanding German writer of naturalistic plays, began his career as playwright for the Freie Bühne. In Russia, Constantin Stanislavski and Vladimir Ivanovitch Nemirovitch-Danchenko organized the Moscow Art Theater. Their restaging of *The Sea Gull* by Anton Chekhov brought the playwright and the company world acclaim. Their production of *The Lower Depths* by Maxim Gorki epitomized naturalism on stage. David Belasco advanced the naturalistic movement in the United States. Belasco's description of the interior of the "Polka" saloon in *The*

Girl of the Golden West offers an excellent example of naturalism on the stage shortly after the turn of the century:

> *Scene: A large, square board-walled apartment—the natural color of pine wood after the first freshness has worn off—many knotholes in the boards. These pine boards to be the real thing, and all doors, windows, properties and accessories exactly such as would have been used in a Western saloon at this period. The ceiling or roof must appear real. Facing audience up L.C. is the bar, which must be characteristic. This bar is gaudy—has fancy glasses, as they took very long drinks. Many colored liquors were in bottles for "show." A pair of scales to weigh out gold dust stands at one end of the bar. Behind bar, water, a pail to wash glasses in, little towels, etc., in fact, the full paraphernalia of a bar of the day. Over the bar may be the sign of gilt lettering: "A REAL HOME FOR THE BOYS!" Some bottles of brandy, whiskey, cigar boxes are on bar. The till is directly under the front bar and contains silver one-bit and two-bit pieces. Mexican silver dollars and money up to a plug of gold ($50.00). Dice box stands on bar to shake for drinks.*
>
> *There are several cigar boxes containing special cigars on a small shelf under the back bar. Rance requires a characteristic cigar, quite large. The Girl has a special box which she keeps in reserve for special occasions. These are "the dollar Havanas." There are chewing tobacco boxes, plug tobacco boxes, cigar boxes, all containing the practical materials. In front of bar and to the L. corner is a small whiskey keg, made in such a way that the top can be withdrawn without having any outward appearance that it is other than an ordinary whiskey keg. This is where the Girl and the Boys place their wealth for safe keeping. Gold dust, coins, in fact everything of value. On the front bar there is an old cigar box small enough to be placed in the above-mentioned keg. It contains stamps and a few small coins. On the back bar all the necessary articles for mixing their so-called fancy drinks—a shaker, a mixing glass, in fact everything which should go on a bar of this period and locality.*
>
> *There is a little sprinkling of sawdust on floor in front of bar—also a little wooden box with sawdust on it.*
>
> *L. is a small, square opening into large dance hall. Drawn aside are bear pelts which hang over this opening to L., and can be pulled together. Above this, opening to L., is a balcony, with a railing on each side, as though to command alike a view of the*

dance hall and of the gambling room. It is reached by a small ladder and is unoccupied. The red calico curtains with which it is decorated are drawn. There is a garland of cedar and bittersweet over it and a fawn skin with a stuffed head straddling the on-stage railing. Somewhere near bar is a stuffed grizzly bear wearing a little green parasol in its paw and an old silk hat.

At back C. is the exterior entrance. Door has a latch and bar to barricade it. When the door opens it shows a reflection of the same lamp we saw in the exterior.

There is a wooden box tacked onto door, marked "Letter-Box." The fireplace is down R., a regular old-timer, genuine, the sheet-iron all dented in, a huge whole pine back log in it, well smoked, and a little blaze of wood in the fore-ground, piled up against back log.

Down R. are elk antlers fastened on wall, on which are hung a curious collection of hats and caps which belong to the characters assembled at the "Polka." On the floor, under antlers, are three saddles of various primitive patterns, and three little wads of folded blankets to go under them, red, grey, and blue, washed out by wind and rain. Two bags of some sort of provisions stand to R. near saddles—bridles, robes, etc., all these thrown carelessly in the corner.

The chairs are of common pine, unpainted. Down R. a faro table, containing all the paraphernalia—chips, card case, tabulating cards, ashtrays, small scale for weighing gold dust, etc. Five chairs are placed around it, a reclining chair at upper end.

L. a poker table, three chairs and a deck of cards. Kerosene lamps of the most primitive order are fastened to brackets on the walls. Gaudy window curtains of gay calico are drawn back from windows so that not a hint of them is seen from the outside. No rugs or carpets. L. is a large scale.

Tacked onto the back wall is a "Reward" notice, printed as though issued from Wells-Fargo headquarters. It reads: "$5,000 REWARD FOR THE ROAD AGENT RAMERREZ OR INFORMATION LEADING TO HIS CAPTURE. (Signed) WELLS-FARGO." The rest is in smaller type, which cannot be read from the front.

There is a small platform for a musicians' stand in the R.U. corner, with a railing and a sheetiron shield attached in such a way that it can be sprung up by working a trick on the floor, shielding the player from any danger of being shot during a quarrel. An old box is used for a seat.

Over this platform, where the CONCERTINA PLAYER sits

with his leg sprawled out, is a flashy lithograph of the period—a woman full length, in short skirts and Spanish costume—under which is advertised "Espaniola cigarros."

R. of the C. door is an old whittled-up desk made from a large packing-box. A smaller box is used for a seat. This is where the boys write their letters, getting their paper, quill pen and ink from bar.

*A wildcat skin is nailed on the R. flat, directly over the mantel. Below this and up stage is a wooden peg on which hangs a lariat. A playing-card—the Queen of Spades—is discovered, on the floor near the faro table. An old weather-beaten reclining chair is down in the L. corner, directly under the ladder leading to the balcony. Cans of provisions and casks are standing up in the L. corner, near bar. Strings of red peppers and onions are hanging from the ceiling. The whole effect is Western and of the period of '49.**

Interest in naturalism began to wane when the practitioners of realism absorbed and modified its principles and when a new wave of playwrights, designers, and producers, weary of both naturalism and realism, advanced the principles of symbolism and expressionism.

9. The Big Four

Although such plays as *The Inspector General* by Nikolai Gogol, *Fashion* by Anna Cora Mowatt, *Charley's Aunt* by Brandon Thomas, *The Importance of Being Earnest* by Oscar Wilde, *Cyrano de Bergerac* by Edmond Rostand, and the satirical operettas of Gilbert and Sullivan continue to be revived with a degree of regularity today, only a few of the thousands of plays written during the nineteenth century hold an interest for the twentieth-century theatergoer. Of the hundreds of playwrights who wrote during the nineteenth century, only the following can still truly speak to a twentieth-century audience:

---

* From David Belasco, *The Girl of the Golden West* (New York: Samuel French, 1915), pp. 15–18. Copyright, 1915, by David Belasco. Copyright, 1933, by David Belasco Literary Trust, Benjamin F. Roeder, Trustee. Copyright, 1942 (in renewal), by Reina Belasco Gest. Reprinted by permission of the publisher.

a. Henrik Ibsen

Henrik Ibsen was born on March 20, 1828, in Skein, Norway. His father, Knud Ibsen, was a well-to-do businessman who was highly respected in the community. Speculation in various schemes, however, depleted his fortune in 1836, and the family had to move to a nearby farm, Venstop, which is operated today as a museum dedicated to the memory of the playwright. In 1843, Ibsen, then fifteen years old, set out to earn his living. He traveled to Grimstad where he became an apprentice to an apothecary. Seven years later, he left Grimstad for Christiania, now Oslo, to attend the university where he planned to major in medicine. As a result of reading Cicero's orations in preparation for the matriculation examination, Ibsen was moved to write his first romantic tragedy, *Catiline.* The play came to the attention of the public when it was published by friends and admirers of the budding playwright. A second play, *The Warrior's Tomb,* followed and was staged with some success. In 1851, Ole Bull, the violinist, invited Ibsen to join the Bergen Theater as stage manager and poet. Here Ibsen remained for six years, learning his craft and seeing his plays staged. During that time, he wrote several romantic historical dramas based upon Norwegian folklore and legend. In 1857, Ibsen was granted a small stipend to enable him to travel abroad and study the theater in other countries. The following year he accepted a position with the Christiania Theater as director and playwright. Four years later, he penned *Love's Comedy,* his first play that satirized the manners of his society. The play outraged the conservatives in the Christiania community because Ibsen revealed the hypocrisy of love and marriage as practiced in middle-class society. Two years later, the playwright was granted another stipend to travel abroad so that he could broaden his knowledge of theater. He did not return to Norway until twenty-seven years later. During his stay in Italy, he wrote *Brand* and *Peer Gynt.* From 1868 until 1876, he lived in Dresden and wrote *The League of Youth,* a political comedy in prose, and *Emperor and Galilean,* a study of paganism and Christianity. Except for a stay in Rome from 1880 to 1885, Ibsen lived in Munich until he returned to Norway in 1891. During the time he lived in Germany and Italy, he wrote the realistic dramas for which he is famous: *The Pillars of Society* (1877), *A Doll's House* (1879), *Ghosts* (1881), *An Enemy of the People* (1882), *The Wild Duck* (1884), *Rosmersholm* (1886), and *Hedda Gabler* (1890). *The Lady from the Sea,* which Ibsen wrote in 1888, is the first of the symbolic plays that include: *The Master Builder* (1892), *Little Eyolf* (1895), *John Gabriel Borkman* (1896), and *When We Dead Awaken* (1899).

Henrik Ibsen was a master at creating the well-made play. Each drama is deliberately constructed with scenes that are carefully selected and arranged for maximum effect. The dialogue is terse and free from artificial asides, without soliloquies that are unrelated to the action of the play. The language is appropriate to the character and his position in life. Unlike the well-made play developed by Scribe and Sardou, Ibsen's well-made play is based upon the behavior and environment of the protagonist. The opening scene in *A Doll's House* provides an example of everyday happenings that reveal both the relationship between husband and wife, and the character of Helmer and Nora. The dialogue not only sets the tone of domestic tranquillity and advances the plot, but, in addition, tells us something about Nora and Helmer as individuals in their own right, and as individuals living as partners in a marital relationship. The situation is carefully developed to tell us a great deal about the conflict that will arise later between Nora and Helmer:

NORA:
Hide the tree well, Helene. The children mustn't get a glimpse of it till this evening, after it's trimmed. (*To the Delivery Boy, taking out her purse.*) How much?

DELIVERY BOY:
Fifty, ma'am.

NORA:
There's a crown. No, keep the change. (*The Boy thanks her and leaves. Nora shuts the door. She laughs softly to herself while taking off her street things. Drawing a bag of macaroons from her pocket, she eats a couple, then steals over and listens at her husband's study door.*) Yes, he's home. (*Hums again as she moves to the table right.*)

HELMER:
(*From the study.*) Is that my little lark twittering out there?

NORA:
(*Busy opening some packages.*) Yes, it is.

HELMER:
Is that my squirrel rummaging around?

NORA:
Yes!

HELMER:
When did my squirrel get in?

NORA:
Just now. (*Putting the macaroon bag in her pocket and wiping her mouth.*) Do come in, Torvald, and see what I've bought.

HELMER:
Can't be disturbed. (*After a moment he opens the door and peers in, pen in hand.*) Bought you say? All that there? Has the little spendthrift been out throwing money around again?

NORA:
Oh, but Torvald, this year we really should let ourselves go a bit. It's the first Christmas we haven't had to economize.

HELMER:
But you know we can't go squandering.

NORA:
Oh yes, Torvald, we can squander a little now. Can't we? Just a tiny, wee bit. Now that you've got a big salary and are going to make piles and piles of money.

HELMER:
Yes—starting New Year's. But then it's a full three months until the raise comes through.

NORA:
Pooh! We can borrow that long.

HELMER:
Nora! (*Goes over and playfully takes her by the ear.*) Are your scatterbrains off again? What if today I borrowed

a thousand crowns, and you squandered them over Christmas week, and then on New Year's Eve a roof tile fell on my head, and I lay there—

NORA:
(*Putting her hand on his mouth.*) Oh! Don't say such things!

HELMER:
Yes, but what if it happened—then what?

NORA:
If anything so awful happened, then it just wouldn't matter if I had debts or not.

HELMER:
Well, but the people I'd borrowed from?

NORA:
Them? Who cares about them! They're strangers.

HELMER:
Nora, Nora, how like a woman! No, but seriously, Nora, you know what I think about that. No debts! Never borrow! Something of freedom's lost—and something of beauty, too—from a home that's founded on borrowing and debt. We've made a brave stand up to now, the two of us; and we'll go right on like that the little while we have to.

NORA:
(*Going toward the stove.*) Yes, whatever you say, Torvald.*

Ibsen is regarded as the father of modern drama because his plays, particularly those which begin with *The Pillars of Society,* mark the beginning of serious drama about modern man and the society in which he lives. The social problems of the late nineteenth century may not be pertinent today, but the problems encountered by many individuals who seek to determine their role in society,

---

* From *A Doll's House,* in *Four Major Plays* by Henrik Ibsen, a new translation with foreword by Rolf Fjelde, pp. 43–44. Copyright © by Rolf Fjelde. Reprinted by arrangement with The New American Library, Inc., New York.

who seek to achieve their aspirations, and who seek to achieve self-realization, are ever constant. For example, the rights of women have been certainly broadened since Ibsen wrote *A Doll's House.* However, a successful marriage that permits each partner to grow in the relationship is still dependent upon mutual love and respect. Today, venereal disease is openly recognized as a social problem. However, it is doubtful whether the families of victims of this disease are any more ready to face the reality of the situation today than is Mrs. Alving in *Ghosts.* Today, the mentally ill or the neurotic may openly seek the help of a psychiatrist. However, it is conceivable that there are many Hedda Gablers who would rather resort to self-destruction than admit that they are in need of psychiatric assistance. The inspiration that an older man derives from a young girl may seem to be a gross exaggeration in *The Master Builder*, but the cult of youth still leads many Decembers to woo Mays. In a day and age that placed great value upon respectability at any cost, it is little wonder that Ibsen's plays were considered to be shocking, embarrassing, disgusting, and sordid. Although Ibsen wrote of another society and of problems related to that milieu, his heroes and heroines offer examples of modern man trapped by the conventions imposed by society, shaped by his environment, influenced by heredity, and motivated by instinct and human nature.

b. Johan August Strindberg

In the closing moments of *The Father,* the Captain, strapped in a straitjacket, and Laura, his domineering and calculating wife, taunt each other for the last time:

LAURA:
(*goes over to the sofa*). Adolph! Look at me! Do you really think I am your enemy?

THE CAPTAIN:
Yes—I do. I believe you all are my enemies! My mother—who didn't want to bring me into the world because childbirth would give her pain—was my enemy when she sapped the nourishment from the first seed of life in me and made a misfit of me. My sister was my enemy when she forced me to be subservient to her. The first woman

I embraced was my enemy, for she gave me ten years of a sickness in return for the love I gave her. My daughter became my enemy when she had to choose between you and me. And you, my wife—you are and have been my deadly enemy—for you never let go your hold on me until no life was left in me . . .

LAURA:

I don't know that I ever gave a thought to doing what you imagine I did. I wouldn't say I may not have had some vague urge within me to get you out of the way—and if you see anything resembling a plan in what I have done, it might have been there although I was not conscious of it. I have never really reflected over what has been taking place: it has all developed along the lines you yourself laid down. Even if I should not be innocent, before God, and in my conscience, I feel I am. You weighed on my heart like a stone that pressed and pressed until at last I tried to shake off the oppressive burden. That is no doubt what happened; and if I have struck you down without meaning to, I ask you to forgive me.

THE CAPTAIN:

All that sounds credible enough! But how does that help me? And where does the fault lie? Perhaps in our spiritual, Platonic marital relations. One used to marry a woman for love; but nowadays one enters into partnership with a business or professional woman—or one shares one's bed and board with a mistress! And then one has illegal intercourse with the partner—or one casts a stigma upon the mistress! But what becomes of love—healthy, sensuous love? It dies as a result! And what happens to the offspring of this sort of love in shares, payable to the bearer, without any mutual responsibility? And who is the bearer when the crash comes? Who is the physical father of the spiritual child?

LAURA:

Let me say that your suspicions about the child are entirely groundless.*

---

* From *The Father* by August Strindberg. *Seven Plays by August Strindberg,* translated by Arvid Paulson, pp. 53–54. Copyright © 1960 by Bantam Books, Inc.

The Father was the first of several plays that Strindberg penned about the sex-duel between male and female, lover and mistress, husband and wife. Each play mirrors the deterioration of Strindberg's marriage to Siri von Essen. The playwright and the actress were married in 1877 after she had divorced her husband so that she could pursue a career in the theater. At first, Strindberg encouraged her theatrical ambitions and frequently coached her in the preparation of her roles. However, as she became more involved in the bohemian life associated with the theater, Strindberg became resentful, jealous, and accusing. As the failing marriage began to assume the proportions of a public scandal, Strindberg used his talents to record his views on marriage and the relationship between man and woman. *The Father* is the story of a husband and wife who attempt to best each other when a decision must be made in regard to the education of their daughter. The wife, cordial to and considerate of everyone else, psychologically undermines and, ultimately, mentally destroys her husband when she implies that the child is not his in order to have her wishes prevail. *Miss Julie,* Strindberg's next play, is a demonstration of the love-hate theme. *Miss Julie* is the pathological study of a well-to-do young woman who both loves and hates men. Her sexual drives are without restraint. She celebrates her broken engagement to a member of her own social class by seducing her chauffeur. At the conclusion of the play, she commits suicide. The play was banned in Denmark after its initial performance at the University of Copenhagen in 1889. The first public performance of the controversial drama occurred three years later when the Freie Bühne ventured a production of the play. *Comrades,* a third play, continues the theme of the conflict between the sexes. Unlike *The Father* and *Miss Julie, Comrades* is a comedy that satirizes the idea of the equality of the sexes. The conclusion of the play is a reversal of the conclusion of Ibsen's *A Doll's House.* In *Comrades,* the husband slams the door on the wife, declaring that he will continue their relationship when he meets her as a comrade at a café. *The Creditors* relates the story of a wife who, having rid herself of one husband, now proceeds to use the same techniques to shed husband number two.

In 1891, the Strindbergs were divorced amid a great deal of attending publicity and acrimony. Embittered by the court's decision to award the custody of their children to his wife, Strindberg wrote *Mother Love* and *The Link* to point up the effect of a stormy marriage upon the children, and the hold of the children upon a marriage. A second marriage in 1893 to Frida Uhl, an emancipated young woman who was a talented journalist, also terminated in the divorce courts in 1897. During the years of 1894–1897, Strindberg suffered a mental breakdown. In 1901, the year of his marriage to Harriet Bosse, a professional actress, Strindberg wrote *The Dance of Death,* the last of the plays dealing with the war between the sexes and the love-hate theme.

After his recovery in 1897, and with the exception of *The Dance of Death,* Strindberg turned to the writing of two types of plays: symbolistic dramas and historical dramas. *There Are Crimes and Crimes* inaugurated the surrealistic and expressionistic plays that include *Easter, To Damascus, The Dream Play, The Spook Sonata,* and *The Great Highway.* Insofar as it is possible to dramatize the abberations of the mind, each play is an extension of the playwright's inner self. Strindberg's historical plays, often thought to be among the best in the theater, include *Gustav Vasa, Gustav Adolph,* and *Queen Christina.*

Strindberg was born in 1849. The fourth child of a large family, his childhood was an unhappy one. His father was a businessman who married Strindberg's mother after she had borne him two children out of wedlock. Strindberg was thirteen when his mother died, and his father remarried shortly thereafter. In 1867, Strindberg entered the University of Uppsala where he remained less than a term because he lacked the needed funds. He obtained a position as a schoolteacher but soon withdrew from the profession because he could not cope with the demands of teaching. A second attempt to seek a higher education ended in failure because he could not pass the qualifying examination in chemistry. He then turned to acting and joined the Royal Theater in Stockholm. In 1871, Carl XV granted him a small stipend because of his enthusiasm for Strindberg's play *The Outlaw.* Unfortunately, this windfall was soon terminated by the death of the king. In 1874, he was appointed to the Royal Library as an assistant librarian. Five years later, he won some recognition with a novel, *The Red Room.* A series of short stories entitled *Marriage* brought charges of heresy. Shortly thereafter, Strindberg embarked upon the writing of his plays with a love-hate theme. A proponent of naturalism and expressionism, Strindberg spent virtually his entire professional lifetime striving to attain the recognition he ultimately received. Producers of commercial theater rejected his plays because the public considered him a misogynist. The playwright was dependent upon such theatrical visionaries as André Antoine, Otto Brahm, and Max Reinhardt to popularize his plays in Europe. Although *The Father* was written in 1887, American and English audiences did not see the play until twenty-five years later. Even today, his plays are considered to be strong theatrical fare. However, there is no doubt that his themes are ageless and that his contribution to the development of psychological drama is incalculable.

c. Anton Pavlovitch Chekhov

In October, 1896, theatergoers crowded the Alexandrinsky Theater in St. Petersburg (now Leningrad) to honor their favorite comedienne. She had selected to play Madame Arkadina, the leading role in *The Sea Gull* by Anton Chekhov, for her benefit performance. However, the actress was dropped from the cast at the last moment and without notice to the public. Consequently, a hostile audience vent its irritation upon the play and the company with jeers, catcalls, and boos. Even though subsequent audiences reacted more favorably, the management soon withdrew the play from its repertory. A dejected playwright wondered whether or not he should pursue a career in the theater, although he had met with considerable success in writing several vaudeville skits: *The Bear, The Marriage Proposal, The Wedding,* and *The Anniversary*. In December 1898, the Moscow Art Theater, under the direction of Nemirovich-Danchenko and Stanislavski, presented the seventh play of its first season, a revival of *The Sea Gull*. Chekhov had reluctantly granted permission to revive the play only because Nemirovich-Danchenko had evinced complete faith in the merits of the play and in the playwriting talents of the dramatist. Additionally, Nemirovich-Danchenko was convinced that *The Sea Gull* would break the chain of box-office failures that threatened the very existence of the Moscow Art Theater. In contrast to the nine rehearsals that had preceded the initial presentation of the play at the Alexandrinsky Theater, the Moscow Art Theater company gave *The Sea Gull* twenty-six rehearsals. As the first act progressed, the producer, the director, and the actors could not determine whether or not the audience was responding to their efforts. When the curtain was lowered at the end of the first act, the actors stood waiting to hear the sound of applause. There was a momentary silence. Next, a thunderous ovation! The Moscow Art Theater company then knew its future was assured. Chekhov was not present to share in the triumph of this opening night. The playwright was in Yalta, nursing his tuberculosis. The news of his success reached him by telegram.

Chekhov's literary career paralleled his years as a medical student at the University of Moscow. When Chekhov, the grandson of a serf who had purchased his freedom, was graduated in 1884, he had already written hundreds of short stories, sketches, and articles for a weekly literary magazine. His first play, *The Fatherless,* was written when he was seventeen years old, and his first important one-acter, *On the High Road,* was written when he was twenty-four. It was suppressed in 1885 by the censor because of the unflattering picture of Russian provincial society. Two years later, his first major play, *Ivanov,* was produced at the Korsh Theater in Moscow. It was revised by the playwright for production by the Alexandrinsky Theater, St. Petersburg, in 1889. Considered by many authorities to be incomplete in terms of plot and character development, *Ivanov* is the story of a self-centered man whose self-pity leads him to a tragic end. Unlike the other major plays, *Ivanov* depends upon the behavior of its central character for interest, rather than upon the interaction of individuals within a group. Written in 1899 expressly for the talents of the Moscow Art Theater company, *Uncle Vanya* offers a study of unrequited love. Helene is unhappily married to the Professor who is absorbed in his books. Vanya loves Helene who is attracted to Astrov who, in turn, is infatuated with Helene. Sonia, the Professor's daughter by his first marriage to Vanya's sister, loves Astrov. In Act II, Vanya, sensing that life may be passing him by, declares his love for Helene:

VANYA:

In a minute or two the rain will be over, and everything in nature will be refreshed and sigh with relief. Only I shall not be refreshed by the storm. Day and night I feel suffocated by the thought that my life has been irretrievably lost. I have no past—it has all been stupidly wasted on trifles—while the present is awful because it's so meaningless. My life, my love—look at them—where do they belong? What am I to do with them? My feeling for you is just wasted like a ray of sunlight falling into a well—and I am wasted too.

HELENE:
When you talk to me of your love I feel quite stupid and I don't know what to say. Forgive me, there's nothing I can say to you. (*Starting to go out.*) Good-night.

VANYA:
(*barring her way.*) And if you only knew how I suffer when I think that near to me, in the very same house, another life is being wasted—your life! What are you waiting for? What confounded philosophy is holding you back? Understand, do understand. . . .

HELENE:
(*looks at him intently.*) Ivan Petrovich, you are drunk!

VANYA:
Maybe, maybe . . .

HELENE:
Where's the doctor?

VANYA:
He's in there . . . He's staying the night with me. It may be, it may be . . . Anything may be!

HELENE:
So you have been drinking again today! Whatever for?

VANYA:
At least it gives the illusion of life . . . Don't prevent me, Helene . . .

HELENE:
You never used to drink and you never used to talk so much . . . Do go to bed! You bore me.

VANYA:

(*impulsively kissing her hand.*) Dearest . . . You wonderful woman!

HELENE:

(*with annoyance.*) Leave me alone. This is really hateful! (*goes out.*)

VANYA:

(*alone.*) She's gone. (*A pause.*) Ten years ago I used to meet her at my sister's house. She was seventeen then and I was thirty-seven. Why didn't I fall in love with her then and ask her to marry me? It could have been done so easily! She would have been my wife now . . . Yes . . . and we two might have been awakened by this storm; she would have been frightened by the thunder and I would have held her in my arms and whispered: "Don't be afraid, I'm here." Oh, what a wonderful thought! how enchanting! it actually makes me laugh with happiness . . . but, oh, God! my thoughts are in a tangle . . . Why am I so old? Why won't she understand me? Her fine phrases, her easy moralizing, her silly, facile ideas about the ruin of the world —how utterly hateful it all is to me! (*A pause.*) And how I've been cheated! I adored the professor, the gouty old invalid, and I worked like an ox for him! Sonia and I squeezed all we could out of this estate . . . Like close-fisted peasants we traded in linseed oil, dried peas, and curds, we saved on our food so that we could scrape together halfpence and farthings and send him thousands of rubles. I was proud of him and his learning, he was the breath of my life! Everything he wrote or uttered seemed to me the work of a genius . . . And now what, good God? He's retired down here, and now you can see what his life really amounts to. Not a page of his writing will survive him . . . he's completely unknown, a nonentity! A soap bubble! And I've been cheated . . . I see it now . . . stupidly cheated . . ."

---

* From *Uncle Vanya,* by Anton Chehov, *Chehov Plays,* trans. by Elisaveta Fen (London: Penguin Books, Ltd., 1959), pp. 205–207. Copyright © Penguin Books, Ltd. Reprinted by permission of the publisher.

The soliloquy that ends the scene includes interrupted inner thoughts that must be conveyed to the audience by the actor. These moments of silence, for example, which occur in the lines "Not a page of his writing will survive him . . . he is completely unknown, a nonentity! A soap bubble! And I've been cheated . . . I see it now . . . stupidly cheated . . ." must be silently communicated by the actor to provide the rationale for that which is spoken by the actor. Frequently this moment of meaningful silence is also indicated by the word "pause."

In 1901, the year of his marriage to Olga Knipper, one of the leading ladies of the Moscow Art Theater company, Chekhov wrote *The Three Sisters.* The play tells the story of three sisters whose inability to rise above the mundane aspects of everyday life prevents them from achieving their dreams and aspirations for a richer life. Three years later, Chekhov wrote *The Cherry Orchard.* The theme is not unlike that of *The Three Sisters.* Madame Ranyevskaia, the leading character, cannot learn to enjoy the ways of a new society because she cannot release herself from the nostalgic past. The play was premiered on January 17, 1904, the day of the playwright's forty-fourth birthday. The playwright died six months later, a victim of tuberculosis that plagued him from the time he was a young adult.

In contrast to the works of other prominent playwrights of the time, Chekhov's plays are without plot. There is no story or a series of happenings to sustain the interest of the audience. Rather, it is character and the relationship between people that provide the plays of Chekhov with what little plot each play has. Out of the card-playing, the amateur theatricals, the wining and dining, the social calls by neighbors, and the trivial, there emerges a play that is life itself. To conclude, the works of Chekhov are impressions of a segment of Russian society at the turn of the century, on the eve of revolution, destined to disappear from the Russian scene.

d. George Bernard Shaw

George Bernard Shaw was born in Ireland in 1856. Like many other adolescents of his day, he left school at the age of fourteen to seek employment to support himself and to supplement the family income. In 1876, Shaw decided to leave Dublin and join his mother, a music teacher, in London. Here he continued to educate himself by attending lectures and reading avidly, rather than by attending a university. An interest in socialism led Shaw to embark upon a literary career. He began by writing five novels, which were published by socialist magazines. Through the friendship of William Archer, a noted nineteenth-century critic and translator of plays, Shaw obtained a position as book reviewer for the *Pall Mall Magazine*. Three years later, he joined the staff of *The Star* and gained a reputation as a music critic. In 1891, Shaw wrote *The Quintessence of Ibsenism* in an effort to popularize the works of the playwright and to arouse interest in the establishment of the Independent Theater by Jacob T. Grein. Grein's purpose in launching this theatrical endeavor was similar to that which had motivated Antoine to establish the Théâtre Libre in Paris. Grein wanted to provide a showcase for English playwrights whose works had been rejected by commercial theater managers, and he wanted to introduce English theatergoers to the works of foreign playwrights. The Independent Theater opened March 9, 1891, with a production of Ibsen's *Ghosts*. Both the press and the public were shocked by the subject matter of the play. Weeks passed before the furor abated.

Shaw wrote his first play, *Widowers' Houses,* in order to end Grein's search for a play by a native playwright. The play stunned property owners and provoked heated discussions among the upper classes because of Shaw's attack upon the wealth derived from the ownership of property in slum neighborhoods. The playwright followed *Widowers' Houses* with, as he describes them, two other "unpleasant plays": *The Philanderer,* which dealt with sexual relations, and *Mrs. Warren's Profession,* which ascribed the causes of prostitution to the economic ills of society rather than to the nature of the individual; and three "pleasant plays": *Candida, Arms and the Man* (later an operetta, *The Chocolate Soldier,* by Oskar Straus), and *You Never Can Tell.* Thereafter, Shaw wrote the following major plays: *The Devil's Disciple, Caesar and Cleopatra* (recently musicalized as *Her First Roman*), *Man and Superman, The Doctor's Dilemma, Androcles and the Lion, Pygmalion* (or, that epitome of American musicals, *My Fair Lady*), *Heartbreak House,* and *Saint Joan.* Shaw's last play, *Buoyant Billions,* was written when the playwright was ninety-two years old. In 1925, Shaw was awarded the Nobel Prize for Literature.

In a comedy of ideas, the playwright espouses a point of view that is derived from a consideration of the pros and cons of a given topic. A slim plot provides a framework for those moments when the playwright can proselytize his viewpoint. The characters seem to be human and real because they are forceful in presenting their opinions, but, in truth, the characters are merely spokesmen for the playwright. The dialogue, which is highly opinionated and more rhetorical than conversational, nevertheless gives credence to the unrealistic and exaggerated situations depicted on stage. The cascade of words, the brilliant structure of sentences and paragraphs, the energy and vitality of the speakers, serve to obliterate the artificiality of the scene on stage. For example, *Man and Superman* is Shaw's interpretation of the battle between the sexes. His premise is that it is the female who pursues the male, not the male who pursues the female, because the female needs the male to fulfill her creative function, child-bearing. Man has the innate capacity, by virtue of his ability to procreate, to produce a superman who, in turn, will enhance the society in which he lives. For this reason, man permits woman to pursue him, overtake him, overpower him, and finally, lead him to the altar. Shaw expresses part of his premise in Act I in a scene between John Tanner, M.I.R.C. (Member of the Idle Rich Class), and Octavius, an artist:

TANNER:
> Tavy: that's the devilish side of a woman's fascination: she makes you will your own destruction.

OCTAVIUS:
> But it's not destruction: it's fulfilment.

TANNER:
> Yes, of her purpose; and that purpose is neither her happiness nor yours, but Nature's. Vitality in a woman is a blind fury of creation. She sacrifices herself to it: do you think she will hesitate to sacrifice you?

OCTAVIUS:

Why, it is just because she is self-sacrificing that she will not sacrifice those she loves.

TANNER:

That is the profoundest of mistakes, Tavy. It is the self-sacrificing women that sacrifice others most recklessly. Because they are unselfish, they are kind in little things. Because they have a purpose which is not their own purpose, but that of the whole universe, man is nothing to them but an instrument of that purpose.

OCTAVIUS:

Don't be ungenerous, Jack. They take the tenderest care of us.

TANNER:

Yes, as a soldier takes care of his rifle or a musician of his violin. But do they allow us any purpose of freedom of our own? Will they lend us to one another? Can the strongest man escape from them when once he is appropriated? They tremble when we are in danger, and weep when we die; but the tears are not for us, but for a father wasted, a son's breeding thrown away. They accuse us of treating them as a mere means to our pleasure; but how can so feeble and transient a folly as a man's selfish pleasure enslave a woman as the whole purpose of Nature embodied in a woman can enslave a man?

OCTAVIUS:

What matter, if the slavery makes us happy?

TANNER:

No matter at all if you have no purpose of your own, and are, like most men, a mere breadwinner. But you, Tavy, are an artist: that is, you have a purpose as absorbing and as unscrupulous as a woman's purpose.

OCTAVIUS:

Not unscrupulous.

TANNER:

Quite unscrupulous. The true artist will let his wife starve, his children go barefoot, his mother drudge for his living at seventy, sooner than work at anything but his art. To women he is half vivisector, half vampire. He gets into intimate relations with them to study them, to strip the mask of convention from them, to surprise their inmost secrets, knowing that they have the power to rouse his deepest creative energies, to rescue him from his cold reason, to make him see visions and dream dreams, to inspire him, as he calls it. He persuades women that they may do this for their own purpose whilst he really means them to do it for his. He steals the mother's milk and blackens it to make printer's ink to scoff at her and glorify ideal women with. He pretends to spare her the pangs of child-bearing so that he may have for himself the tenderness and fostering that belong of right to her children. Since marriage began, the great artist has been known as a bad husband. But he is worse: he is a child-robber, a blood-sucker, a hypocrite, and a cheat. Perish the race and wither a thousand women if only the sacrifice of them enable him to act Hamlet better, to paint a finer picture, to write a deeper poem, a greater play, a profounder philosophy! For mark you, Tavy, the artist's work is to shew us ourselves as we really are. Our minds are nothing but this knowledge of ourselves; and he who adds a jot to such knowledge creates new mind as surely as any woman creates new men. In the rage of that creation he is as ruthless as the woman, as dangerous to her as she to him, and as horribly fascinating. Of all human struggles there is none so treacherous and remorseless as the struggle between the artist man and the mother woman. Which shall use up the other? that is the issue between them. And it is all the deadlier because, in your romantic cant, they love one another.

OCTAVIUS:

Even if it were so—and I don't admit it for a moment—it is out of the deadliest struggles that we get the noblest characters.*

---

* From George Bernard Shaw, *Man and Superman* (Baltimore, Md.: Penguin Books, 1952), pp. 61–62. Copyright The Society of Authors, London, agent for the Bernard Shaw Estate.

Thereafter, John is chased by Ann until the inevitable moment when he capitulates to her charms. A man of "moral passions" who desires to improve society through reforms, John gives way to the "passion" of the life force in his realization that, through the reproduction of the species, a superman may be created. Generally, only three of the four acts of *Man and Superman* are performed. Act III, the "Don Juan in Hell" act, is usually omitted because it breaks the continuity of the John-Ann conflict, and because its inclusion makes the performance too lengthy, thereby causing the interest of the audience to wane. In recent years, however, Act III has been successfully performed as an independent offering.

Shavian comedy is primarily concerned with man's tendency to destroy himself through his inhibitions, his follies, his foibles, and his institutions. In each of his plays, Shaw attacks that which he believes prohibits the individual from realizing his worth, that which deters society from improving conditions, that which averts civilization from moving forward. Government, imperialism, capitalism, war, peace, parents, marriage, divorce, prostitution, medicine, poverty, sex, feminism, business—even speech and spelling—are scrutinized by the playwright as possible causes for the disruption of the life force. Like Aristophanes, Molière, and Ben Jonson, George Bernard Shaw utilizes the techniques of comedy to call our attention to a need for a rational approach to the business of living—if, indeed, we are to continue living.

B. CUES FOR THEATERGOERS: ANALYZING THE PLAY

A play is a story written for actors to perform on a stage in the presence of an audience. Therefore, in writing his play, the playwright must take into consideration the elements of drama, the techniques of acting, the dynamics of play production, and the response of the audience. In selecting his theme, the playwright must consider the contemporary scene if the play is to provide a meaningful experience for the theatergoer. In developing his theme, the playwright must adhere to the time allotted for presentation, whether the theme has the magnitude of *King Lear* by Shakespeare or the simplicity of *Never Too Late* by Sumner Arthur Long. In creating a character, the playwright must reveal an understanding of human emotions and an awareness of psychological behavioral patterns that motivate conflict and action. In fashioning his dialogue, the playwright must advance his plot through words that are appropriate to the personality and social status of the characters. In addition, the playwright must write dialogue that actors can speak with ease and fluency. In planning changes of locale and special effects, the playwright must recognize the limitations of the physical stage in producing the play. Playwriting is a complicated and demanding art that warrants examination in order to understand and to appreciate the creative effort of the playwright. Therefore, for optimum enjoyment of the theatergoing experience, theatergoers should consider:

1. Does the playwright utilize the elements of drama effectively?
2. Does the structure of the play allow for a logical development of the theme and the plot?
3. Does the playwright create characters with whom the theatergoer can identify and empathize?
4. Does the dialogue advance the plot, reflect the situation, reveal the personalities of the characters, and sustain the mood of the play?
5. Does the play suggest the concept of a particular play form?

1. Does the playwright utilize the elements of drama effectively?

a. Situation

Situation is the circumstance that triggers the action out of which arise conflict, suspense, surprise, and emotion. In *Oedipus Rex* by Sophocles, for example, a curse on the city causes Oedipus to embark on a quest to appease the gods. In *Hamlet* by Shakespeare, a restless ghost motivates the brooding prince to seek revenge for his father's sudden death. In *Le Bourgeois Gentilhomme* by Molière, a rise in social status inspires Monsieur Jourdain to indulge himself to the point of becoming ludicrous. In *Mourning Becomes Electra* by Eugene O'Neill, the return of General Mannon sets in motion the acts of violence that have tragic consequences for the Mannon family. In *You Can't Take It with You* by George S. Kaufman and Moss Hart, a marriage proposal causes the heroine to examine the eccentricities of her family realistically. In *A Streetcar Named Desire* by Tennessee Williams, loneliness compels Blanche to visit her sister and brother-in-law. In *Death of a Salesman* by Arthur Miller, financial and professional failure leads Willie Loman to re-evaluate his life. In *Born Yesterday* by Garson Kanin, Brock's search for status leads to the refashioning of Billie Dawn. In *Rosencrantz and Guildenstern Are Dead* by Tom Stoppard, Hamlet's behavior at court results in a royal summons that greatly affects the future of Hamlet's two friends. In *The Great White Hope* by Howard Sackler, the defeat of a white champion by a black man causes a search for a "white hope" who will inflict defeat upon a black champion. Once the underlying situation propels a play into motion, new situations develop, each contributing to the expansion of theme and plot, each intensifying the action, each heightening the conflict that must be resolved.

b. Action

Action is the course followed by the protagonist in attaining his goal. Action is the incident that arises and the situations that develop. Action is structure, the forward movement of the plot toward the play's highest point of interest, the climax, and the play's logical conclusion, the resolution. In *Oedipus Rex,* action is the search for the unclean thing that has brought a blight upon the city. In *Hamlet,* action is the attempt to catch the conscience of the king to avenge the murder of Hamlet's father. In *Le Bourgeois Gentilhomme,* action is the enjoyment of life. In *You Can't Take It with You,* action is the pursuit of happiness and individuality. In *A Streetcar Named Desire,* action is the quest for understanding and acceptance. In *Death of a Salesman,* action is the re-examination of life as it pertains to values, relationships, and a career. In *Born Yesterday,* action is the education of Billie Dawn. In *Rosencrantz and Guildenstern Are Dead,* action is the meaninglessness of life and the inevitability of death. In *The Great White Hope,* action is the fight against racial prejudice. Additionally, action is thought that excites and motivates the protagonist to pursue his course. For example, memory and conscience motivate Willie Loman's tragic end in *Death of a Salesman.* Finally, action is the physical movement of the characters on stage. Dance accompanies recitation by the Greek chorus. Pantomime reveals the validity of Hamlet's suspicions. Spectacle climaxes Monsieur Jourdain's rise in society. A raid by the F.B.I. shatters a social evening in *You Can't Take It With You.* Suicide ends the life of the heroine in *The Great White Hope.* Action, then, is the life force of a play. It is the heart and bloodstream that keeps the play alive, the conflict pulsating.

c. *Conflict*

Conflict is the struggle between two opposing forces. Conflict arises when the protagonist meets opposition to his determined course of action. The opposition may come from external forces such as fate, society, environment, and other individuals. In *Oedipus Rex,* fate militates against the probability that the protagonist will achieve his goal without incurring tragic consequences. In *Hamlet,* other individuals, namely Claudius, Polonius, Laertes, Rosencrantz, and Guildenstern, conspire to prevent Hamlet from avenging his father's death. In *Le Bourgeois Gentilhomme,* the mores of French family life prevent Monsieur Jourdain from becoming a sophisticate. In *A Streetcar Named Desire,* the reduced status of her environment contributes to the downfall of Blanche. In *Death of a Salesman,* age and a changing social and economic order threaten Willie Loman's dream of success. In *The Great White Hope,* white society schemes against the rise of a black hero figure. Additionally, opposition may come from internal forces, such as the nature and character of the protagonist himself. In *Oedipus Rex* and in *The Great White Hope,* pride prevents each protagonist from yielding to the forces that militate to defeat him. In *Hamlet,* introspection and indecisiveness hinder the protagonist from following an immediate course of action. In *Mourning Becomes Electra,* incestuous desires bar the protagonists from enjoying a normal emotional life. In *Death of a Salesman,* self-deception keeps the protagonist from adjusting to the demands of his society. In *A Streetcar Named Desire,* fantasy deludes Blanche into living in a world of illusion. In

You Can't Take It With You, conformity and rugged individualism nearly destroy the relationship between the members of a family. Inevitably, the opposing forces meet head-on and the conflict must be resolved. In tragedy, the protagonist is generally defeated and loses his life as a consequence. In comedy, the protagonist wins, but at the cost of conforming to life!

d. Emotion

Emotion is the natural consequence of action and conflict. It is the shout of joy, the moan of sorrow, the sigh of love, the cry of hate, the growl of anger, the gasp of fear that emanate when the protagonist embarks on a course of action to resolve the conflict. Emotion is the vocal expression and the physical manifestation of the agitation of inner thoughts and feelings. Emotion is expressed in the words and the situations written by the playwright. It is depicted and voiced by the actor and in the behavior and feelings of the characters. For example, in *The Trojan Women* by Euripides, a humiliated and crushed Hecuba, Queen of Troy, laments the destruction of her city and the enslavement of her people. In *King Lear* by Shakespeare, a vengeful Edmund strikes out in anger and anguish at a world that accepts no moral responsibility for illegitimate children. In *The School for Husbands* by Molière, an arrogant and lusting Sganarelle ridicules a society that enjoys a relaxed manner of living. In *Uncle Vanya* by Chekhov, a lonely and desperate Vanya, in a state of complete hysteria, attempts to kill the professor. In *Saint Joan* by Shaw, a zealous Joan inspires the leaders to join her in the battle against the English. In *Angel Street* (*Gaslight*) by Patrick Hamilton, a frightened Mrs. Manningham conspires with Detective Rough to trap a maniacal murderer, her husband. In *Private Lives* by Noel Coward, an urbane Elyot and a sophisticated Amanda joyously quarrel their way to sexual happiness and fulfillment. In *Ceremonies in Dark Old Men* by Lonne Elder III, a crafty and sensuous Blue Haven pours out his ambivalent and violent responses to a mistress who demands that he marry her. In *1776* by Peter Stone and Sherman Edwards, a newly married Thomas Jefferson cannot concentrate on the business of drafting the Declaration of Independence because he yearns for his bride. Emotion, then, is one of the catalytic agents that involves the theatergoer with the play. Although he is not on stage, the viewer is drawn into the action and the conflict through identification and empathy with the emotions that motivate the character. If the playwright does not provide the theatergoer with the opportunity for emotional involvement, then the playgoing experience is frustrating and unrewarding.

e. Suspense

Suspense is the anxiety displayed by the protagonist in pursuing his course of action and in his surmounting the opposition. Suspense is a delaying technique used by the playwright to develop the theme, the plot, the characters, and to whet the interest of the theatergoer. In *Oedipus Rex,* Sophocles sustains the suspense of Oedipus discovering that which the theatergoer already knows by making Oedipus's search a thorough and prolonged quest. One clue uncovers another; one incident begets another. The theatergoer soon forgets that he knows the outcome of the legend as he unwittingly joins Oedipus in his search of self. Little wonder, then, that *Oedipus Rex* is often hailed as the greatest detective story ever written. In *Born Yesterday,* Garson Kanin sustains the suspense of Billie Dawn becoming a free agent until that moment when she is intellectually ready to confront Brock with her newly acquired knowledge. In *You Can't Take It with You* the playwrights sustain the suspense of a familiar story by expounding and dramatizing a philosophy of living through the behavior of lovable but eccentric characters. In *Rosencrantz and Guildenstern Are Dead,* Tom Stoppard sustains the suspense of the two protagonists meeting their death by combining the familiar and the unfamiliar. Scenes from *Hamlet* are interwoven with scenes written by Stoppard to give meaning to the life and death of Hamlet's two friends. In *The Great White Hope,* Howard Sackler sustains the suspense of the ultimate defeat of the black champion by a careful arrangement of selected scenes that are emotionally charged and increase in emotional intensity, building to a shattering climax. Suspense is the mounting excitement that comes from the theatergoer's involvement and identification with the action. Suspense is the waiting and the wondering, the apprehension and the unpredictability, the doubt and the uncertainty, the heaving and the sighing, the expectancy and the reality of what happens throughout the play.

f. Surprise

Surprise is the reaction of the protagonist to the occurrence of the unforeseen situation and to the shock of discovery of the truth. Surprise is the response of the audience to the logical but unanticipated behavior and emotional reaction of the protagonist, and to the sudden change in plot development by the playwright. Surprise is a technique used by the playwright to sustain attention throughout the play and to excite response to the development of plot and character. *Hamlet,* Act III, offers several examples of Shakespeare's use of surprise to reveal character, motivate action, and develop plot. The first example occurs in Scene 2 when Hamlet surprises Claudius and the court with the presentation of a play, the plot of which resembles the murder of Hamlet's father by Claudius. Confronted with the realism of the plot and the performance, an astounded Claudius cries out for "some light" as though he were choking on the truth of the presentation. In performance, the surprise of the king is reflected in the reaction of the court, whose members scurry away at Claudius's bidding. A second example occurs when Hamlet comes upon a distraught and conscience-stricken Claudius kneeling in silent prayer. The avenging Dane raises his sword to kill his uncle, but restrains himself to rationalize:

> Now might I do it pat, now he is praying,
> And now I'll do't. And so he goes to heaven;
> And so am I revenged. That would be scanned;
> I, his sole son, do this same villain send
> To heaven.
> O, this is hire and salary, not revenge.
> He took my father grossly, full of bread;
> With all his crimes broad blown, as flush as May;
> And how his audit stands who knows save
> heaven?
> But in our circumstances and course of thought,
> 'Tis heavy with him. And am I then revenged,
> To take him in the purging of his soul,

When he is fit and seasoned, for his passage?
No!
Up, sword; and know thou a more horrid hent.
When he is drunk asleep, or in his rage,
Or in the incestuous pleasure of his bed;
At gaming, swearing, or about some act
That has no relish of salvation in't;
Then trip him, that his heels may kick at heaven,
And that his soul may be as damned and black
As hell, whereto it goes. My mother stays;
This physic but prolongs thy sickly days. *(exit)*

Hamlet, Act III, Scene 3

It is a moment in which the playwright superbly blends suspense—will or will not Hamlet murder Claudius? When will the opportune moment arise again?—and surprise—that Hamlet, determined to avenge the murder of his father, allows Claudius's state of grace to deter him from completing the action. "The Queen's Closet" scene, Scene 4, continues the dramatic use of surprise by the playwright. Hamlet surprises Polonius whose movements behind the arras and whose muffled cry for help is mistaken by the prince for the actions and voice of Claudius. Hamlet makes a pass through the arras and kills the old man. An overwrought Hamlet then castigates an astounded Gertrude for her role in the murder of her husband. Suddenly, the ghost materializes and admonishes Hamlet for his treatment of Gertrude and urges him to get on with his "almost blunted purpose." The act concludes with Hamlet dragging the body of Polonius off stage. It is an action that shocks the audience because of its positive feelings for the old man and because the action reveals the criminal depths to which the noble Dane has fallen. Thereafter, the fortune of Hamlet takes a turn: he becomes the hunted rather than the hunter. The element of surprise is, in part, responsible for his rise and tragic fall.

In summary, surprise accents the rising action, intensifies the conflict, and underscores the resolution. Surprise reveals emotion and inner thoughts. Additionally, surprise aids the audience in identifying with the protagonist: the cry of astonishment by the protagonist or the dramatis personae is almost always an outburst of emotion inwardly experienced by the audience.

2. Does the structure of the play allow for a logical development of the theme and the plot?

Play structure is the organizational design that emerges when we sense that a play has been well plotted by the playwright. It pertains to the manner in which the playwright arranges his material. It embraces the means by which the playwright builds his play to an appropriate climax and resolution. It involves the exploration of theme, the variations of which provide insight and meaning. It touches upon the progression and development of character, showing us what the character is and what he becomes as a result of his experience. Play structure includes the alignment of incidents and the forward movement of the plot. It embraces the use of exposition throughout the play, the uncovering of the initial incident or crisis that instigates the action, the plotting and planning of incidents that rise to and follow the climax. It allows for the action to cover the events of a day, a month, a year, a decade, or a century, but it demands that the action be completed within the performance time. It allows for either continuous or episodic development of plot and action with act and scene divisions to indicate a passage of time, to allow for scene changes, and to permit the audience to relax and discuss the performance. It permits the playwright to write a tragedy, a comedy, a farce, a melodrama, a fantasy, or a musical. It is not concerned with whether or not the treatment is romantic, sentimental, realistic, naturalistic, or absurd. It asks only that an organizational structure make the play-viewing experience a meaningful and logical one.

Hadrian VII by Peter Luke offers an example of a play whose structure provides the audience with a logical development of theme, plot, and character. The first scene of the play lays the foundation for what happens in subsequent scenes. In this opening scene, the playwright introduces all the major characters, as well as the threads of action that compose the plot. The leading character is Frederick William Rolfe, a talented eccentric with delusions of grandeur, who has been rejected as an applicant for the priesthood. He is visited by two bailiffs who have come to remove his possessions, which are to be sold at auction to pay off his creditors.

He curtly dismisses the bailiffs, refusing to give up his meager belongings. When his landlady, Mrs. Crowe, offers to help him because she is interested in him as a man, Rolfe angrily rejects her advances calling her "a rapacious concupiscent female." He receives a letter from the archbishop that irrevocably denies him entrance into the Church. He cries out to God for help. His emotional outburst is broken by the entrance of Agnes, a charwoman. She consoles Rolfe by persuading him to eat, and she attempts to offer him some physical comfort by putting a coin in the heater. The newspaper that she brings contains the news that the Pope is dead. It is this event and her chance remark that "it's about time they had an English Pope" that starts Rolfe writing his book, *Hadrian the Seventh.*

Suddenly, the lights begin to change and the scene seems to repeat itself as Mrs. Crowe announces that Rolfe has two visitors. When the door opens, the visitors, Dr. Courtleigh, Cardinal and Archbishop of Pimlico, and Dr. Talacryn, the Bishop of Caerleon, enter. Both bear a close resemblance to the two bailiffs. The clergymen have come to summon Rolfe to accept Holy Orders. When the scene ends, Rolfe is bound for Rome. We know that he will become Pope and we know that his reign will be filled with travail. Earlier in the scene, he is visited by Mr. Jeremiah Sant, the editor of a rabble-rousing newspaper, *The Tory Protester,* and a fanatic dedicated to the persecution of Roman Catholics. The climax of the play occurs when Sant assassinates the Pope. As the funeral procession engages the attention of the audience, Rolfe, holding his manuscript, suddenly appears downstage to observe the workings of his imagination. In short, the shot that is fired by Sant is the means by which Rolfe is brought back to reality and the audience shocked into the realization that they have witnessed a dramatization of Rolfe's book—the story of a man who experiences love and compassion through fulfillment of his dream to be accepted as a dignitary of the Church. The play ends with the return of the two bailiffs who confiscate Rolfe's belongings, part of which is the manuscript that he describes as "a probable masterpiece."

The structure of Mr. Luke's adaptation of *Hadrian VII* permits the audience to experience a common human desire—the realization of an unattainable dream. The world of reality is interwoven with the world of fantasy through the development of situations that are possible but highly improbable and through the inclusion of personages from the real and the unreal world. The play reaches a logical conclusion, one that the playwright has prepared the audience for in the development of the conflict between Rolfe and Sant, when the Pope is assassinated. It is logical that the dream is ended. The audience, aware of Rolfe's delusions, leaves the theater satisfied that the protagonist has triumphed at least in fancy, if not in fact.

The chart on page 245 illustrates the underlying structure of the majority of plays.

3. Does the playwright create characters with whom the theatergoer can identify and empathize?

Death of a Salesman offers an example of a play with which many theatergoers feel a high degree of self-identification. The ambitions, the dreams, the frustrations of the Loman family are the ambitions, the dreams, the frustration of an everyday American family. Willie Loman is a common man, a salesman whose hard-sell techniques are ineffective and old-fashioned in a world whose wares are advertised and promoted by Madison Avenue. We meet Willie at a time when he is frightened by the uncertainty of the future, stunned by the failure of his sons to succeed, and shaken by the discovery that the American dream is a nightmare. Biff, the apple of Willie's eye, is a personable young man who, at the age of thirty-two, is a ne'er-do-well still on the brink of finding himself. Biff has never lived up to Willie's expectations because Biff has never been anything but a very average young man and because he has never been able to overcome his shock at discovering that his father is not a perfect man, not a hero, not a flawless idol. Hap, Biff's younger brother, is a second Willie, youthful and enthusiastic about the future, quick to sell and use his personality to achieve the same dream that has enticed his father to a tragic end. Linda is the helpless bystander, the faithful wife and mother who gives all, asks little, and receives less. From this portrait of an American family facing a crisis, there emerges a penetrating study of the relationship between man and his society, father and son, husband and

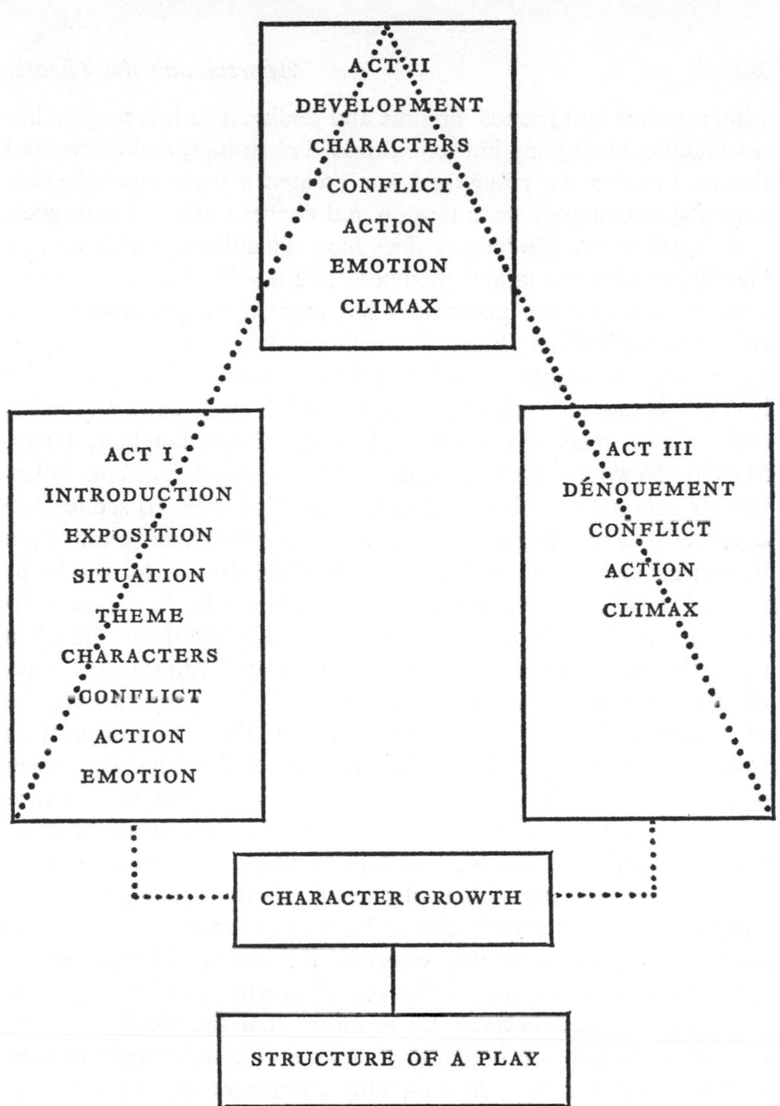

KEY: The dotted line represents the rise and fall of the action as it approaches the highest point of interest, the climax, and as it moves toward the dénouement.

The boxes represent the act division usually found in the modern full-length play and the function of each act in a three-act play. The theatergoer should note, however, that the function will vary from play to play, from playwright to playwright; that the climax, for example, may not occur well into the third act, perhaps not until the very end of the play.

wife, relatives and friends, dreams and reality. The theatergoer has no difficulty identifying himself with Willie's values, ambitions, and dreams because the playwright has created a well-rounded character that commands the attention and concern of the theatergoer.

In contrast, the theatergoer does have difficulty empathizing and identifying with the family members in Jules Feiffer's play, *Little Murders,* because the playwright has created recognizable family types but not flesh-and-blood characters with whom the theatergoer can personally identify. Carol Newquist is a possessive father who believes that no man, save perhaps himself, is sufficiently masculine and virile to meet the drives and needs of his daughter, Patsy. Marjorie Newquist, his wife, is cute and coy, capable of emasculating her son and not above using her feminine wiles to seduce her daughter's fiancé. Kenny, their son, is an effeminate young man who meets every emotional crisis by heading straight for the bathroom. His sister is, in the words of the playwright, ". . . all consuming . . . tall, blonde, vibrant, the All-American Girl," a molder of men. Alfred, her fiancé, is quiet and withdrawn, a daydreamer who faces the vicissitudes of daily living by turning the other cheek. The play is concerned with the thesis that each of us is at heart a little murderer, that in our relationships with each other and in our responses to everyday events, we commit innumerable little murders that make the society in which we live an acceptable, albeit a violent, one. Unfortunately, the characters are too contrived, too psychologically disturbed, too lacking in human warmth to arouse our sympathy and enlist our concern. The theatergoer observes the shattering effect of the strange knocks on the door, the mysterious shots from out of nowhere, but the theatergoer does not feel because he is aware that the playwright has created types who are potentially capable of committing and supporting violence rather than creating characters who become the perpetrators of violence because of what has happened to them. The theatergoer may be shocked and surprised by the sudden demise of Patsy, but he is not emotionally moved by her death because he recognizes that the senselessness of her death has been introduced to bring about the metamorphosis of Alfred. *Little Murders* is a provocative and disturbing play that shakes the theatergoer intellectually, but leaves the theatergoer unmoved emotionally because the family members are deliberately fashioned types rather than human beings with whom the theatergoer can identify.

The theatergoer will be able to judge the success of the playwright in creating a well-rounded character by the degree to which the theatergoer can identify and empathize with the character. The theatergoer will realize that the intellectual capacity of the character is of no consequence—provided that the character and the theatergoer share the innate capacity of man to reason. The theatergoer will observe that the kinds of emotional desires manifested by the character are of no consequence—provided that the character and the theatergoer share similar emotional drives. The theatergoer will agree that the educational level of the character is of no consequence—provided that the character and the theatergoer share a common interest. The theatergoer will sense that the prestige or position of the character in his milieu is of no consequence—provided that the character and the theatergoer share a common ambition. The theatergoer will learn that the economic level of the character is of no consequence—provided that the character and the theatergoer share a common need. In short, the theatergoer will discover that the playwright has created characters with whom he can identify and empathize when the playwright has established a commonality that binds the character with the theatergoer, one that permits the theatergoer to better understand himself through identification with the human strengths and weaknesses of the character.

4. Does the dialogue advance the plot, reflect the situation, reveal the personalities of the characters, and sustain the mood of the play?

As in life, dialogue in a play is a conversation between two or more persons. It is the literary device used by the playwright to tell the story and to reveal the thoughts and feelings of the characters. It is the means by which the playwright presents the past, states the present, and suggests the future. The lines spoken by the characters must be true to the characters who speak them, as well as true to the situation from which the lines flow. For example, in

The Silver Cord by Sidney Howard, a mother-in-law discusses the future plans of the young couple with her daughter-in-law whom she is meeting for the first time. Mrs. Phelps is a well-to-do widow whose oldest son, David, married Christina, a biologist, while they were both on vacation abroad. After much innocuous conversation about Europe, Mrs. Phelps continues:

MRS. PHELPS:
Tell me, Christina, you think David *is* well, don't you?

CHRISTINA:
Yes, perfectly.

MRS. PHELPS:
He didn't seem quite himself just now.

CHRISTINA:
Perhaps he was embarrassed.

MRS. PHELPS:
With me? His own mother?

CHRISTINA:
Wouldn't I have accounted for it?

MRS. PHELPS:
How silly of me not to remember that! Tell me what your plans are—if you have any plans, which I hope you haven't, because I've been making so many for you and such perfect ones.

CHRISTINA:
Well, as a matter of fact, we haven't many, but what we have are pretty definite.

MRS. PHELPS:
Really! Are they really? What are they?

CHRISTINA:
Well, we're going to live in New York, of course.

MRS. PHELPS:
Why "New York, of course"? It seems to me that you might choose a pleasanter place to live in than New York.

CHRISTINA:
No doubt of that, Mrs. Phelps. But it does seem a good place for David to work and . . .

MRS. PHELPS:
Oh, I can't agree with you!

CHRISTINA:
I shouldn't have thought there could be two ways about New York for Dave any more than for me.

MRS. PHELPS:
For you?

CHRISTINA:
It's where my appointment is.

MRS. PHELPS:
Your appointment?

CHRISTINA:
At the Rockefeller Institute.

MRS. PHELPS:
So that's what takes Dave and you to New York? Your geology.

CHRISTINA:
Partly. Only it isn't geology. It's biology.

MRS. PHELPS:
Of course. Geology is about rocks, isn't it?

CHRISTINA:
Largely.

MRS. PHELPS:
And biology?

CHRISTINA:
Well—about Life.

MRS. PHELPS:
(*getting it clear.*) So you're a student of Life, my dear. I do wish David had called you that instead of the other.*

---

* Reprinted with the permission of Charles Scribner's Sons from *The Silver Cord*, pages 24–27, by Sidney Howard. Copyright 1926, 1927 Sidney Howard; renewal copyright 1954, 1955 Leopoldine B. D. Howard.

The general tone of the dialogue is one of polite discussion replete with all the social amenities. Upon closer examination, however, one can sense the smoldering undercurrent of negative feelings harbored by Mrs. Phelps. The seeming addle-brained confusion of biology and geology on the part of Mrs. Phelps evokes laughter, but emphasizes the hostility and frustration experienced by the older woman in not being able to control the plans of the newlyweds. This seemingly polite encounter between the two women foreshadows the tug-of-war that will occur between the professional mother and the professional woman as each struggles for possession of a son and husband.

The theatergoer will discover that the nature of dialogue varies with play types and with playwrights. For example, in comedy, the dialogue is usually bright, witty, epigrammatic, stimulating, and sophisticated. In farce, the dialogue is peppered with puns, jokes, facetious comments, and humorous non sequiturs. In melodrama, the dialogue is laconic, cryptic, diabolical, veiled, and incisive. In tragedy, the dialogue is figurative, lyrical, rhetorical, euphonious, and emotional. The theatergoer will also discover that the personality of the playwright and his attitude toward life will color the conversation spoken by the characters. In listening to the dialogue of a play, the theatergoer will generally find, however, that the purpose of dialogue is the same in all plays, namely, to advance the plot and, at the same time, reveal character. With repeated playgoing experiences, the theatergoer will learn to discern whether or not the playwright has fulfilled the purposes of dialogue in writing his play.

5. Does the play fulfill the concept of a particular play form?

Although it is not the fashion to classify a play as a "tragedy, comedy, history, pastoral, pastoral-comical, historical-pastoral, tragical-historical, tragical-comical-historical-pastoral, scene individable, or poem unlimited," to recall the categories listed by Polonius in *Hamlet,* still, the theatergoer is frequently attracted to spending an evening in the theater because the play *is* a farce, a comedy, a melodrama, a tragedy, or some modern variation of one of those classic forms. Generally, the theater critic does not judge the merits of a play on the basis of the playwright adhering to the characteristics of a particular form, although the critic might very well compare the play with other works of the same type. And, while playwrights might wince at the criticism that makes a negative comparison, few playwrights will deny the producer's use of such terms as "hilarious farce," "scintillating comedy," "exciting melodrama," "moving tragedy," to attract the theatergoer to the box office. Rightfully, of course, the creative effort should not be stifled by playwriting rules and regulations; the playwright should be encouraged to write his play as he sees and senses it. With each attendance at the theater, however, the theatergoer will discover that each play does follow a particular play form, that the form remains constant while the content changes in accordance with the viewpoint expressed by the playwright, and that an understanding of the form will increase the theatergoer's enjoyment of the play and his appreciation of the skill of the playwright.

a. Tragedy

A tragedy is a serious play that generally ends with the defeat and destruction of the protagonist. The protagonist in classical tragedy is generally a man of noble birth, high ideals, and fierce determination. In the *Poetics,* Aristotle describes the protagonist in tragedy as one who is neither overly virtuous nor overly villainous, but one who is capable of both good and bad actions, one who is capable of human error. In Greek tragedy, the downfall of the protagonist is usually the result of an error in judgment caused by an overwhelming pride that brings the tragic hero into conflict with supernatural powers over which he has no control. In classical tragedy, the fate of the tragic hero is sealed, predetermined, inevitable; the protagonist cannot escape the fate that has been decreed by the gods. In Elizabethan tragedy, the downfall of the protagonist is usually the result of a flaw in character, one that brings the tragic hero into conflict with human forces. In Elizabethan tragedy, the fate of the tragic hero is inevitable, but of his own choice and making; he cannot, however, succeed beyond that which is in conflict with the human forces around him. In modern tragedy, the tragic protagonist is a common man of unusual and uncommon qualities that are in conflict with the forces of the society in which the protagonist lives. The fate of the protagonist in modern tragedy is also inevitable; he cannot win out over the economic, environmental, and social forces that dominate his life. The language of classical and Elizabethan tragedy is the language of poetry; the language of modern tragedy is highly selective prose. Tragedy is a fighter's show that has all the heroic aspects of the fighter who fights well, in good style, but in vain. In tragedy, the protagonist rises to and above the occasion to achieve his notion of the ideal. Ironically, the ideal of the protagonist, usually a just and worthy one, is not always the ideal of the world in which the protagonist lives. Tragedy should inspire the theatergoer because it reveals man at his finest moment, when his determination to overcome knows no obstacles or bounds. In viewing a tragedy, the theatergoer should sense pity for the protagonist in his plight, fear of the inevitable outcome, and admiration for the glorious manner in which the protagonist conducts himself. The theatergoer should leave the theater emotionally purged, relieved that the ordeal of the protagonist is finished, elated by the wonder and will of man to overcome.

b. Comedy

A comedy is a humorous play that generally ends happily for the hero. The comic protagonist is usually a recognized member of everyday society: a lawyer, a professor, a politician, a show-girl, a businessman, a librarian, an artist, a housewife, an executive, or any other representative of John Q. Public. The subject matter of comedy is life, or more specifically, any incongruity in character, society, or situation that interrupts the normal course of everyday existence. The conflict in comedy is one that arises out of a point of view that is in opposition to the well-being of the individual or the society in which he lives. The situation in comedy is true to life, one that stems from the action and character of the hero. Something within the nature of the comic hero causes him to take flight and to remove himself from the everyday world. For the moment, the comic hero, high above the life line, views the world through rose-colored glasses, peering at the world as he wants to see it. In time, he is brought to earth by shafts of laughter fashioned by the playwright. Additionally, the situation in comedy may be deliberately contrived to produce a humorous effect, or the situation may dramatize an idea that emphasizes the incongruity of a prevailing concept. The language of comedy resembles everyday conversation, although it is highly colored by the inclusion of barbed remarks, witty retorts, bright epigrams, sly innuendos, joyous banter, and stimulating repartee that produce laughter. In viewing a comedy, the theatergoer will discover that comedy, despite the humorous treatment by the playwright, is serious business because it is concerned with our faults, foibles, and follies. Comedy dangles the comic hero before us so that we may see the incongruity in our behavior in the matter of living, the absurdity in our pursuit of a course that is contrary to our well-being, the humor in our perversity to occasionally step out of line. In watching a comedy, the theatergoer will discern the importance of timing in delivering humorous dialogue, the absolute seriousness that accompanies the performance of comic action, the expertise in executing comic stage business, the objective comic spirit that permeates the writing and the performance of the script. In reading comedy, the theatergoer will learn that comedy wears many hats: *the comedy of character,* which stems from a belief or notion of the comic hero; *the comedy of manners,* which exposes the mores and morals of high society; *the romantic comedy,* which is concerned with affairs of the heart; and *the comedy of ideas,* which provokes thoughtful laughter and discussion of an idea proposed by the playwright. After viewing a comedy, the theatergoer should leave the theater intellectually amused and aware of what fools we mortals are in the business of living and enjoying life.

c. *Farce*

A farce is a delightful concoction of merriment devised by the playwright to beguile and entertain the theatergoer. The people in farce are comic types—not well-rounded characters—who can trace their ancestry to the stock characters invented and developed by Molière, Shakespeare, Jonson, the *commedià dell'arte* actors, Plautus, Terence, Menander, and Aristophanes. The subject matter of farce is the airy somethingness of daily living, the much ado about little facts of life, the tempest-in-a-teapot differences of opinion, the importance of trivia in decision making. The conflict in farce arises out of simple minds and simple wills to undo and outwit one another. If the conflict seems to be complicated, it is only because a cascade of incidents occurs as a result of a simple misunderstanding, a chance remark, a case of mistaken identity, an acceptance of the illogical as fact. The action in farce is fast and furious, a mad dash upstairs and a wild chase downhill. Comic physical violence spanks the posteriors of the combatants. Custard pies decorate the faces of the participants. Disguises allow for mixups and deceptions. The language is the vernacular, plus jokes, gags, wisecracks, clichés, and puns. All is caricature, overstatement, and exaggeration to regale the theatergoer with lavish laughter. The theatergoer will discover, however, that a basic truth underscores the exaggerated complications in farce, and that a credible situation prevents the theatergoer from throwing up his hands in total disbelief. Thus, it is possible in *The Doctor in Spite of Himself* by Molière that a woodcutter, threatened with his life and at odds with his wife, agrees to pass as an eminent physician, and that a father, frightened by his daughter's inability to speak, accepts the "physician" without question. It is conceivable, therefore, in *Three Men on a Horse* by John Cecil Holm, that a timid greeting-card writer, bored with the dullness of daily commuting, helps pass the time by selecting the winners of the daily double, and that a group of gamblers, down on their luck, kidnap the writer and thereby enrich their pockets by placing bets on his selections. It is possible in *Charley's Aunt* by Brandon Thomas that a young man, deeply in love but hampered by the conventions of his society, consents to pose as his roommate's aunt to be near the girl of his dreams. Only a grain of truth, a tightly structured plot, and rapid pace prevent the preposterous happenings in farce from disintegrating on stage. It is not until he leaves the theater that the theatergoer realizes the assault on his common sense, the degree to which he has suspended credibility, the success of the playwright in duping the viewer into accepting a possible but highly improbable situation. The theatergoer goes along with the playwright because he has been provided with an evening of mirthful entertainment, one that has tickled his ribs and his funnybone, thus provoking convulsive laughter.

d. Melodrama

A melodrama is a serious play that contains calculated and sensational effects to excite and thrill the theatergoer. The protagonist in melodrama is usually a man who is determined to pursue a course of action that may result in his death. He may be a man of impeccable virtue, resolute in his decision to triumph over an evil that threatens his life, or he may be a man of unscrupulous ethics, equally resolute in his decision to destroy the good that is an obstacle to his ambitions. In either case, the protagonist faces strong opposition to his course of action. The conflict in melodrama, therefore, understandably reflects that between good and evil, right and might, virtue and villainy. The action in melodrama is ever forward, quick moving, greatly accelerated as the climax nears. The threat of physical violence is ever present. Death looms prominently in the background. The sensational situations increase in number and in emotional intensity in order to titillate the senses of the theatergoer. The dialogue is sharp and pointed, laconic in statement, menacing in tone, secretive in purpose, accusative in choice of word. Expletives are plentiful; ominous warnings are frequent. A combination of the Greek words "melo," meaning song and dance, and "drama," melodrama was introduced to theatergoers at the end of the eighteenth century. Originally conceived as a play form that utilized music freely to heighten the dramatic action on stage, melodrama developed as a play that placed emphasis on sensational incidents with exaggerated appeals to sentiment rather than as a play with emphasis on character. Popularized by the plays of René Guilbert de Pixerécourt, August von Kotzebue, and Dion Boucicault, melodrama became the rage of the nineteenth century. Although melodrama on television and in the motion picture still employs music to heighten dramatic effect, melodrama on stage omits the use of music, but retains the exaggerated appeals and the sensational incidents to hold the attention of the audience. Good, however, still triumphs over evil whether the play is a mystery such as *The Mousetrap* by Agatha Christie, a court trial such as *The Caine Mutiny Court Martial* by Herman Wouk, a domestic drama with political overtones such as *Watch on the Rhine* by Lillian Hellman, or a pseudo-biographical drama such as *The Great White Hope* by Howard Sackler.

e. Musical Comedy

The American musical comedy, an integration of spoken dialogue with song, music, and dance, represents the perfection of a form of entertainment that has its roots in (1) the use of spectacle in the production of Aristophanic comedy, (2) the musical divertissements mounted in the courts of the Tudor and Bourbon kings, (3) the development of the ballad-opera in the English theater, (4) the appeal of the minstrel show, the revue, and vaudeville, and (5) the availability of exceptional entertainers whose special talents were needed to fill the demands of this unique form of entertainment. The widespread popularity of the American musical is attested to in the world-wide productions of such current favorites as *Fiddler on the Roof, Man of La Mancha,* and *Hair.* The appeal of the musical in the United States is indicated by the long runs of such musicals as *Oklahoma!, My Fair Lady, The Sound of Music, Hello Dolly!,* and *The Fantasticks;* the repeated revivals of such musicals as *Finian's Rainbow, Pal Joey,* and *West Side Story;* and the establishment of the Musical Theater of Lincoln Center, New York City, which each summer revives one or two popular musicals of the past. The cheerful optimism of the musical, the tuneful songs and music, the lavish production numbers, and the exceptional talent of the performers assures the theatergoer of escapist entertainment, and undoubtedly accounts for the attraction of so many eager and enthusiastic theatergoers to the box office.

The hero in musical comedy is an ordinary man from an ordinary walk of life; he is an actor in *Showboat* by Oscar Hammerstein II, and Jerome Kern; a playboy in *Girl Crazy* by Guy Bolton, John McGowan, and Ira and George Gershwin; a Presidential candidate in *Of Thee I Sing* and a President in *Let Them Eat Cake,* both by George S. Kaufman, Morrie Ryskind, and Ira and George Gershwin; a public enemy in *Anything Goes* by Guy Bolton, P. G. Wodehouse, Howard Lindsay, Russel Crouse, and Cole Porter; vaudeville performer in *Babes in Arms* by Richard Rodgers and Lorenz Hart; a dumb blonde and her friend in *Gentlemen Prefer Blondes* by Anita Loos, Joseph Fields, Leo Robin, and Jule Styne;

a supervisor and a factory worker in *The Pajama Game* by George Abbott, Richard Bissell, Richard Adler, and Jerry Ross; a gambler and a Salvation Army lass in *Guys and Dolls* by Jo Swerling, Abe Burrows, and Frank Loesser; a socialite in *Call Me Madam* by Joseph and Dorothy Fields and Irving Berlin; adolescents and parents in *Bye Bye Birdie* by Michael Stewart, Lee Adams, and Charles Strouse; and a patriot in *1776* by Peter Stone and Sherman Edwards. The hero in musical comedy is a stock character, predictable in his behavior, uncomplicated in thought and feeling, related to the hero we find in farce.

Occasionally, however, a well-rounded musical comedy hero gives an extra dimension in human emotions and behavior to this otherwise light-hearted form of popular entertainment. The hoofer and the society matron in *Pal Joey* by John O'Hara, Richard Rodgers, and Lorenz Hart; the fashion editor in *Lady in the Dark* by Moss Hart, Ira Gershwin, and Kurt Weill; the professor and the flower girl in *My Fair Lady* by Alan Jay Lerner and Frederick Loewe; the daughter and the mother in *Gypsy* by Arthur Laurents, Stephen Sondheim, and Jule Styne; the barker in *Carousel* by Oscar Hammerstein II, and Richard Rodgers; the farmer and his wife in *The Most Happy Fella* by Frank Loesser; the mayor in *Fiorello* by Jerome Weidman, George Abbott, Jerry Bock and Sheldon Harnick; the philosopher in *Man of La Mancha* by Dale Wasserman, Joe Darion, and Mitch Leigh; the younger generation in *Hair* by Gerome Ragni, James Rado, and Galt MacDermot; and the accountant and the elevator girl in *Promises, Promises* by Neil Simon and Burt Bacharach, offer examples of the musical comedy hero and heroine who are complex human beings.

The book, or the libretto, is the story of a musical comedy. Although the plot is as complicated as the plot in farce, the story is usually easy to follow. Often it involves nothing more than a series of humorous escapades that provide opportunities for song and dance. In the end, always a happy one, the misunderstandings, the mishaps, the inconveniences are explained, resolved, and forgiven because of the good character and good intentions of the musical comedy hero. The rosy world depicted in musical comedy seldom dissolves into a world of harsh reality. Consequently, the conflict in a musical comedy almost always arises out of a contrived situation that manages to hold the interest of the theatergoer because of the songs and dances that, on the one hand, entertain the theatergoer, and, on the other, prevent the conflict from being resolved until the propitious moment. The dramatic action consists of a number of related scenes that invariably end in a musical number that permits the performer to display his talents. The physical action is apt to be exuberant, exhilarating, and rambunctious because of the singing and dancing talents of the chorus and the stars, and because of the comic talents of the comedians. The language of musical comedy is prose and song. The spoken dialogue includes expository material that establishes and reveals character, explains and advances the action, provides comic routines for the comedians. Music underscores the spoken dialogue, thus providing the spoken word with an emotional connotation that it does not have without the reinforcement of music. Additionally, music establishes and reiterates the theme, constantly building and emphasizing the mood. Similarly, song provides an outlet and a display of emotions, a means of developing and revealing character, a way of repeating the theme, a vehicle for the talents of the performer. Dance enlivens the action, dramatizing the theme, plot, and character, through movement devised by the choreographer.

Lavish and elegant costumes appeal to the eye of the theatergoer and spectacular and wondrous scenic effects arouse and stimulate his emotions. Rapid and efficiently managed set changes give the illusion of being transported from one locale to another with no difficulty. Small wonder, then, that the book is frequently of little consequence to the theatergoer. In musical comedy, it is personality, talent, song, dance, music, costume, set, and special effects that excite and capture the interest and emotions.

f. Absurdist Drama: A Variation on a Play Form

"Absurdist drama," if it is not too absurd to assign such a category to the plays written by Samuel Beckett, Eugene Ionesco, Jean Genêt, Arthur Adamov, Fernando Arrabal, Günter Grass, N. F. Simpson, Harold Pinter, and Edward Albee, is drama in which the theatergoer is confronted with the notion that life is without meaning and purpose, and that life will only have meaning and purpose when man faces up to the meaninglessness of his existence and his institutions. Inasmuch as the tragic consequences of the absurdity of the human condition are realized through humorous and sensational devices that provoke chills and laughter at the meaninglessness of man and his institutions, "absurdist drama" represents a variation of a play form. It is, by its philosophical content, its treatment, and its resolution, tragic comedy, tragic farce, tragic melodrama, but never, except for its viewpoint, pure tragedy. The protagonist in "absurdist drama" is not as quickly recognized nor as easily identified as he is in tragedy, comedy, melodrama, or farce because the focus of attention is on mankind, an aspect of mankind, or a representative of mankind, rather than on an individual. The characters seem to be symbols, personifications of social institutions, representatives of the accepted verities, not complex human beings. The action in "absurdist drama" is static. Nothing happens, or does it? The play ends as it begins, or did it ever begin? The language of "absurdist drama" is prose, words as they are spoken in real life with and without meaning, words as they are arranged and spoken by music-hall comedians, words as they appear on the toilet wall. Although the literary and theatrical devices are many and vary from playwright to playwright, the philosophy remains the same: man leads a meaningless existence because his life and his world are dominated and controlled by meaningless institutions that he has created. Many theatergoers find the Theater of the Absurd depressing and pessimistic. Comparatively few disagree that its drama provides an exciting and stimulating evening in the theater.

The theatergoer today has ample opportunity to view the plays of past and present-day playwrights. Although New York City is the acknowledged center of the professional theater in the United States—some consider it to be the trend- and style-setter for theatrical production throughout the world—other major American cities are beginning to establish and support professional acting companies that offer a balanced program of plays. For example, the Minnesota Theater Company, a professional company organized by Sir Tyrone Guthrie, has offered the residents of Minneapolis and St. Paul an opportunity to enjoy the works of Shakespeare,

Molière, Anton Chekhov, George Bernard Shaw, Bertolt Brecht, Thornton Wilder, Tennessee Williams, and Arthur Miller. The Arena Stage, Washington, D.C., has premiered *The Great White Hope* by Howard Sackler and *Indians* by Arthur Kopit, among others. The Alley Theater, Houston, Texas; American Conservatory Theater, San Francisco, California; Seattle Repertory Theater, Seattle, Washington; Studio Arena Theater, Buffalo, New York; Long Wharf Theater, New Haven, Connecticut; Virginia Museum Theater, Richmond, Virginia; Center Stage, Baltimore, Maryland; and Theater Atlanta, Atlanta, Georgia, are other examples of resident professional companies that present plays, old and new, to local theatergoers. Additionally, theatergoers can always take advantage of theater fare produced by nearby colleges and universities. Community theater organizations make it possible, too, for theatergoers living in areas where there is no professional theater to enjoy the semi-professional's production of many current plays. An extensive summer theater program throughout the nation offers the traveling theatergoer a wide variety of established masterpieces and recent commercial successses. The American tourist in Canada, for example, can see superb theater entertainment at Stratford, Ontario; and many of the "straw hat" theaters in the East house tryouts prior to the New York opening. In short, there is no dearth of theatrical fare across the nation; the theatergoer has ample opportunity to discover the universality and the relevancy of both the classic and contemporary play. Somewhere each night, actors gather to perform a play. Somewhere each night, an audience gathers to watch the actor and listen to the words of the playwright. The theater is both a timeless and classless art, one that is available to the theatergoer wherever he may be.

C. THEATER SPOTLIGHTS

I. *Theater Terminology:* Define the following:

afterpiece	fantasy	sides
entr'acte	folk play	promptbook
chronicle play	ground cloth	traveler
expressionism	Noh play	unities

II. *Theater Who's Who:* Identify the following:

Jean Anouilh	Rachel Crothers	Luigi Pirandello
S. N. Behrman	George S. Kaufman	Robert Sherwood
George M. Cohan	Clifford Odets	
Noel Coward	Sean O'Casey	

III. *Theater Investigation:* Discuss the following:

1. For many decades, Parisian theatergoers crowded the "Grand Guignol." What was it? What purpose did it serve? Why did it ultimately fail?
2. Bertolt Brecht was a prominent twentieth-century German playwright whose plays enjoy frequent revival. What is the Brecht style of playwriting? What production style evolved as a result of the mounting of his plays?
3. Defend or refute the assertion that nineteenth-century melodrama paved the way for the rise and popularity of the motion picture.
4. What happened to the "comedy of manners," or for that matter, the "tragedy of the common man"?
5. Our times seem right for melodrama and farce, but not for comedy and tragedy. Why do you agree or disagree with this point of view?
6. Cite specific examples to support the observation that the plays of the nineteen sixties, like those of the nineteen thirties, are "dramas of protest."

IV. *Theater Projects:* Prepare the following:

1. Dramatize a current event in the manner of *Ethiopia, Triple A Plowed Under, 1935, Power,* and *One Third of a Nation,* plays produced by the Federal Theater.
2. Dramatize a short story you believe would make a good play.
3. Select a human-interest story from a newspaper that you believe contains the elements of a play and do as follows:
   a. state the theme in one sentence
   b. describe the setting
   c. briefly describe each of the characters

d. outline the plot
e. write the play

V. ***Theater Bibliography:*** Read the following:

Esslin, Martin. *The Theatre of the Absurd.* New York: Anchor Books, Doubleday, 1961.

Gassner, John. *Directions in Modern Theatre and Drama.* New York: Holt, Rinehart and Winston, Inc., 1956.

Golden, Joseph. *The Death of Tinker Bell.* Syracuse, N.Y.: Syracuse University Press, 1966.

Himelstein, Morgan Y. *Drama Was a Weapon.* New Brunswick, N.J.: Rutgers University Press, 1963.

Kerr, Walter. *How Not to Write a Play.* New York: Simon & Schuster, 1955.

Styan, J. L. *The Dramatic Experience.* London: Cambridge University Press, 1965.

V

Theater Off Stage: Play Production

BOTTOM:
Are we all met?

QUINCE:
Pat, pat; and here's a marvellous convenient place for our rehearsal. This green plot shall be our stage, this hawthorn brake our tiring-house; and we will do it in action as we will do it before the Duke.

SHAKESPEARE, *A Midsummer Night's Dream,* Act III, scene 1.

A. SETTING THE SCENE: THE PROFESSIONALS OFF STAGE

The press agent focuses our attention on the personality and the talent of the actor and on the literary skill of the playwright, but the finished product—the professionally mounted and performed play—represents the creative imagination and the combined efforts of many talents. The producer, for example, draws upon his creative sense to guide him in selecting a desirable script. His visual concept of the play becomes a reality through the efforts of the skilled personnel whom he employs to stage and design the production. His business acumen comes to the fore in securing money to finance the production and in promoting audience response at the box office. The director analyzes and stages the script, breathing life and meaning into the theme through his interpretation of the playwright's work. He endows the characters with human strengths and weaknesses through his grasp and knowledge of human nature. He vitalizes the printed words through the movement and gestures of the actor. He extracts a performance from the actors through an understanding of the craft of the actor. The designers reinforce the playwright's words and the director's interpretation with visual representations. The set designer provides an environment for the action. The costume designer clothes the actor in raiment that reflects time and reveals character. The lighting designer illuminates the setting and reinforces the mood developed by the director. The theater, unlike other arts, is a collaborative art that employs the combined talents of the producer, the playwright, the director, the actor, and the designers to catch the conscience of the audience. Each practitioner contributes his special talent to activate the script without compromising his individuality and without obscuring or infringing upon the creativity of his fellow artist.

1. The Producer

a. The Producer in the Greek Theater

The responsibilities of the producer in the theater today, and the organization of his staff of business executives and artists, stem from theater practices that have evolved from the time that Pisistratus organized the City Dionysia Festival in 534 B.C. On that occasion, Athens functioned as the producer, fulfilling its responsibilities by inviting Thespis and his company to perform for the Athenian citizenry. In subsequent times, especially during the reign of Pericles, an organizational structure developed that clearly defined both the role and the responsibilities of the city-state, the producer, and the playwright in producing the play. The city-state provided the theatergoing occasion by declaring a religious festival in honor of the god Dionysus. The Archon, or chief magistrate of the city-state, and his ten assistants selected the plays from those submitted by the competing playwrights. The Archon then assigned to each playwright a chorus and a *choregus.* The *choregus* was a wealthy citizen who assumed the cost of training and costuming the chorus, the cost of hiring the musicians and supernumerary actors, and the cost of production equipment. The *choregus* accepted the appointment with honor and pride, because he viewed the assignment as a matter of civic and religious duty. It is quite probable that the costs were great and that the *choregus* spent a large amount of money in producing the play when one recalls that three actors, fifteen chorus members, and several musicians comprised the company performing one tragedy. The playwright generally directed his play and performed the role of the protagonist. After Sophocles set the precedent of assigning an actor to the lead role, the city-state assumed the costs of paying the three lead actors. On the opening day of the festival, Athenians were treated to the *proagon,* a kind of preview of what could be expected during the days of the festival. The playwrights, the actors, the *choregi,* the chorus, and the musicians paraded through the city. On the last day of the festival, prizes were awarded and the plays were discussed. Punishment was meted out to those who had in any manner disturbed the festival proceedings. The Didascalia, a theatrical record of the festival, listed the name of the Archon and that of each playwright. The chart on page 266 represents the organization of the Greek theater.

b. The Producer in the Roman Theater

Roman government officials began to take a more tolerant view of the theater with the development of dramatic literature by such playwrights as Livius Andronicus, Lucius Accius, Plautus, and Terence, although the building of permanent theaters was forbidden by law and the acting profession was deemed to be despicable. Roman officials were also quick to note the enthusiastic response of the populace to the new form of entertainment and to utilize the theater as another means of distracting the attention of the public from the political events of the day and the need for social and economic reforms. Although gladiatorial contests, chariot races, simulated sea battles, and animal fights continued to enthrall and excite Roman spectators—audience members did not hesitate to

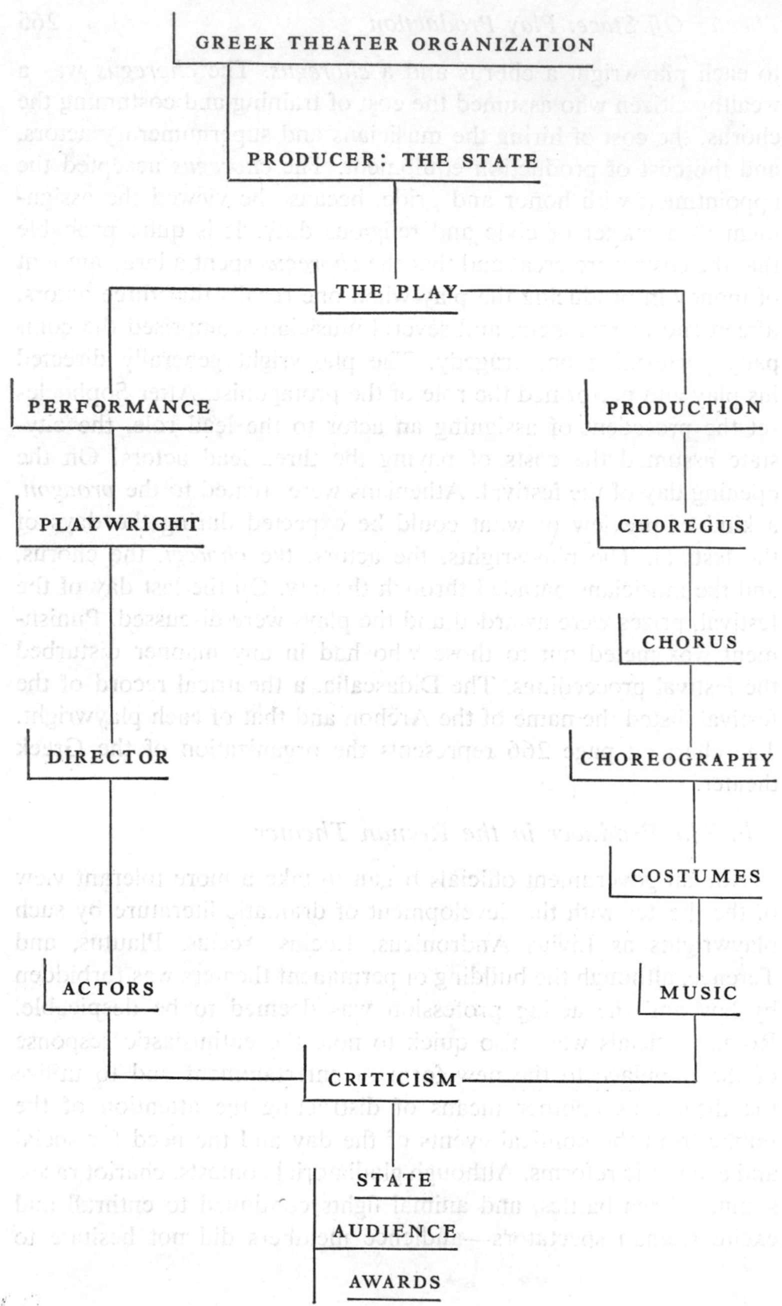

GREEK THEATER ORGANIZATION
PRODUCER: THE STATE
THE PLAY
PERFORMANCE
PRODUCTION
PLAYWRIGHT
CHOREGUS
CHORUS
DIRECTOR
CHOREOGRAPHY
COSTUMES
ACTORS
MUSIC
CRITICISM
STATE
AUDIENCE
AWARDS

leave during a performance of a play to hurry to a sports competition that was in progress nearby—the number of days allotted to dramatic presentations increased from five to eleven at the end of the third century B.C. and to forty or more during the Augustan era. Of the 175 declared holidays during the fourth century A.D., however, 100 days were set aside for dramatic presentations. Appropriations from public funds were made by the Senate for production of the plays and the spectator was admitted free of charge upon presentation of a ticket that entitled him to a reserved seat. The matter of producing the play was placed in the hands of a government official who, in turn, contracted a manager of a troupe of actors, generally captives owned by the manager, to "deliver" a show for a specified sum of money. It is likely, therefore, that the manager selected the script, something guaranteed to please the audience, and which the manager probably purchased outright from the playwright, who may or may not have been a member of the company. Although a claque of enthusiasts were hired to applaud and laugh at the right moment, or to boo and play down the effectiveness of a production offered by a rival manager, the play did not always succeed and the actors were punished by the manager. Occasionally, a wealthy citizen financed the costs of a production or sponsored a dramatic presentation to win political favor with the populace, or to display his wealth to the community. Ostensibly a part of a festival honoring a god, the plays had no religious significance, but represented holiday entertainment for the mob. However, if, at the conclusion of the festival, government officials noted any mishap that might desecrate the spirit of the festival, then the game competitions, the spectacles, and the plays were performed once again.

Through the practice of appropriating public funds, Greek and Roman civilizations set the precedent for governmental participation in, and subsidization of, the theater. Through the designation of officials and the assignment of responsibilities, the Greek and Roman theater created the producer. Through the need to limit governmental expenditures for the festival and through the need to involve members of the upper class in the theatrical venture, the wealthy Greek and Roman citizen was encouraged to become either a direct participant in the production, or a patron who contributed to the financial costs of the presentation. Finally, through the declaration of festivals, the Greeks and Romans established the theatergoing experience we emulate today.

c. The Producer in the Medieval Theater

The Church began to function as a producer when it elected to dramatize the Easter Mass to make the Resurrection a more meaningful religious experience for the simple villagers who did not comprehend Latin, the language of the Church. The resulting emotional effect upon the congregation encouraged the Church to increase its use of theatrical techniques as a means of teaching the truth and glory of the Christian religion. Priests, nuns, and choirboys were pressed into performing the roles of Biblical characters, although the Church abhorred and condemned the acting profession. The presentations were staged and supervised by members of the clergy. A miniature by Jean Fouquet depicting the martyrdom of St. Apollonia, the patron saint for those suffering from toothache, reveals a priest functioning as prompter, director, and stage manager. Staff in one hand and promptbook in the other, the priest stands in the midst of the action, presumably giving directions and cues to the actors! Costumes were furnished by the clergy and the cathedral became a theater for the production and presentation of liturgical drama, a body of dramatic literature developed by priests and nuns from their dramatizations of religious ritual and scripture. Eventually, however, the Church was confronted with a problem that eclipsed the original intent to indoctrinate the people with religious dogma. The involvement of the laity in acting and staging the scripts resulted in the interjection of everyday happenings and the use of the vernacular into the service. In addition, the increased introduction of theatrical techniques tended to obscure and obliterate the religious significance of the performance. The service gradually became a form of entertainment for the congregation. Too, the auditorium of the church could not accommodate the large crowds that were now drawn to attend the worship. The Church resolved this ironic twist by shifting the presentations from within the church to the steps outside the church and by finally ordering its clerics to withdraw from active participation in the production and presentation of religious drama.

The town council and the guilds assumed the obligations of the producer when the Church withdrew as sponsor of liturgical drama. The authority of the town council approximated that which had been exercised by high government officials in the Greek and Roman theaters. The council selected and arranged the Biblical episodes to form a unified whole, or a cycle of playlets that dramatized a Biblical theme. Moreover, the town council allocated money for expenditures, planned the route of the procession, designated the placement of stations for viewing and performance, publicized the event, and charged each guild with the burden of mounting the episode which it had been assigned by the council. In effect, the town council operated in the manner of the modern producer who conceives the overall production, but who charges his artistic and technical personnel with the responsibility for preparing the script for presentation to an audience. Each guild then functioned as an independent production organization. Actors were drawn from the guild membership and were rehearsed by a guild member. Occasionally, professional actors were hired to enhance the performance of the episode. Actors were signed to an iron clad contract that assured punctuality at rehearsals and exemplary behavior during the performance. Guild members constructed the pageant wagon on which the episode was staged, invented machinery for special effects, devised and secured the props, and made the costumes. Frequently, the Church came to the aid of the guild and provided appropriate costumes for special Biblical characters. Accurate records of expenditures were maintained by guild officials and guild members were taxed to meet the cost of production.

When one recalls that the Chester cycle, for example, consisted of twenty-five playlets, that each playlet was produced by a different guild, that three days were required to perform the complete cycle, and that the event involved an entire community and its resources, one can begin to comprehend the necessity for the division of responsibilities between the town council and the guilds. One can also appreciate the need for cooperation from both groups. Someone had to plan the event and coordinate the efforts of the participants; that became the responsibility of the council. Someone else had to execute the plan and fulfill the purpose of the event, a celebration of Corpus Christi day; that became the responsibility of the guilds. Obviously, the complexity of the plan demanded cooperation and coordination if the production was to serve the religious needs of the community. The pooling of administrative ability and creative talent by the council and the guilds is an excellent example of the collaborative effort that must exist between the producer and his staff.

Religious organizations also functioned as producers of religious drama during the medieval period. A notable example is the *Confrèrie de la Passion.* Consisting of amateur actors who were dedicated to the perpetuation of religious drama in Paris, the *Confrèrie* was organized in 1402. Officially recognized by Charles VI, the *Confrèrie* maintained a permanent theater in the Hôpital de la Trinité. In 1518, the organization was granted a monopoly on all theatrical production in Paris. It was forbidden to continue the production of religious drama in 1548; thereafter, the *Confrèrie* functioned primarily as a landlord and a dictator of theatrical fare for Parisians. The organization either refused to rent the premises of the Hôtel de Bourgogne, which it had built in 1548, or it discriminated in its choice of lessees. The influence exerted by the *Confrèrie* in the matter of public taste was broken when Cardinal Richelieu encouraged Montdory to found the Théâtre du Marais. However, the *Confrèrie* retained its formidable hold on the French professional theater until 1675, when Louis XIV rescinded the monopoly it had enjoyed for over a hundred years.

d. The Producer in the Elizabethan and Restoration Theaters

With the return of the professional actor at the opening of the sixteenth century, and with the growing interest in the theater during the same period, the role of the producer was assumed by the professional acting company. The professional Elizabethan acting company, such as the Lord Chamberlain's Men or the Lord Admiral's Men, was a compact organization, self-sufficient and capable of fulfilling all the duties of the producer. Led by men whose keen business instincts were complemented by the artistic talents of their progeny or in-laws—Richard Burbage, England's first great actor, was the son of James Burbage, and Edward Alleyn was the son-in-law of Philip Henslowe—the professional acting company either leased or owned its own theater or theaters. At one point in its career, the Lord Chamberlain's Men operated The Curtain and The Globe, while the Lord Admiral's Men controlled and operated The Rose, The Swan, The Fortune, and The Hope. Generally, the housekeeper, the official company title for the owner–manager, made the initial financial investment required to lease or build a theater. The actor and the playwright accepted a share in the company as monetary compensation for their services and talents. Payment was made after operating expenses had been deducted. The actors usually wore contemporary dress, whether or not it was appropriate for the scene; however, elaborate costumes were designed and manufactured for atypical or foreign characters. The cost of the material as well as the cost of labor was deemed an operational expense and deducted before the net profits were computed. Similarly, the cost of props and special stage machinery was charged against gross profits. The playwright wrote for specific members of the company and he was paid a flat sum for his creative efforts. He received an additional proportionate amount of the profits if he performed a part. Master actors were expected to train and tutor apprenticed actors. The play was generally staged by the playwright and the prompter diligently made written notes in the script of all stage business. A copyist prepared the individual parts for the actors. The housekeeper was responsible for sending the manuscript to the Master of Revels for official approval. The play was put into rehearsal when notification was received that the play had been accepted without alteration and a license had been granted. A careful delegation of responsibilities that required the cooperation of the housekeeper, the actor, and the playwright made it possible for the professional Elizabethan acting company to perform the functions of the producer.

The composition of the two Restoration professional acting companies, the Duke of York's Men and the King's Men, were similar to that of the two Elizabethan acting companies. The housekeeper of each of the Restoration acting companies, however, was a more powerful and dominant figure in matters involving artistic and financial policy. This increase in power and status probably stemmed from the fact that each housekeeper had been instrumental in obtaining the immediate reopening of theaters when Charles II ascended the throne in 1660. Capitalizing on the King's enthusiasm for the theater and on his felt need to find employment for the destitute actors who had suffered the wrath of the Puritans during the Commonwealth, Sir William D'Avenant and Thomas Killigrew succeeded in persuading Charles II to grant each a theater patent. This assured them control over theater production in London. Empowered to build new theaters, D'Avenant and Killigrew effected a change in theater architecture by approving plans for indoor theaters that featured a deep apron, a raked stage, and a proscenium frame that included two doors on each side of the stage. The new theaters, the Drury Lane and the Dorset Garden, resembled those being built on the Continent. An avid interest in opera led Sir William D'Avenant to use music in his productions, including the plays of Shakespeare. Earler, Sir William had been responsible for the production of the first English opera, *The Siege of Rhodes*. Although the permanent actors were granted a share in the company as a means of determining their portion of the company's profits, many actors were hired for a specific period for which they were paid a stipulated wage. Eventually, the actor was allotted at least one benefit performance during the course of a year. Actresses, a new addition to the English stage, were paid a fixed salary. The housekeeper in the company was permitted to retain several shares and he could, if he so desired, sell them to non-theatrical investors called "Adventurers," so named because of their fortuitous interest in the theater. The fixed salary of the playwright was augmented by a benefit performance every third night, particularly if his play proved to be successful at the box office. When the run of the play ended, the play became the property of the company and the playwright could not expect any additional remuneration from the housekeeper. In time, the housekeeper lost control of his company because his sale of shares to non-theatrical persons resulted in new policies that antagonized the actor. In response, the actor broke away from the company and formed his own acting group.

e. The Producer in the Seventeenth-Century French Theater

In France, the seventeenth-century professional acting company also functioned as a producing organization. Leadership, however, rested in the hands of a popular and ambitious actor whose talents attracted the attention of theater-oriented and cooperative government officials. For example, Cardinal Richelieu encouraged Montdory and his troupe to open the Théâtre du Marais in competition with the troupe of actors at the Hôtel de Bourgogne; King Louis XIV commanded Molière to establish his troupe in Paris, offering the talented actor and playwright the use of the Petit-Bourbon. All actors and actresses in the company were designated shareholders and each held a full or part share in the night's profits according to his importance in the company and his maturity as an actor. The actor was paid immediately after each performance, a treasurer and auditor attesting to the accuracy of the expenses that had been incurred. New members of the troupe were trained by the more experienced actors. The neophytes were expected to continue the character interpretation and the traditional stage business that had been developed by the senior actor. An "orator," or company manager, publicized the play and at the conclusion of a performance he announced the next attraction. Although the playwright was permitted at times to share in the profits during the run of the play, he generally sold his play outright for a stipulated fee after the company had gathered to hear a reading and to determine the merits of the play. Since the actors were usually hired to play certain roles or types, the parts were frequently assigned to those players associated with such parts. Consequently, once the play was approved by the company, it was a foregone conclusion that so-and-so would essay such-and-such a role. The initial staging was undertaken by the playwright; subsequent staging depended on the memory of the actors and on the notations that had been made by the stage manager or prompter. Production details were relatively simple and inexpensive, except for the elaborate productions staged at the Court of Louis XIV. Moreover, the small stages in both the Hôtel de Bourgogne and the Théâtre du Marais, a converted tennis court, were not conducive to production on a grand scale. Nor did the presence of numerous spectators on stage permit the use of complicated sets and lavish production. Costumes were furnished by the actor rather than by the company, because attire was considered part of the actor's equipment.

Despite the fact that the seventeenth-century professional acting company in France operated as a producing organization, it was not in complete control, nor was it free to develop out of trial and error. Rather, it was another unit of French society, manipulated by high-ranking government officials as one approach toward solving the problem of national unity. Hovering in the background was His Majesty Louis XIV, *Roi Soleil,* benefactor and "super-producer." With a purpose reminiscent of that which had motivated Pisistratus to inaugurate the Great Dionysia Festival, and with the tight rein reminiscent of that which had been exercised by the Chief Archon and his assistants in the Greek theater, Louis XIV influenced the activities of the French professional acting company because he wished to promote the development of the French professional theater, to improve the quality of French dramatic literature, and to provide a source of entertainment for the Court. Exercising his royal prerogative, Louis XIV permitted the actors to use his theaters in the Palais Royal and in the Petit-Bourbon. He gave monetary assistance to the impoverished acting companies and he pensioned actors and actresses. In the interest of raising the quality and standards of French dramatic literature, he generally sustained the churlish criticisms of the French Academy, which was relentlessly determined to force playwrights to adhere to its interpretation of the rules of classical playwriting. For example, the King did support Molière in his quarrel with the Church over *Tartuffe,* but Louis did little about modifying the requirement set by the French Academy as a condition for Molière to qualify as a member—the Academy demanded that the playwright renounce his profession as an actor in return for membership. The King commisioned Corneille, Racine, and Molière to write for the Court, and His Majesty frequently performed in royal entertainments. He advanced the cause of scene design and play production in the French theater when he permitted Cardinal Mazarin to hire Giacomo Torelli and Gaspare Vigarani, two noted Italian designers of the time. In 1673, Louis XIV closed the Théâtre du Marais, ordering its actors to join Mme. Molière and her troupe at the Théâtre du Guenegaud, which she had purchased after the death of Molière. Seven years later, the King united the Théâtre du Guenegaud and the Hôtel de Bourgogne companies. He charged the new acting company, the Comédie-Française, with the responsibility for regularly reviving the works of the leading playwrights of France. He agreed to provide the new company, often called La Maison de Molière, with an annual subsidy of 12,000 livres. Louis XIV was not only the grand monarch, but the grand producer, a model for lesser monarchs to emulate.

f. The Actor–Manager as Producer

With the recognition of the theater as a cultural and social force in the community, the responsibilities of the producer were assumed by the actor–manager. In 1682, a politically troubled and beset Charles II effected an amalgamation between the Duke's Men and the King's Men when the latter company failed as a result of mismanagement. Moreover, neither company could sustain the loss of profits that resulted from the fierce competition for a dwindling audience of post-Restoration playgoers, or from the failure to discover the key to the entertainment needs of a changing society. The United Company, the result of the amalgamation, survived until 1695. At that time, Thomas Betterton rebelled against the management of Christopher Rich, a non-theater person, and obtained permission from King William to organize a second company. The new company, under the management of Betterton, opened with William Congreve's *Love for Love,* Betterton playing the lead role. During the ensuing ten years, a transitional period that witnessed the shift from the brittle and glittering comedies of the Restoration to the popularity of sentimental comedy, Betterton's presentation of legitimate drama successfully met the competition offered by Rich's presentation of ballets, musicals, and novelty acts imported from the Continent. In 1710, actors Colley Cibber, Robert Wilks, and Thomas Doggett formed a partnership to operate the Drury Lane. Cibber selected the plays, and Doggett kept the records of expenditures. Wilks, and later Barton Booth who replaced Doggett in the partnership, headed the acting company. In 1714, actor John Rich, son of the now deceased Christopher Rich, opened a new playhouse in Lincoln's Inn Fields. To meet the competition of the company at the Drury Lane, Rich offered the theatergoer pantomime, a dumb-show divertissement that employed elaborate effects to capture the imagination of the audience. However, it was not until David Garrick acquired a half-ownership of the Drury Lane patent in 1747 that the actor blossomed as producer in the English professional theater.

Virtually all the major actors in the eighteenth and nineteenth centuries became actor–managers, owners of theaters, and artistic directors who instituted many theatrical reforms. In Germany, Konrad Ekhof, Friedrich Schröder, and Carolina Neuber combined their acting assignments with managerial duties, and each contributed to the growth and development of the German eighteenth-century theater. In France, the great Talma expressed his republican sympathies by leaving the Comédie-Française and founding Le Théâtre Français de la Rue de Richelieu where he introduced many changes. Later, the great French tragedian headed the Comédie-Française when it was reorganized by Napoleon. In the nineteenth century, Benoit Constant Coquelin and Sarah Bernhardt withdrew from the Comédie to pursue careers as actor–managers and, on occasion, the two French stars would join forces and perform together. Lucien Germain Guitry, another very successful French actor of the time, became the manager of the Théâtre de la Renaissance, a theater operated by the "Divine Sarah." In the United States, Louisa Lane Drew (maternal grandmother of the Barrymores), John Lester Wallack, and Lawrence Barrett were highly regarded as actor–managers during the nineteenth century. The mercurial and talented Dion Boucicault functioned as actor, director, manager, and producer, introducing realism to American audiences as well as the policy of organizing road companies of established successful plays performed on Broadway. Boucicault was also instrumental in the enactment of the first copyright law in the United States designed to protect writers. The Syndicate, an association of American theater magnates, met its match in Minnie Maddern Fiske, an outstanding American actress–manager whose career extended into the twentieth century. In Russia, Stanislavski and Nemirovich-Danchenko formed the Moscow Art Theater.

In England, numerous actors and actresses followed the example of David Garrick and became actor–managers. John Philip Kemble, brother of Mrs. Sarah Siddons, managed both the Drury Lane and Covent Garden during his career in the theater. A polished and dignified performer whose classical style lost favor when the romantic manner of Edmund Kean captured the imagination of London theatergoers, Kemble introduced many innovative costume and scenic reforms in his productions of the plays of Shakespeare. Kemble encouraged William Capon, his scene painter, to design sets that were historically accurate, thus initiating a trend that culminated in the elaborate spectacles that characterized the productions offered by Henry Irving and Beerbohm Tree at the end of the century. Kemble's career as a manager was troubled by the infamous "O-P" riots that ensued when Kemble sought to raise the admission prices to meet the mounting production costs at the new Covent Garden theater. On sixty performance nights, theatergoers gathered in front of, and within, the vast theater to interrupt the performance with shouts of "O-P, O-P, O-P, Old Prices!" This demonstration of public displeasure forced Kemble to rescind the increase in the cost of admissions. In 1823, Charles Kemble, actor–manager of Covent Garden and father of the scintillating English actress, Fanny Kemble, offered London theatergoers their first historically authentic production of a play by Shakespeare. Kemble's production of *King John* was correct in its scene, costume, and prop details, and represented the work of James Robinson Planche, a designer and playwright whose work advanced the techniques of realism in the nineteenth-century English theater. At mid-century, Madame (Lucia Elizabetta Bartolozzi) Vestris, Samuel Phelps, and Charles Kean claimed the attention of theatergoers. Madame Vestris revolutionized the standard practice of using wing and border sets by introducing the box set in her production of *London Assurance* by Dion Boucicault. The petite actress–manager, a former singer and dancer, further startled London theatergoers by curtailing the length of the evening performance. She closed the doors of her Olympic Theater promptly at eleven o'clock. Phelps's meticulous attention to production details and his insistence upon ensemble acting were instrumental in the successful presentation of thirty-two Shakespearean plays over an eighteen-year period. The authentic historical production details in the Shakespearean plays presented by Charles Kean made the actor–manager a worthy rival of Phelps. Moreover, the exquisite beauty of the productions aroused the interest of theatergoers at a time when audiences were clamoring for dramatic offerings more closely related to their times.

It was Charles Kemble who initiated the policy of the long run when a play proved an attraction at the box office. The trend toward historical accuracy and everyday realism gathered additional momentum when Squire Bancroft and Marie Wilton, his wife, became actor–managers and producers of the plays written by Tom Robertson. Actors were hired to perform special roles and the salary of the actor was increased when the Bancrofts abolished the custom of benefit nights. The Bancrofts were the first to offer a single play as a program and to establish regularly scheduled midweek and Saturday matinees. In the last quarter of the nineteenth century, Henry Irving epitomized the successful actor–manager. With Ellen Terry as his leading lady and a company of superior supporting actors, Irving dominated the English stage for nearly thirty years. Under his management, the Lyceum theater became the foremost playhouse in London, noted for Irving's artistic and spectacular productions of Shakespearean plays. Additionally, Irving introduced the practice of lowering the house lights at the beginning of the presentation, the shifting of scenery out of view of the audience, and experimenting with colored lights to illuminate the stage and to enhance the mood. Both Irving and Bancroft were knighted by Queen Victoria for their contributions to the growth and development of the English theater.

g. The Theatrical Syndicate

Certainly all the men who headed acting companies from the time the theater became a public institution, and certainly all the actors who became successful managers and producers, were in part businessmen who enjoyed the challenge of operating a financially prosperous and artistically successful theater. Otherwise, their ventures in the theater would not have withstood the economic pressures of the time—and sometimes they didn't—nor would the theater have developed and thrived if each actor–manager–producer had not been willing to undertake the financial risk in operating a theater and producing a play. A theater is a costly white elephant if it remains without tenants over too long a period of time; and the costs of production have always been notoriously high, considering that all might be lost after the first performance.

The commodity, the play, has always been and remains an uncertain one until performed before an audience. The actors and designers may or may not be the right combination, or available, to "manufacture" the commodity. The buyer, the theatergoer, may or may not respond to the commodity. He is fickle in his tastes and restless in his search for entertainment. He is gullible by nature, easily swayed by the opinion of friends and critics. His response at the box office may reflect a quest for social status as much as an avid interest in the theater. Consequently, the presence of the businessman–producer in the late nineteenth-century American theater was not a new phenomenon in the professional theater. He had always been an integral part of theater production and operation, whether as a trade guild advertising its wares and skills in celebration of Corpus Christi day, or as an actor, for example Edwin Booth, investing his lifetime earnings to open a magnificent new theater. What was new, however, was his attempt to operate the theater as "big business" in order to control theatrical production in the United States.

By 1900, Charles Frohman was the foremost producer in the United States. At the height of his career, his theaters in New York and London alone were assessed at five million dollars. He furnished employment to thousands of people, and his yearly payroll was thirty-five million dollars. In addition, his advertising and transportation costs ran into the millions. Manufacturing stars was a Frohman specialty. The process included (1) hiring an actor whose talent lent itself to stardom, (2) casting an actor in a play by an established playwright who could write a play around the talent of the actor, and (3) mounting a publicity campaign that established a relationship between the actor's role on stage and his life off stage. Frohman believed that his process would cut short the lengthy period of training necessary to achieve stardom and would provide a company of new stars with whom a generation of new playgoers could identify. In 1892, Charles Frohman put his "process" into operation when he persuaded John Drew to leave the management of Augustin Daly. Maude Adams and William Gillette were other American actors who joined the Frohman management.

In 1896, Frohman organized the Theatrical Syndicate in order to conduct his business on a national scale. His associates in the venture were Mark Klaw and Abraham Lincoln Erlanger who controlled a large chain of theaters in the South; Samuel F. Nixon and J. Frederick Zimmerman who operated a chain of theaters throughout Pennsylvania and Ohio; and Al Hayman, co-owner of the Empire theater and a string of theaters throughout the West. The American Theatrical Syndicate's stated aim was to bring order to the chaotic conditions that prevented a profitable road tour. The Syndicate promised minimum trouble, effort, and expense to independent managers and stars who agreed to the terms of the Syndicate. Usually one of the terms was a large percentage of the profits.

Under the supervision of Erlanger, the Theatrical Syndicate became a quest for real estate and a means of crushing competition. Theater owners in cities outside New York were forced either to agree to the demands of the Syndicate, or to close their doors because of the lack of attractions. In many instances, the theater owner lost his property and the theater was closed until the Syndicate could acquire ownership and reopen it. To counteract this tactic, the Shubert Brothers refurbished many old playhouses and built new ones, thus forcing some communities to support two theaters instead of one. The entrance of the Shubert Brothers into the fray led to an even more powerful trust that was not broken until fifty years later. At the time, however, the Brothers were considered the lesser of two evils, and many actors and managers accepted Shubert booking.

h. The Producer Today

In the twentieth-century American theater, the producer is the person who selects and initiates the mounting of a play, obtains financing for the production, supervises the artistic approach to the play, and publicizes and sells the play to an audience. A producer may be an individual such as David Merrick, Saint Subber, or Harold Prince; a partnership such as Feuer and Martin, APA-Phoenix, or Albert W. Selden and Hal James; a group such as The Repertory Theater of Lincoln Center, The Minnesota Theater Company, or The Negro Ensemble Company. A producer chooses a script for production because he believes that the script is stage-worthy and that the literary and artistic merits of the script warrant that it be produced. A producer selects a script because he is familiar with the work of the playwright, or has previously been the producer for the playwright. A producer decides upon a script because he has the services of a star performer whose talents are suitable for the leading role. A producer evinces interest in a script because he believes it will be a sure-fire hit, or because it has already enjoyed rave notices elsewhere. For example, *The Great White Hope* was a successful attraction at the Arena Stage in Washington, D.C., before it was produced in New York City; and *Hadrian VII* was a successful production at the Mermaid Theater in London before it crossed the ocean to Broadway. In reverse order, *Hair, Fiddler on the Roof, Our Town,* and *Man of La Mancha* among others were successful plays on Broadway before they were produced abroad.

To finance the costs of production, the producer must either invest his personal funds or secure financial backing from other sources. Individuals, recording companies, and motion picture companies have been known to "angel" play productions. After the script has been selected and the needed monetary investment obtained, the producer organizes both an artistic and business staff to assist him in producing the play. Generally, the producer selects a director and designers whose talents he believes will do justice to the script and to his reputation in the theater. Although the producer is usually involved with casting the play and with approving the work of the designers, he depnds upon the compatibility of the director and the designers to resolve the artistic problems inherent in producing the play so that he can focus his attention upon the business aspect of marketing the play. Of course, there are exceptions to this procedure. Harold Prince, for example, both produced and directed *Cabaret* and *Zorba*. The complexities involved in mounting and marketing a production are so manifold, that the producer, a member of the League of New York Theaters, heads a tightly structured organization, as indicated in the following chart:

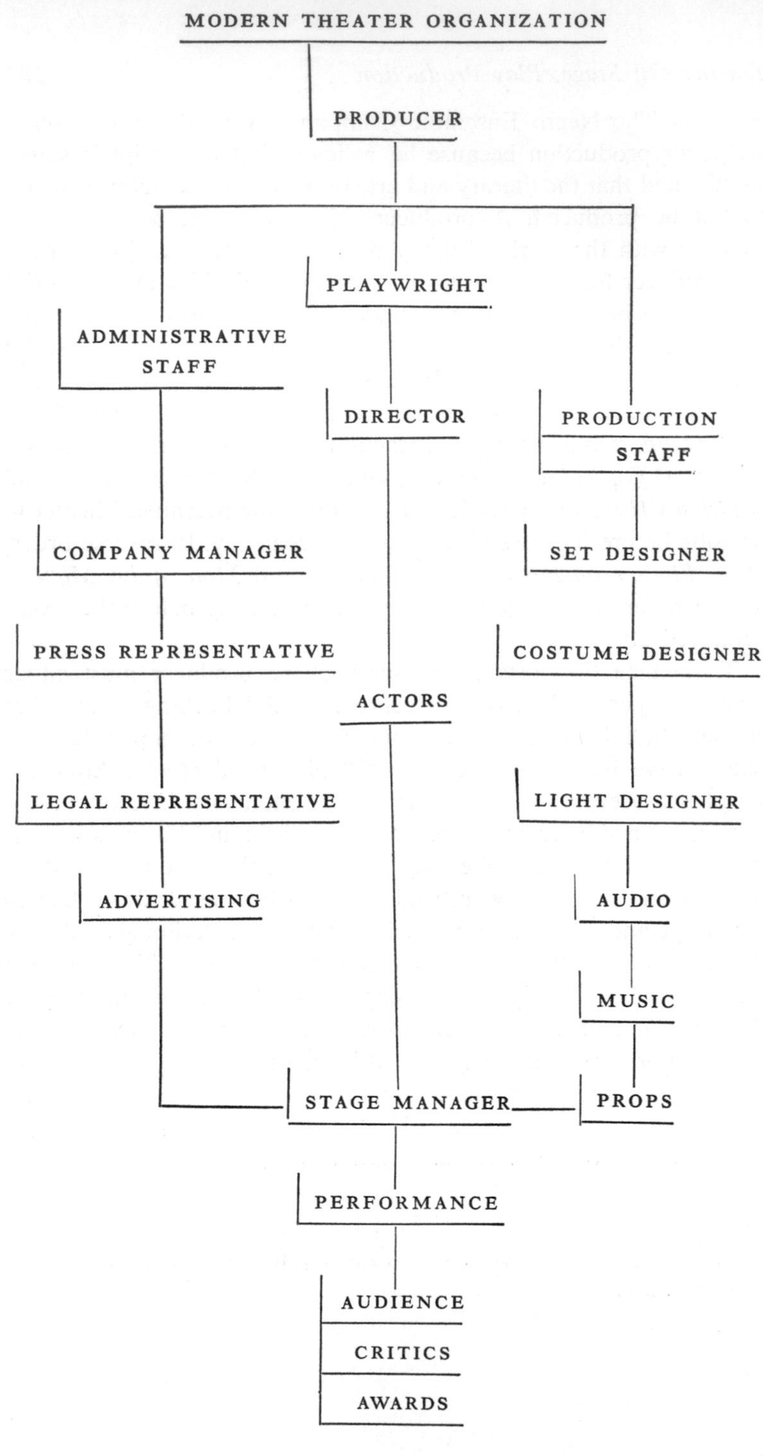
MODERN THEATER ORGANIZATION
PRODUCER
PLAYWRIGHT
ADMINISTRATIVE STAFF
DIRECTOR
PRODUCTION STAFF
COMPANY MANAGER
SET DESIGNER
PRESS REPRESENTATIVE
COSTUME DESIGNER
ACTORS
LEGAL REPRESENTATIVE
LIGHT DESIGNER
ADVERTISING
AUDIO
MUSIC
STAGE MANAGER
PROPS
PERFORMANCE
AUDIENCE
CRITICS
AWARDS

2. The Director

In one theater era or another, the director has been the playwright, the cleric, the guild member, the actor, the stage manager, and the prompter. Aeschylus, Sophocles, Euripides, and Aristophanes established the precedent for the play being staged by its playwright. The Romans continued the tradition begun by the Greeks. After the initial staging by the playwright, the stage manager or prompter took over the restaging of the play when it was revived. Sometimes the leading actor contributed to the restaging through his recall of what had transpired in the previous production. In the medieval theater, the cleric served as the *maître de jeu,* the master of the action in the liturgical play being staged. Each guild appointed a member as superintendent to attend to the organization and production of the Biblical episode. Shakespeare doubled as playwright and director for his company; Ben Jonson worked with Inigo Jones in the staging of masques at the Court of James I. In France, Molière tripled as actor, playwright, and director. From the middle of the eighteenth century to the latter quarter of the nineteenth century, the actor assumed the responsibility for staging the production, although in many instances the playwright continued to supervise the initial staging of his play. In the Age of Great Actors, David Garrick, Konrad Ekhof, Friedrich Schröder, John Philip Kemble, William Charles Macready, Charles Kean, Edwin Booth, and Henry Irving applied their theatrical genius to directing the play. Their aims, however, were to achieve reforms in rehearsal procedure and historical accuracy in costume and scene design, rather than to develop the director as a true *maître de jeu,* one who would integrate all the elements of play production and performance into a unified entity.

The director began to achieve identity as a skilled craftsman, one adept at interpreting the script through an integration of all the elements of play production and performance, when Georg II, Duke of Saxe-Meiningen, introduced his troupe of unknown actors to Berlin theatergoers on May 1, 1874. The performance and production of Shakespeare's *Julius Caesar* by the Meininger, as the troupe came to be identified, astounded the audience because the settings were historically accurate, the costumes authentic, and the acting coordinated to achieve an ensemble effect. There were no stars in the Meininger, because the Duke believed that the star system was detrimental to the presentation of a unified whole. Actors were expected to sublimate their professional ambitions and status in the company to meet the needs of the play. The Duke demanded that the gifted actor acquiesce in the matter of casting, that he play minor roles as well as leads, and that, if it served the demands of the play, the actor graciously accept and perform a walk-on role. The crowd scenes in particular captured the attention and admiration of the theatergoer because the crowd seemed to be something more than merely a collection of actors standing around on stage. Under the watchful and creative eye of the Duke and his assistant, Ludwig Chronegk, each actor was taught, trained, and drilled in appropriate stage business that was carefully rehearsed and deliberately arranged and coordinated to emphasize the significance of the mob in the action of the plot. The result was the epitome of ensemble acting, evidence of a guiding hand that made the play the focus of attention rather than an occasion for displaying the talents of a gifted actor, as was often the case in the productions staged by Edwin Booth. From 1874 to 1890, the Meininger toured Germany, Russia, Austria, Holland, Belgium, Switzerland, England, Denmark, and Sweden, setting new criteria in play production and performance, and supporting the growing recognition that the director served a distinct function in the theater. In France, André Antoine applied the Duke's approach to mounting a production when the Théâtre Libre was opened in 1887. In Germany, Otto Brahm emulated the directorial techniques developed by Georg II and André Antoine. In Russia, Stanislavski was influenced by his observations of the Meininger when he organized the Moscow Art Theater. In England, Harley Granville-Barker exerted strong directorial control in his productions at the Cort Theater. David Belasco was the prototype of the director in the American theater. Adolph Appia and Edward Gordon Craig attested to the distinct function of the director in the legitimate theater. Finally, the evolution of the director as an interpretative artist in the theater reached its zenith with the creative genius of Max Reinhardt.

Initially, the director studies the script in order to evolve a directorial concept that he can use as a guide in dramatizing the essence of the play for the audience. He must extract that essence from the work of the playwright and translate it into a concrete concept that will enable him to serve as spokesman for the playwright. To this end, he probes the theme to learn how the playwright has developed it through his arrangement of scenes and the behavior of the characters. He analyzes the structure of the play so that he can understand the meaning of each scene and the relationship of one scene to another. He dissects the behavior of each character to comprehend the motivation underlying the behavior. He senses the mood of the play, carefully noting nuances as they occur throughout the script. He researches the period in which the play is set so that he is conversant with the social, economic, and political panorama against which the action occurs. His creative imagination enables him to envision the finished production on stage. This directorial concept that he develops as a result of a careful analysis of the play becomes his frame of reference as he leads the actors and the designers through the rehearsal period to the finished production before a live audience.

In preparation for staging the script, the director plots the physical action in his copy of the play. He begins by examining the work of the playwright to discover the natural action that accompanies the development of plot and the revelation of theme and character. He notes the entrances and the exits of the characters and he considers the instructions written by the playwright. The director then reviews each scene to discover inherent physical action that will help him dramatize the meaning of the play. For example, a scene that is built around an everyday ritual demands physical movement that identifies the ritual but which is purposely arranged or redesigned by the director to project the meaning of a scene. Scenes that involve eating must not only include the physical action that is involved with serving and consuming a meal, but must be staged in a manner that permits the director to focus attention on character and plot development during the scene. The dining scenes in *Life with Father* by Howard Lindsay and Russel Crouse, *Ah, Wilderness!* by Eugene O'Neill, and *A Streetcar Named Desire* by

Tennessee Williams are examples of the necessity to adjust the physical action of an everyday ritual to the dramatic demands of the play. Additionally, the director considers the relationship between the characters in the scene and attempts to evolve a pattern of movement that illustrates the relationship or that reveals the behavioral pattern of each character. In plotting the physical action of the entire play, the director draws upon his directorial concept to guide him in selecting significant movement that does justice to the essence of the play. In the margins of his copy of the play, the director records symbols and diagrams of the action that he has planned. He will use this copy in rehearsals with the actors. In the course of plotting the action, the director uses the floor plan submitted by the set designer in order to relate the action to the setting and to clarify his groupings before he goes to the rehearsal. The director attends the rehearsal with his "homework" well prepared, but not without a willingness to adjust his thinking to the creative needs of the actor, and consequently, to the dramatic needs of the play.

In preparation for rehearsing the actors, the director analyzes each character in the script. He must understand the importance of each character in the play and in each scene in which the character appears. He must comprehend the personality of each character and sense the basis for the emotional drives of each character. He must mentally project the life of each character off stage in an effort to grasp his behavioral pattern on stage. He must be able to perceive what makes each character function, why he does or does not grow as the result of what happens to him in the course of the play. The director must find ways to reveal the nature of the character to an audience. The director begins the rehearsals of a play by reading the script with the actors. At the first rehearsal, the director discusses his directorial concept with the actors. In subsequent rehearsals, the director blocks the physical movement of the play. The next phase finds the director and the actor working together to achieve a performance that is in accord with the meaning of the play and its production. In working with the actor, the director must draw upon his knowledge of human emotions and human strengths and weaknesses to guide the actor in rendering a meaningful interpretation of the role. The director should encourage freedom of interpretation within the limits of his concept of the play. The director should neither create the role for the actor nor should he stifle his interpretative sensitivity. Rather, the director should draw upon his knowledge of the actor's craft to guide the actor in creating a role. In short, the director must remember that in rehearsing the actor, his aim is twofold: he must extract from the actor a characterization that meets the demands of the play and a performance that utilizes the creative talents of the actor.

In the final stages of rehearsal, the director divorces himself from staging the play and rehearsing the actors in order to weave the entire production together. He calls for a dress parade so that he and the costumer can inspect the wardrobe worn by the actors. He joins the set designer and the lighting designer in a series of technical rehearsals to finalize the cues for scene, sound, and light changes. In subsequent rehearsals, he works the cast and the crews together to synchronize their efforts. He makes only those adjustments in the performance of the actors, the staging of the play, or the running of the performance that manifest themselves as a result of performing the production before a preview audience.

A member of the Society of Stage Directors and Choreographers, the director receives a flat fee for his services. Depending upon his reputation in the theater, he may also receive a percentage of the weekly box-office receipts and a percentage of the net profits if the show enjoys a long run. Periodically, he is expected to spot-check the performances, and he may be asked to approve cast replacements and to direct the road company production. The director severs his connection with the show after opening night, leaving the stage manager in charge of subsequent performances.

3. The Designers

The costume designer, the set designer, and the lighting designer assist the director in his visual dramatization of the play. The costume designer selects fabrics and colors to fashion appropriate clothing for the character written by the playwright, performed by the actor, and interpreted by the director. The costumer adapts his patterns to the physique of the actor and actress, no small task when one remembers that actors, like all humans, come in assorted sizes, shapes, and heights. The dress, coat, hat, cape, or accessory generally reveals the personality of the character, his status in life, his relationship with others. The finished costume is an external manifestation of how the character feels inwardly as well as a manifestation of his place in, and his response to, the society in which he lives. The set designer makes of "airy nothingness," the physical stage, a three-dimensional environment before which the characters come to life, the action takes place, the actors perform. The set establishes the boundary of the physical action on stage and turns space into reality, albeit a theatrical one. The set becomes the home of the costumed actors. The lighting designer bathes the stage in light that illuminates the performance of the actors and the action staged by the director. From thousands of watts of electricity, the lighting designer creates an atmosphere and a mood that express the theme of the play, the emotional interpretation of the director, and the climate of the locale. Light envelops the costumed actors as they move about in their environment. Each designer is a skilled practitioner in his respective field. Each is a free agent in using his talent, imagination, and creativity to design the production. In expressing his originality, each designer is limited by the need to accommodate the director in achieving his visual concept of the play, and by the need to adapt his designs to achieve harmony with the creativity of his fellow designers.

a. The Set Designer

When the house lights are dimmed and the curtain rises, the set commands the attention of the audience and provides the theatergoer with his first contact with the play. The physical environment on stage represents the image conjured by the description of the time and place stated in the program. The theatergoer discovers the "elegant drawing room" with its softly tinted paneled walls, its tastefully selected period furniture, its brightly lighted crystal chandeliers. The theatergoer beholds "a palace room" with its gilded carved throne and chair, its sumptuous tapestries, its highly polished floors. The theatergoer observes "a shabby cabin" with its rickety porch, its creaking steps, its forlorn desolate countryside in the background. The theatergoer identifies "a walk-up apartment house" with its worn red brick façade, its poorly curtained windows, its adjacent construction scaffolding. The theatergoer inspects "a saloon" with its half-curtained window front, its long massive bar, its mirrored wall with shelves of bottles on either side. The theatergoer responds with applause in appreciation for what he sees before him. The set designer's "picture" has spoken a thousand words. What was once a printed description, a floor plan, a sketch, or a mental concept of a finished drawing room is now a reality, the fruition of the set designer's visual interpretation of the playwright's script.

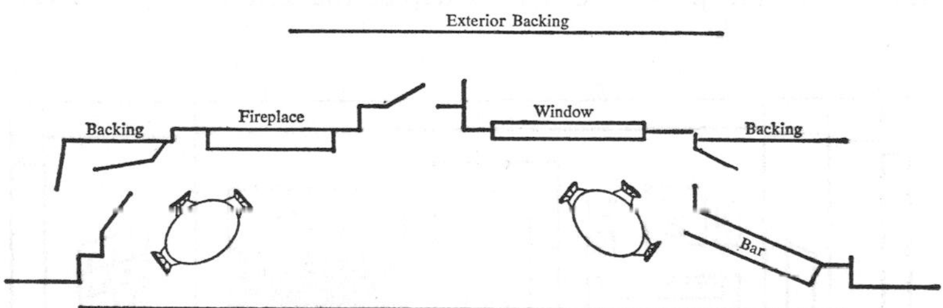

Floor plan of Act I, Frederick Jackson, *The Bishop Misbehaves* (New York: Samuel French, Inc., 1935). Copyright, 1935, by Frederick Jackson. Copyright, 1935 (acting edition), by Frederick Jackson. Reprinted by permission of the publisher.

The set designer approaches his task of designing the interiors and the exteriors of a play by reading it as though he were a member of the audience. His impersonal approach at this point is to see the play as a theatergoer and not as a professional craftsman connected with producing the play. He then analyzes the play as a set designer to determine the scenic needs of the script and to reconcile his initial impressions wtih the environmental needs of the play. He translates the set description into a floor plan that takes its form from his initial concept. The floor plan is a kind of blueprint that outlines the walls of the set and includes the placement of furniture. The floor plan is used by the director when he is plotting the movement of action. It is used by the lighting designer when he is planning the placement of lighting equipment. Technical crews use the floor plan to assemble the set on stage. Moreover, the initial planning includes a consideration of scenic changes, which must not impede the flow of the production and must be adapted to the physical limitations of the stage. It is in this early step of designing that the set designer must envision the totality of the finished production and provide for solutions to any complications that may prevent the achievement of that totality.

When he has devised a floor plan that he believes will be acceptable to the director, the set designer draws a sketch of his concept of the environment. The sketch generally represents an important moment in the play in order to depict the relationship between

Perspective sketch based on floor plan, Act I, of Frederick Jackson, *The Bishop Misbehaves* (New York: Samuel French, Inc., 1935). Copyright, 1935, by Frederick Jackson. Copyright, 1935 (acting edition), by Frederick Jackson. Reprinted by permission of the publisher.

the action and the set. The architectural details reveal the set designer's awareness of the period and his ability to adapt the architecture of the time to the theater. The decor, although not presented in detail, indicates his awareness of the furnishings characteristic of the period. The sketch includes those characters who appear in the scene in order to indicate the relative sizes of the actor and the set. The sketch is generally done in water color. The colors, however, represent the effect that the set designer hopes to achieve, rather than the actual colors that will be used in the finished set. The costumes worn by the characters in the sketch are not usually those created by the costume designer but are included by the designer to reinforce his impression of the scene. If the set designer is not pressed for time, he also builds a model of the set. The floor plan and the sketch and/or model are presented to the producer and the director for their approval. The presentation may be made at a conference when the costume designer and the lighting designer are in attendance. It is at this point that the producer, the director, the set designer, and the lighting designer must agree that one and all are in visual accord.

To qualify for membership in the United Scenic Artists Union, the set designer must prove his competency in costuming, lighting, and designing. As part of the examination, he is required to submit sketches and drawings from which a set can be constructed. Similar to the union requirement made of the costume designer, the set designer is required to obtain a signed contract before he can submit designs to a producer. His fee is based on his reputation as a designer and the complexity of the production. He is expected to select, design, and secure all the properties pertinent to the play. He must be available for consultation throughout the rehearsal period. He generally severs his connection with the production when the play is premiered, although he may be asked to submit and execute designs for a road company.

b. The Lighting Designer

The lighting designer in the professional theater is a member of the United Scenic Artists, Local 829 of the Brotherhood of Painters, Decorators, and Paperhangers of America. He may hold either a Lighting Associate Membership, which permits him to work on lights exclusively, or he may hold membership as a set designer, which qualifies him to design the lights for his own set. In either case, the lighting designer reads the play many times to discover how the element of light can contribute to the visual effectiveness of the play. His first obligation is to make the actor and the action visible to the audience. His next obligation is to observe the time

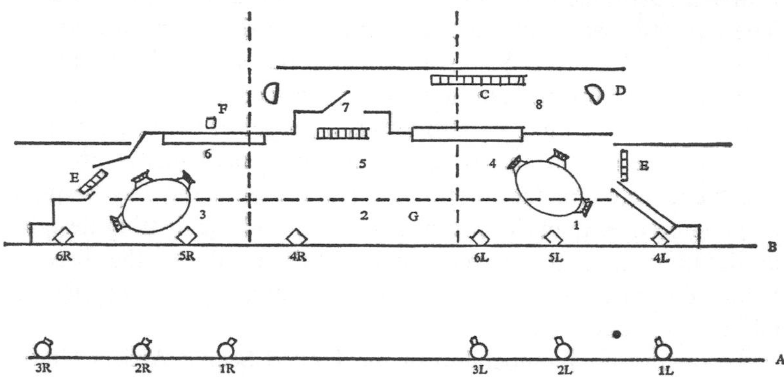

The Floor Plan as used by the Lighting Designer to Light Major Acting Areas

A Auditorium Ellipsoidal Spots to light right and left of actor in downstage areas.

B Teaser Fresnel Spots to light right and left of actor in upstage areas

C Floor strips

D Flood lights

E Overhead strips

F Special Fireplace

G 1-2-3-4-5-6-7-8: Major Acting Areas

- - - Imaginary line dividing stage into major lighting areas

{ Generally light areas beyond set provide special effects and additional illumination to important areas of action on stage, for example bar, tables, entrances, etc.

From Frederick Jackson, *The Bishop Misbehaves* (New York: Samuel French, Inc., 1935). Copyright, 1935, by Frederick Jackson. Copyright, 1935 (acting edition), by Frederick Jackson. Reprinted by permission of the publisher.

of year and day in which the play takes place, as well as the switching on and off of hand-operated mechanical devices such as lamps and chandeliers. His third obligation is to use the qualities of light—intensity, color, distribution, movement—to evoke the mood of the play, to emphasize the dramatic composition of the stage picture, and to enhance the atmosphere of the set. The lighting designer presents his concept to the producer, the director, the set designer, and the costume designer for their consideration. He uses the floor plan of the set and the physical structure of the stage and the auditorium to locate the placement of lighting equipment. He observes the rehearsals of the play to discover the important areas of action. When he devises his lighting plan, he remembers to focus his instruments so that those areas are emphasized through light. In contrast, other areas may be de-emphasized, thus applying the artistic principle of lightness and darkness to the stage picture. He examines the sketches of the costume designer, and he considers the effectiveness of the choice of materials selected and whether the texture and the color of the materials will prove dramatically effective when lighted on stage. The lighting designer predicts the probable effectiveness of the makeup of the actor when lighted on stage. The lighting designer generally organizes and instructs the crew that will run the show and he is responsible for preparing a chart that lists dimmer readings, cues, and changes of lighting throughout the show. His assignment is terminated when the play reaches Broadway, and his fee is based on the number of settings and the complexity of the production.

c. The Costume Designer

In preparation for his conference with the producer, the director, and the set and lighting designers, the costume designer studies the script to determine the costume needs for the play, and how the costumes can contribute to the visual mounting of the play. Despite the fact that the play may be a classic, typical of a certain period, or the representative work of an established playwright, the costume designer reads the play as though it were a fresh work, one that is being performed for the first time. From the time of the play and the locale of the action, he determines the silhouette of the costume and its relationship to the environment in which the character lives. He discerns the attitude of the playwright toward life by examining the theme of the play and the manner in which the playwright explores this theme. He speculates how his costumes can express the attitude of the playwright. The costume designer examines the structure of the play to determine the dominant mood of each scene. He notes how his costumes can enhance and visualize the mood as it develops and changes throughout the play. The costume designer scrutinizes each character to determine his personality, his relationship with others, his importance in the play, or his importance in a particular scene. He considers how his costumes can reveal these facets of human nature and human relationships. Finally, the costume designer crystallizes his impressions and his thinking by preparing costume sketches that reveal his approach to costuming the play. He discusses his designs with the producer, the director, the set and lighting designers, making certain that his costume concept of the play is in accord with the artistic thinking of his colleagues.

After the director has approved the preliminary sketches and the costumer has the assurance that his concept is in accord with the total visual concept of the play, the costume designer is ready to get down to the business of planning his costumes in detail. He begins by noting the number of characters in the play and the number of costumes required by each character, without regard to the importance of his role. He notes the scenes in which each character appears, what he wears in the scene, whether or not there is a costume change within the scene, and whether the change takes place within view of the audience or off stage. He checks the script to determine whether the playwright has allowed sufficient time for the change off stage, and he dwells on the arrangements he will have to make to overcome any quick off-stage changes. He consults with the director to determine whether or not the change on stage can be incorporated into stage business invented by the director, and he designs the costume with this possibility in mind. He divides his list of costumes according to those worn by male and female members of the cast; and he keeps a record of the number of costume plates he makes, although only one plate is necessary for a costume that is to be duplicated and worn by several members of the cast. In addition to a costume plot that contains the title of the play, the name of the actor, the name of the character, the required costumes worn by the character, and the scene in which the costume appears, the costume designer prepares a costume chart that displays the silhouette of each costume worn throughout the entire production.

It is important that the costume designer understand human nature and that his understanding is reflected in his designs. The costumer must design from the viewpoint that he is creating a wardrobe for a live person; otherwise the costume will be meaningless and contribute little to the dramatic effectiveness of the production. It is necessary, therefore, that the costumer grasp that which motivates the character or provokes his responses, the image he has of himself, the perceptions others have of him, and his significance to the play. From his conclusions and the evidence he finds in the script, the costumer designs raiment that reflects and reveals the emotional needs and the conflicting tensions within the character. If the play is a period piece, the costumer has the additional problem of including his awareness of the nature of the character in the silhouette of the time. If the play is a contemporary piece, the costumer must adapt current modes of fashion to what is theatrically effective without raising questions of accuracy and authenticity. In conceiving a costume, the costumer must think in terms of line, color, and texture, all of which must coincide with the visual concept enunciated by the director and accepted by the other designers. The costumer, therefore, frequently consults with the scene designer to determine whether or not the costumes are in accord with the environment, and he confers with the lighting designer to determine whether or not the texture of the materials will be effective when lighted. Inasmuch as our clothing represents aspects of our personality and our response to the world in which we live, the costume worn by the actor should reveal aspects of the personality of the character and the response of the character to the world in which he lives. The work of the costumer, therefore, is to create the fashion world of the play, one that is true to the character, true to the time, and true to the style of the production.

To design for the professional theater, the costume designer must join the United Scenic Artists Union. Membership is achieved by passing an examination administered by the union. Under union rules, the costumer is prohibited from submitting any designs until he has been signed to a contract. The contract generally states the fee and the billing the designer is to receive in advertisements and play programs. The fee is based on the number of designs required by the production. The costume designer terminates his connection with the production when the show opens, although he may be recalled to supervise the replacement of costumes or to redesign the costumes for a road tour.

Costume Chart—The Bishop Misbehaves, Act I *

Character	*Costume*
Red Eagan	Dark trousers; belt; worn work shoes; striped shirt; narrow dark tie; bar-apron.
Donald Meadows	Evening suit; dark hat; raincoat.
Hester	Evening dress; light raincoat.
Mrs. Waller	Evening dress; fur stole; jewelry; compact; evening bag.
Mr. Waller	Evening suit; hat; coat.
Lady Emily Lyons	Simple dark dress; black lace scarf for hair; three-quarter coat; carries umbrella.
The Bishop of Broadminster	Dark hat and coat; clerical garb.
Collins	Regulation chauffeur's uniform.
Frenchy	Dark trousers; odd jacket; cap; dark plaid shirt.

4. The Stage Manager

The producer hires the stage manager to work with the director during the rehearsal period and to assume the responsibility for

---

* From Frederick Jackson, *The Bishop Misbehaves* (New York: Samuel French, Inc., 1935). Copyright, 1935, by Frederick Jackson. Copyright, 1935 (acting edition), by Frederick Jackson. Reprinted by permission of the publisher.

Waller at Fireplace after hanging coat etc on pegs.
Mrs W. X DR - sit.

20 THE BISHOP MISBEHAVES ACT I

try in the world, England. If this was America, now—

MRS. WALLER. I do hope the chauffeur hurries. I'm afraid we're going to be very late. ①

WALLER. Well, what if we are? More people will see us coming in. ②

MRS. WALLER. How far did the gentleman say the garage was? ③

WALLER. *(Sitting above table)* About a mile. ⑤

RED. *(Enters* L. *carrying a small round tray on which are a bottle of champagne and two glasses)* 'Ow's this, sir? *(Crosses to table* R.*)* ④

WALLER. *(Looking at the bottle)* Looks all right. Open it.

RED. Yes, sir. *(Stands* L. *of table, bending over the bottle to open it.* MR. *and* MRS. WALLER *watching him.)*

DONALD. *(Enters* L.C. *in hat, coat and mask. He goes quickly down* L., *his gun leveled)* Hands up! All of you. (MRS. WALLER *rises with a slight scream.* RED *turns quickly with the champagne bottle in his hand.* WALLER *rises slowly, looking at* DONALD.) Quick now and no nonsense!

WALLER. Say—what is this—a joke?

DONALD. No joke! Put 'em up. (WALLER'S *hands go up.*) I'm a crack shot and I know just where to place the bullets.

RED. *(Makes a move toward* DONALD, *the bottle raised)* Why, you bloody crook, you— (WALLER *makes a slight move toward* DONALD.)

DONALD. *(Fiercely)* Stop where you are! Or somebody is going to get badly hurt. Now do what you're told—I've no time to waste.

MRS. WALLER. Guy! Are you going to stand there—

DONALD. *(To her—savagely)* Shut up! *(To* RED*)* You, barman, put down that bottle and strip the jewels off her. Quick now!

① Remove compact, etc. Fix make up.
② Boast a little.
③ Remove cigarette - note edge of concern in voice.
④ X D bar - place bottle on bar X to window - adjust curtain several times as though signalling to Donald. XUC door - adjust shade - return to bar - get glasses.
⑤ XDRC to sit table
⑥ Read label. Emphasize name as though knowledgeable about wines, etc.
Set glasses - place bottle between legs - face Mr & Mrs Waller.
Donald enters quietly - tiptoe down left. Others follow.
⑦ He can't believe it! Looks at Mrs. W. as though some prank on her part. Red remains in crouched position - then hands in air - bottle above like Indian club.
8. Wave the bottle overhead as though just in vaudeville routine!
⑨ Red - bottle in both hands. Turn look at Mrs. W. Turn to Donald as though "Really, must I?" - Mrs. Waller - hands to throat - frightened at "strip" - Emphasize - Mrs. Waller. Step forward - Donald. Wave back into place.
10 Red X to table - place bottle X to Mrs W - R

Promptbook with director's notes.

1. Printed directions may be those written by the playwright or a recording of the movements given by director of original staging.

2. Notes in margin represent direction and notes given by director of a current production. Director's notes are usually recorded by the stage manager. From Frederick Jackson, *The Bishop Misbehaves* (New York: Samuel French, Inc., 1935). Copyright, 1935, by Frederick Jackson. Copyright, 1935 (acting edition), by Frederick Jackson. Reprinted by permission of the publisher.

running the show after the director terminates his connection with the production. The stage manager arranges and conducts the casting procedure while the producer and the director sit in the auditorium to observe and judge the auditions. He maintains a personnel folder on each actor for publicity releases and administrative requirements. He calls the rehearsal and posts notices to inform the actors of any changes in rehearsal plans. He is expected to begin the rehearsal in the absence of the director and he is required to set the stage in preparation for the rehearsal. During the rehearsal, the stage manager records all directions and instructions given to the actors by the director. These notations are entered in the stage manager's copy of the script, and this becomes the master copy of the production. The master copy, which in a sense becomes the history of the play, includes the floor plan of the set, a scene shift plot, a lighting plot and lighting cue sheet, a costume and property plot, and a list of sound cues. The master copy also contains a record of the running time of each performance with notations concerning any atypical situations that may have occurred during the performance as well as comments that indicate why the show may not have started on time. During the performance of the play, the stage manager warns the actors of approaching entrance cues. He signals the various crews who are responsible for scene shifts, light changes, and sound accompaniments. Additionally, he must rehearse the understudies and call company rehearsals when, in his judgment, the performance of the actors is at variance with the original intent of the director. The stage manager is second in command when the play is in the throes of rehearsal. He is first in charge when the play begins its run. To work in the professional theater, the stage manager must be a member of Actors Equity.

5. Investing in the Play

On May 17, 1962, the Federal Bar Association of New York, New Jersey, and Connecticut conducted a symposium on financing a theatrical production. In his summary of the legal and business aspects of financing a theatrical production, Paul J. Sherman suggested that the prospective "angel" ask the following questions when contemplating investment in a production:

1. How expensive is the production? What is it likely to cost to open in New York? After the show opens, what will its weekly running expenses be, and what kind of a weekly operating profit margin can be anticipated?
2. What is the division of profits between the producer and the investors? How many weeks at capacity business will the show have to run before the investment is repaid, and the production begins making profits?
3. Has any participation in the profits been given away to the star(s), director or others? Out of whose share is such participation deducted? Will the production participate in the sale of motion picture and other subsidiary rights? Does anyone else cut into the producer's share of such subsidiary?

Mr. Sherman also advises that:

Even more important than the answers to these questions, is the answer to an ever-present riddle in the theater: How good is the script? That, and the reputations and track record of the producer, the director, the star and all the other creative personnel are of paramount importance to successful theater investing. On Broadway, nothing succeeds like success—and plenty of knowhow.*

Since the symposium, the New York State Legislature enacted Article 26-A of the General Business Law and amended the Penal Law. The Article provides for the regulation of theatrical syndication financing, and the amendment pertains to the unlawful charges for theater tickets. *Caveat emptor!* Let the theatergoer, investor, and producer beware!

---

* From Joseph Taubman, ed., *Financing a Theatrical Production* (New York: Federal Legal Publications, 1964). Copyright © 1964, Federal Legal Publications. Reprinted by permission of the publisher.

B. CUES FOR THEATERGOERS

1. The Theatergoer as Critic

From the moment he purchases tickets to the moment he enters the theater, the theatergoer should look forward to seeing the play. He should approach the ritual of theatergoing with a high degree of enthusiasm and anticipation. He should take delight in making whatever plans are necessary to attend the performance, part of which includes planning for appropriate dress. The theatergoer will find that a theater audience, in contrast to the audience found at the motion-picture theater or at the sports arena, is usually not dressed in casual clothing because the occasion still enjoys the religious aura of the theatergoing ritual initiated by the Greeks. On entering the theater, the theatergoer should suspend judgment until after the final curtain if he is to accept and revel in the conventions of the theater. Although the theater holds the mirror up to nature, all is make-believe and merely a representation of life. The theme is a crystallization of the philosophy of life held by the playwright. The plot consists of selected incidents to demonstrate the theme. The characters live a complete lifetime in the space of a few short hours. There is no opportunity for the theatergoer to observe their going forward in time and rectifying the errors of the past. The setting simulates an actual environment. In some instances, the setting can only suggest the environment because of the limitations imposed by the physical stage. The costumes are deliberately fashioned to aid the clarification of character. The movement is purposely arranged to underscore the theme and the action of the plot. Thus, if the theatergoer does not suspend judgment when he enters the theater, the conventions will appear to be merely exercises in deceit. In watching the performance, the theatergoer should remain open-minded, exposing himself to the emotional impact of the play. After the performance, the theatergoer should apply his intelligence to the theatergoing experience, asking himself why he has had a positive, negative, or noncommittal reaction to the experience.

Man is capable of analyzing his reactions to the experience because he is, by nature, a critic. However, if he wishes to refine and sharpen his critical faculties, he can consult the drama reviews of professional critics. In reading the professional review, the theatergoer should understand the organization of the review and he should be able to discern within that organization the criticism of the various components of play production. The organization and contents of the written review are analyzed in the following review of *1776* by Clive Barnes, the drama critic for *The New York Times.*

Analysis of a Play Review

Theater: Spirited '1776'

Founding Fathers' Tale Is a Happy Musical

BY CLIVE BARNES

On the face of it, few historic incidents seem more unlikely to spawn a Broadway musical than that solemn moment in the history of mankind, the signing of the Declaration of Independence. Yet "1776," which opened last night at the 46th Street Theater, most handsomely demonstrated that people who merely go "on the face of it" are occasionally outrageously wrong. Come to think of it, that was also what the Declaration of Independence demonstrated, so there is a ready precedent at hand.

"1776," which I saw at one of its critics' previews on Saturday afternoon, is a most striking, most gripping musical. I recommend it without reservation. It makes even an Englishman's heart beat a little bit faster. This is a musical with style, humanity, wit and passion.

The credit for the idea of the musical belongs to Sherman Edwards, who has also contributed the music and lyrics. The book is by Peter Stone, best known as a Hollywood screenwriter. The two of them have done a fine job.

The critic's opinion.

Mr. Edwards and Mr. Stone have found a wonderful story for themselves in the birth pangs of a nation. Here is John Adams ("obnoxious and disliked," as everyone is agreed) fighting for his dream of freedom, the avuncular Franklin, full of aphorisms, plagued by gout and confident of the good report of history, and then the laconic Virginian, Thomas Jefferson, the great drafter of independence, who, even though he sometimes plagiarized John Locke, wrote with the eloquence of justice. It is a great cast and a great story.

The playwrights and the play.

THE INTRODUCTION

The headline and subheadline quickly tell the reader the critic's reaction to the presentation. In this instance it establishes the main idea and the tenor of the review.

The first few paragraphs answer the who, what, where, when questions of journalism.

In his introduction to his review, the critic generally states his reaction to the entire production as well as stating his opinion of the play. The critic is then expected to defend his statements in the body of the review. In this review, Mr. Barnes is obliged to develop the statements he makes in paragraph two.

THE CRITICISM

Having stated his opinion, the critic then summarizes the plot—sometimes briefly, sometimes in detail.

In this instance, the idea of the plot is stated in one sentence: "Mr. Edwards and Mr. Stone have found a wonderful story for themselves in the birth pangs of a nation." The critic depends upon our knowledge of American history to supply the details, and he recalls the names of patriots to stir our memory of the event and its participants. This leads into a discussion of the play and its elements.

In fairness, my personal comprehension of American history is probably as profound as was that of General Burgoyne. However, it should perhaps be noted that the authors have, on occasion, bent history just a little. The general thrust of their story is undoubtedly honest, but here and there one or two parries have been perhaps exaggerated in the interest of histrionic accuracy.

As even a European schoolboy knows, there were 56 signatures to the Declaration of Independence, not the dozen or so represented here. Assuredly the economics of the theater are to blame, and this is a license, if not poetic at least practical.

The Play

Then again—my memory could be wrong here—I believe that historians consider that Congress's resolution of July 2—all signatures, amendments and holidays to the contrary—was the really vital event. Also I wonder about the author's treatment of Richard Henry Lee, the Virginia patriarch. They present him as a charming fool, and the pawn of Franklin who sends him, in May, back to Virginia to get a resolution through the Virginia Legislature proposing independence. In fairness to the reputation of Mr. Lee, I think it is true that even a month before that he had already written to Patrick Henry suggesting that independence was absolutely essential.

What only is important however, is that the authors have really captured the Spirit of '76. The characterizations are most unusually full for a musical, and even though the outcome of the story is never in any very serious doubt, "1776" is consistently exciting and entertaining, for Mr. Stone's book is literate, urbane and, on occasion, very amusing.

Theme

Characters

Plot

Action

Conflict

For the music it would have been easy for Mr. Edwards to have produced a pastiche of Revolutionary tunes, but this he has studiously avoided. There is admittedly a flavor here, but the music is absolutely modern in its sound, and it is apt, convincing and enjoyable.

Music

THE CRITICISM

Poetic license, the liberty taken by the playwright in deviating from the fact to produce a desired effect, is discussed by Mr. Barnes in his outlining of the plot of *1776*.

It is not unusual, however, for a playwright to "bend" history in order to clarify a situation or to provide additional insight into character.

Johann von Schiller and Maxwell Anderson employed the technique in their plays about Mary, Queen of Scotland. Both playwrights included a scene of confrontation between Mary and Elizabeth. The scene cannot be substantiated historically. On stage, the scene seems logical in terms of the development of plot and character.

In most reviews, the content of the play comes through a direct summary of the plot, theme, characters, conflict, etc. In this review, we learn about the play and its contents through a discussion of the literary term, poetic license.

The authors have, bravely perhaps although in the event it seems perfectly natural, omitted any chorus, so that absolutely everyone in the cast has a significant part to play. This offers a great challenge to the actors and to the people responsible for the staging. In almost every respect this is excellent, although personally I felt that the settings by Jo Mielziner were very disappointing and old-fashioned. Here, with such an adventurous musical, was an opportunity for some outstanding design, but it was an opportunity missed.

Setting

Fortunately the costumes by Patricia Zipprodt were stylishly appropriate—although, as a matter of accuracy, virtually everyone should have been in white wigs, certainly at the signing—and the direction by Peter Hunt and the musical staging by Onna White were both faultless. Mr. Hunt has encouraged his actors to behave precisely as if they were in a play rather than a musical, and Miss White has most adroitly done the rest. Both are helped by a great cast.

Costumes

Direction and Choreography

William Daniels has given many persuasive performances in the past, but nothing, I think, can have been so effective as his John Adams here. This is a beautiful mixture of pride, ambition, an almost priggish sense of justice and yet —the saving grace in the character—an ironic self-awareness. Mr. Stone and Mr. Edwards provided Mr. Daniels with the character to play, but Mr. Daniels plays it to the hilt. Also, notably, he still remains perfectly in character when he sings.

Performance

The divisions of the review are generally indicated by a printer's symbol or a double space after each completed section.

After introducing the review and after discussing the play itself—the plot, the theme, the characters, and the conflict—the critic turns his attention to the actors and the production elements. Although there is no hard and fast rule that one must precede the other, the critic in this particular review comments on the sets, the costumes, and the direction before he comments on the performance of the actors.

The first actors mentioned are usually those who carry the burden of performing the play. Note the colorful adjectives used by the critic in describing the performance and characterizations rendered by the actors.

The other star performer is provided by Howard Da Silva as Ben Franklin. Mr. Da Silva has a voice as sweet as molasses and as mellow as rum, and his humor and good nature are a constant delight. But this is a cast without a weak link. I must mention Clifford David's rapier-sharp arrogance as the Southern Edward Rutledge, Paul Hecht's aristocratic elegance as the loyalist John Dickinson—the Pennsylvanian who, though unable to vote for Independence, did join the Continental Army as a private—Ronald Holgate's brilliantly extrovert and showstopping performance of Richard Henry Lee, and the aptly clumsy poise of Ken Howard as Thomas Jefferson. And then there were the ladies, the beautiful Virginia Vestoff as Abigail Adams, and Betty Buckley as the spirited Martha Jefferson.

Performance

But enough. I cannot mention all 26 of the actors, and yet utter fairness would demand no less. The musical will, I suspect, prove to be the sleeper of the season. Who knows, it might even run until the celebration of the bicentenary in 1976. I rather hope so. Certainly you don't have to be a historian to love "1776."

Reaction

A criticism of the supporting cast members generally follows that accorded the leading actors or stars. Sometimes these observations are briefly stated and include only the name of the actor. In this review, however, the excellence of the entire cast is noted by the accolades heaped upon the actors playing supporting roles. Occasionally, a critic uses this means of singling out a little-known performer who has exhibited exceptional talent.

THE CONCLUSION

The final paragraph of a review summarizes the opinion of the critic, stating in few words his appraisal of the play and its production. The theatergoer must now decide whether or not he wishes to see the show.

2. The Professional Critic

In his time, the critic has been more maligned than praised. For example, consider the following comments:

> Sir Henry Wotton used to say that critics are like brushers of noblemen's clothes.
>
> Sir Francis Bacon, *Apothegms,* No. 64

> Of all the cants which are canted in this canting world, though the cant of hypocrites may be the worst, the cant of criticism is the most tormenting.
>
> Laurence Sterne, *Tristram Shandy,* Book III, Ch. 12

> Reviewers are usually people who would have been poets, historians, biographers, if they could; they have tried their talents at one or the other, and have failed; therefore they turn critics.
>
> Samuel Taylor Coleridge, *Lectures on Shakespeare and Milton*

> Reviewers, with some rare exceptions, are a most stupid and malignant race. As a bankrupt thief turns thief-taker in despair, so an unsuccessful author turns critic.
>
> Percy Bysshe Shelley, *Fragments of Adonais*

> As soon seek roses in December, ice in June;
> Hope constancy in wind, or corn in chaff;
> Believe a woman or an epitaph
> Or any other thing that's false, before
> You trust in critics.
>
> Lord Byron, *English Bards and Scotch Reviewers*

> Dear Critics, whose verdicts are always so new!—
> One word in your ear. There were Critics before . . .
> And the man who plants cabbages imitates, too!
>
> Henry Austin Dobson, *The Ballad of Imitation*

> A wise scepticism is the first attribute of a good critic.
>
> James Russell Lowell, *Shakespeare Once More*

> Criticism is the endeavor to find, to know, to love, to recommend, not only the best, but all the good, that has been known and thought and written in the world.
>
> George Saintsbury, *A History of Criticism*

Despite the barbs, the theatergoer can accept the critic's review as an objective and reliable guide to theatergoing. The critic attends the play in the dual role of theatergoer and critic. Insofar as it is professionally possible, he must suspend judgment until after he has seen the play. He must be reached, touched, and he must experience an emotional reaction if he is to report his experience to the theatergoer. Unlike the theatergoer, the critic cannot accept or reject a play without indicating cogent reasons. In his review, he is expected to justify why he did or did not enjoy the play. He must pinpoint those elements that contribute to the success or failure of the production. Although he is not an integral part of the planned theatrical processes, his role as critic makes him an influential factor in theatergoing. The theatergoer generally respects and cites his opinion, too often denying himself the right to make his own decision. He accepts the words of the critic as gospel, seldom questioning quotations from the critical review that have been taken out of context for purposes of advertising the production. Occasionally, however, the theatergoer will disregard the critic's review and turn a critical failure into a box-office success. For example, *Abie's Irish Rose* by Anne Nichols and *Tobacco Road* by Jack Kirkland were not favorably reviewed by the critics. The theatergoer responded by making both plays two of the longest run hits on the American stage. The difference in the reaction of the theatergoer and the critic was one of dramaturgical merit versus public taste and popular appeal. On the other hand, *All the Way Home* by Tad Mosel, which received both the Drama Critics Award and the Pulitzer Prize, was accorded only half-hearted support from theatergoers and had a comparatively short run on the American stage.

The critic in the professional theater is well qualified to write a criticism that meets the need of the average theatergoer. Frequently, his educational training is rooted in the study of the theater. For example, Walter Kerr, the Sunday critic for *The New York Times,* was graduated from Northwestern University where he majored in speech and drama. Additionally, Mr. Kerr was an associate professor of drama at Catholic University, Washington, D.C., prior to becoming drama critic for *Commonweal* (1950–52) and *The New York Herald-Tribune* (1951–66). Mr. Kerr has also worked in the theater as a professional director. Sometimes the training and experience of the critic stems from a related art. Clive Barnes, whose drama reviews appear daily in *The New York Times,* has had considerable experience studying and evaluating the dance as well as reviewing the merits of music, films, and drama for the *Daily Express* in London. Other critics, such as John Chapman of the *Daily News,* Richard Watts, Jr., of the *New York Post,* and Henry Hewes of the *Saturday Review,* apply their training as journalists and their experience as professional theatergoers to reviewing and criticizing dramatic productions. On October 22, 1935, the New York City drama critics officially formed the New York Drama Critics Circle. At that time, the stated purpose was to award a prize for the best new play by an American playwright, one that had been produced in New York during the theatrical season. Maxwell Anderson was the first recipient of the Drama Critics Prize for his play *Winterset.* In recent years, however, the Circle has taken a broader view in making its award, sometimes honoring a musical or the work of a foreign playwright.

C. THEATER SPOTLIGHTS

I. *Theater Terminology:* Define the following:

agitprop
Belascoism
curtain raiser
epic theater
mansion
mise en scène
theatricalism
multiple setting
raked stage
regiebuch

II. *Theater Who's Who:* Identify the following:

Cecil Beaton
Peter Brook
John Mason Brown
Harold Clurman
Mordecai Gorelik
Sir Tyrone Guthrie

Elia Kazan	Roger L. Stevens
Harold Prince	Stark Young

III. *Theater Investigation:* Discuss the following:

1. We live in a world of social change and moral upheaval. The theater reflects our changing society by a display of nudity on stage and by the use of dialogue that is charged with obscenities. To what extent should our Bill of Rights guarantee and protect the freedom of language and performance on stage?
2. The repertory system, which offers a different production each night, works well for the opera and ballet. Why does this system not work in the commercial and professional theater?
3. New York City has been proclaimed "the theater capital of the world." There is, however, a growing movement to decentralize the theater in the United States. To what extent has it succeeded or failed?
4. Compare the aims of the commercial, community, university, and educational theaters.
5. What evidence is there to support or to refute the statement: "A critic can make or break a play"?
6. Acting companies come and go, regardless of artistic merit. What are the social, economic, and artistic factors that militate against the establishment of a successful and permanent acting company in the United States?

IV. *Theater Projects:* Prepare the following:

1. After reading a play that you have or have not enjoyed, write a criticism for:

   a. Tulane *Drama Review*
   b. *Newsweeek*
   c. Columbia Broadcasting System
   d. *The New York Times*

2. After you have read a play that you would like to produce, prepare:

   a. The artistic aims of the production
   b. A floor plan
   c. A sketch of the set
   d. A light plot

e. A costume chart
f. A promptbook

V. *Theater Bibliography:* Read the following:

Cole, Toby, and Chinoy, Helen K. *Directors on Directing,* New York: The Bobbs-Merrill Co., Inc., 1963.

Gallaway, Marian. *The Director in the Theatre.* New York: The Macmillan Co., 1963.

Larson, Orville K. *Scene Design for Stage and Screen.* East Lansing, Mich.: Michigan State University Press, 1961.

Parker, W. Oren, and Smith, Harvey K. *Scene Design and Stage Lighting.* New York: Holt, Rinehart and Winston, Inc., 1968.

Poggi, Jack. *Theater in America.* Ithaca, N.Y.: Cornell University Press, 1968.

Stagg, Jerry. *The Brothers Shubert.* New York: Random House, Inc., 1968.

Walkup, Fairfax Proudfit. *Dressing the Part.* New York: F. S. Crofts & Co., 1938.

VI
The Theater: A Mirror

The world's a stage on which all parts are played.

THOMAS MIDDLETON, *A Game of Chess*,
Act V, Scene 1

The theatergoer today lives in a world that is frequently at odds with itself. Mighty nations of opposing ideologies diplomatically maintain a show of peaceful coexistence while openly supporting friction between opposing satellite nations. In the flush of independence, rising nations defy the wisdom of elder statesmen and challenge the status quo of world powers. Defeated nations that once sought to dominate the world through military strength now prosper while a victorious nation that courageously faced the enemy now suffers a loss of political power and economic status in the world. In the name of peace, millions of dollars, pounds, francs, rubles, and marks are spent on military defense; one nation competes with another to win, place, and show in the armaments race. While one segment of society luxuriates, another wants for the bare necessities of life. Meanwhile, the boundaries of the world grow smaller as nations take off for the moon.

The theatergoer today lives in a violent society. Religious and political leaders are assassinated because of their association with movements and support of viewpoints of the times. Lives are lost and property is destroyed in civil riots that are a result of economic, social, and racial injustices too long ignored. Police authority is challenged and police protection is questioned. New dimensions and expressions of protest emanate from unexpected classes of society: men of the cloth rebel against the established doctrine of the Church; students rebel against parental authority and university leadership; welfare recipients, social workers, teachers, and other civil-service employees march, demonstrate, and picket to call attention to the justice of their cause or position. Flamboyant and dramatic methods are used by militant minorities to state their cause and, as a consequence, frequently distort the true degree of their support from groups and individuals. The old order is accused of a lack of social commitment to a group or a concept. A tradition-laden era appears to be on the brink of a new era that seeks to reappraise the responsibilities of governmental, religious, educational, and civil institutions, and to provide greater opportunities for wide participation in matters that affect the well-being of the whole of society.

The theater today reflects the myriad aspects of twentieth-century society. History and the assessment of world leaders and their decisions during World War II is the substance of *Soldiers* and *The Deputy,* two semi-documentary plays written by Rolf Hochhuth. A similar investigation is undertaken in the plays *The United States vs. Julius and Ethel Rosenberg* by Donald Freed and *In the Matter of J. Robert Oppenheimer* by Heinar Kippardt. The antipathy to war accounts for such plays as *We Bombed in New Haven* by Joseph Heller, *Viet Rock* by Megan Terry, and a restatement of Shakespeare's *Henry V* at Stratford, Connecticut. The rationale for the protest of the black citizen against the society in which he lives is dramatically stated in *Ceremonies in Dark Old Men,* by Lonnie Elder III, *No Place to Be Somebody* by Charles Gordone, *Dutchman* by LeRoi Jones, and *The Great White Hope* by Howard Sackler. The apathy of an affluent society that tolerates and condones violence is the theme of *Little Murders* by Jules Feiffer. The acceptance of such plays as *The Boys in the Band* by Mart Crowley, *The Madness of Lady Bright* by Lanford Wilson, and *A Patriot for Me* by John Osborne reveal a compassionate understanding of the homosexual. Patriotism, freedom, and statesmanship characterize the spirit of *1776* by Peter Stone and Sherman

Edwards. Government policy and its effect upon a minority of the population in terms of human suffering is the concern of *Indians* by Arthur Kopit. The younger generation has its say in *Hair* by Gerome Ragni, James Rado, and Galt MacDermot. The "new freedom and the new morality" make a case for nudity on stage in *The Prime of Miss Jean Brodie* by Jay Allen; *Oh! Calcutta!,* a musical revue with sketches by numerous playwrights; *Geese* by Gus Weill; and *Scuba Duba* by Bruce J. Friedman. *Che!,* a drama dealing with the Cuban revolutionist, however, experienced the backlash of a segment of society that found the degree of nudity and the accompanying action on stage objectionable. A court order caused performances to be temporarily suspended. In England, however, Parliament has abolished the Lord Chamberlain's licensing authority dating back to the days of Henry VIII, thereby assuring dramatic freedom on stage. The revolt against the Establishment, in this case, the commercial theater, is evident in the stimulating and provocative productions of The Living Theater under the direction of Julian Beck and Judith Malina; The Open Theater under the direction of Joseph Chaikin; and The Performance Group under the direction of Richard Schechner. The excitement and tempo of the times is the source of the vitality of the off-Broadway theater that has introduced new themes by new playwrights to a new generation of theatergoers. The commercial theater, however, continues to supply the more traditionally oriented theatergoer with slick musical comedies and hilarious farce-comedies. The appreciation of our literary heritage is apparent in the revival of the works of the major playwrights of the past. Finally, the "cultural explosion" has resulted in the decentralization of the theater in the United States. Major cities throughout the country now operate and support their own professional companies in new playhouses.

Organized theater is nearly 3,000 years old. It developed from a religious ritual that was a cult of a people. It was molded into an art form by the talents of many people: the producer, the playwright, the actor, the director, the designer, and the technician. It has enjoyed the patronage of kings and commoners. It has survived the wrath of a part of the citizenry as well as the competition of motion pictures, radio, and television. It is an ephemeral art that comes to life when an audience gathers to watch the performance of an actor and to listen to the words of a playwright. It fades when the actor and the audience depart, but frequently lingers in the memory of its patrons. Through the ages, despite political, social, and economic turmoil, somewhere, in some form, there has always been an actor to demonstrate the art of the theater, and there has always been an audience to enjoy the art of the actor and the playwright. It is likely that the Fabulous Invalid will always be with us, since man's need to express himself through performance and man's need to understand and enjoy life is timeless and universal.

Bibliography

Allen, John. *Great Moments in the Theater.* New York: Roy Publishers; London: Phoenix House, Ltd., 1958.

Exciting moments on and off stage from the building of the Globe theater to the establishment of the Shakespeare Festival Theater, Stratford, Canada.

Anthology of the American Negro in the Theater. Compiled and edited with an introduction by Lindsay Patterson. New York: Publishers Co., Inc., 1967.

An excellent critical approach to the role of the Negro in the American theater. Part of a series detailing the cultural and historical backgrounds of black Americans.

Arnott, Peter D. *An Introduction to the Greek Theater.* London: Macmillan & Co., Ltd., 1959.

An easy-to-read general introduction to the Greek theater.

Beare, W. *The Roman Stage.* 3rd. ed. rev. London: Methuen & Co., Ltd., 1964.

A scholarly approach to the Roman theater and its major playwrights.

Boleslavsky, Richard. *Acting: The First Six Lessons.* New York: Theatre Arts Books, 1949.

An excellent dramatic discussion of the principles of modern acting.

Bowman, Walter Parker, and Ball, Robert Hamilton. *Theatre Language.* New York: Theatre Arts Books, 1961.

A dictionary of terms and phrases germane to the legitimate theater.

Bradbrook, M. C. *The Rise of the Common Player.* Cambridge, Mass.: Harvard University Press, 1962.

An informative account of the status of the actor in Elizabethan society.

Burton, E. J. *The British Theater 1100–1900.* London: Herbert Jenkins, Ltd., 1960.

A good reference book for directors, designers, and costumers.

Carlson, Marvin. *The Theatre of the French Revolution.* Ithaca, N.Y. Cornell University Press, 1966.

A detailed and informative study of the French theater during the Revolution (1789–1799).

Cole, Toby, and Chinoy, Helen Krich. *Actors on Acting.* New York: Crown Publishers, 1949.

A source book for learning what notable actors, directors, critics, etc., think about acting.

Corrigan, Robert W. *Theatre in the Twentieth Century.* New York: Grove Press, Inc., 1963.

An anthology of articles by various writers on the playwright, the actor, and the critic.

Duerr, Edwin. *The Length and Depth of Acting.* New York: Holt, Rinehart and Winston, 1962.

A comprehensive account of the development of the art of acting.

Dusenbury, Winifred L. *The Theme of Loneliness.* Gainesville: University of Florida Press, 1960.

A study of the theme of loneliness as found in plays written by O'Neill, Miller, Williams, Hellman, Odets, and Barry.

Gottfried, Martin. *A Theater Divided.* Boston, Mass.: Little, Brown and Co., 1967.

A provocative consideration of the American theater today and the direction in which it is going.

Gould, Jean. *Modern American Playwrights.* New York: Dodd, Mead and Co., 1966.

A collection of biographical sketches of important playwrights in the American theater.

Hartnoll, Phyllis. *The Concise History of the Theater.* New York: Harry N. Abrams, Inc., 1968.

An attractively illustrated history of the theater that includes a survey of the evolution of dramatic literature.

Himelstein, Morgan Yale. *Drama Was a Weapon.* New Brunswick, N. J.: Rutgers University Press, 1963.

An account of the left-wing theater in New York from 1929 to 1941.

Hodge, Francis. *Yankee Theater.* Austin: University of Texas Press, 1964.

A study of the "stage yankee" and the development of American comedy (1825–1850).

Hotson, Leslie. *The Commonwealth and Restoration Stage.* New York: Russell and Russell, Inc., 1962.

An excellent account of what happened when the theaters were supposedly closed from 1642–1660, and the reorganization that took place when they re-opened.

Kernan, Alvin B., ed. *The Modern American Theater.* Englewood Cliffs, N.J.: Prentice Hall, Inc., 1967.

A collection of critical essays written by twentieth-century critics, playwrights, and directors.

Krutch, Joseph Wood. *"Modernism" in Modern Drama.* Ithaca, N.Y.: Cornell University Press, 1953.

An evaluation of the influence of Shaw, Ibsen, Strindberg, and Pirandello upon modern drama.

Laufe, Abe. *Anatomy of a Hit.* New York: Hawthorn Books, Inc., 1966.

In an informative, readable style, the author examines the long-run plays of the commercial theater from 1900 to 1965 and analyzes the elements that spell a successful box office.

Lelyveld, Toby. *Shylock on the Stage.* Cleveland: Western Reserve University, 1960.

A study of the role as played by leading actors of the British and American theater.

Lewes, George Henry. *On Actors and the Art of Acting.* New York: Grove Press, Inc., 1957.

Informative dramatic criticisms that expertly discuss and analyze the art of acting.

Lucas, F. L. *Tragedy in Relation to Aristotle's* Poetics. London: The Hogarth Press, 1953.

A readable discussion of tragedy as it pertains to Aristotle's *Poetics.*

Maney, Richard. *Fanfare.* New York: Harper & Bros., Publishers, 1957.

A lively view of the twentieth-century American theater in New York City as perceived by a top-notch press agent.

Matthews, Brander. *Papers on Acting.* New York: Hill and Wang, Inc., 1958.

A compilation of papers on acting from the Brander Matthews dramatic museum of Columbia University. Includes articles by such personalities as Talma, Irving, and Gillette, as well as notes on leading actors written by Brander Matthews.

Moses, Montrose J. *The Passion Play of Oberammergau.* New York: Duffield & Co., 1930.

History and text of the passion play as presented in Oberammergau, Germany.

Munk, Erika. *Stanislavski and America.* New York: Hill and Wang, Inc., 1966.

An anthology of essays on the Stanislavski "system" as practiced in the American theater.

Nicoll, Allardyce. *The Theatre and Dramatic Theory.* New York: Barnes and Noble, Inc., 1962.

An interesting book that raises the question of whether the theater today meets the needs of the audience.

Novick, Julius. *Beyond Broadway.* New York: Hill and Wang, Inc., 1968.

An informative study of theatrical organizations—professional and otherwise—outside the New York City area.

Parker, W. Oren, and Smith, Harvey K. *Scene Design and Stage Lighting.* New York: Holt, Rinehart and Winston, Inc., 1968.

An instructive approach to the problems of designing the set and lighting the stage.

Poggi, Jack. *Theater in America.* Ithaca, N.Y.: Cornell University Press, 1968.

A compelling study of the economic forces in the American theater from 1870 to 1967.

Rowell, George. *The Victorian Theatre.* London: Oxford University Press, 1956.

A survey of the development of the Victorian theater, including references to actors, playwrights, theater architecture, and production.

Smith, Stephenson S. *The Craft of the Critic.* New York: Thomas Y. Crowell Co., 1931.

"Part II—Play Reviewing" is of special interest to the theatergoer and is fundamentally sound.

Stagg, Jerry. *The Brothers Shubert.* New York: Random House, Inc., 1968.

A biographical study of three brothers who built a theatrical empire that dominated play production in the United States.

Varneke, B. V. *History of the Russian Theater.* New York: The Macmillan Co., 1951.

A history of the Russian theater with emphasis on the development of realism during the nineteenth century.

Weales, Gerald. *American Drama Since World War II.* New York: Harcourt, Brace & World, Inc., 1962.

A critical consideration of major plays and playwrights on the American stage since World War II.

Wilson, John Harold. *All the King's Ladies.* Chicago: The University of Chicago Press, 1958.

An informative and entertaining study of England's first actresses.

Index